John Inglis

Bible Illustrations From the New Hebrides

with notices of the progress of the Mission

John Inglis

Bible illustrations From the New Hebrides
with notices of the progress of the Mission

ISBN/EAN: 9783337095864

Printed in Europe, USA, Canada, Australia, Japan

Cover: Foto ©Lupo / pixelio.de

More available books at **www.hansebooks.com**

BIBLE ILLUSTRATIONS

FROM

THE NEW HEBRIDES

With Notices of the Progress
of the Mission

BY THE

REV. JOHN INGLIS, D.D., F.R.S.G.S.
AUTHOR OF "IN THE NEW HEBRIDES," ETC.

THOMAS NELSON AND SONS
London, Edinburgh, and New York

1890

PREFACE.

THIS volume is totally distinct from my former one. Although on the same subject, and written to some extent on the same plan, it is nevertheless totally different from the other. While I have not followed the order of time in relating events, I have endeavoured to keep up the connection of subjects. I have arranged these so that each chapter may be complete in itself, and that the whole book from beginning to end may be clearly and distinctly understood. In the first part of the book the subject is entirely new: fresh light from the New Hebrides is shed upon texts of Scripture all more or less obscure—then follow sketches of natural history, manners and customs of the natives, short native biographies, heathen and Christian, and a statement of the progress of the Mission. I pray and hope that,

by the blessing of God, the book may be instru-
mental in advancing the Divine glory, in interesting and instructing its readers, and in advancing
the interests of the New Hebrides Mission.

LINCUAN COTTAGE, KIRKCOWAN, WIGTOWNSHIRE, N.B.

December 14th, 1889.

CONTENTS.

I. NAKEDNESS AND CLOTHING—(Genesis ii. 25; iii. 7,

    21; John xxi. 7) 1

II. THE CURSE OF CANAAN—(Genesis ix. 24-27) . . 7

III. BENJAMIN'S MESS—(Genesis xliii. 32-34) . . . 12

IV. WITCHCRAFT FROM A MISSIONARY POINT OF VIEW

    (Exodus xxii. 18) 17

V. GIDEON'S SOLDIERS LAPPING—(Judges vii. 5, 6) . 36

VI. SHIBBOLETH VERSUS SIBBOLETH—(Judges xii. 5, 6). 41

VII. SAMSON AND THE FOXES AND FIREBRANDS, ETC.

    (Judges xv. 1-6) 45

    THE LEVITE AND HIS CONCUBINE—(Judges xx. 29,

    30; xxi. 1-7) . . . .

    SAUL AND THE YOKE OF OXEN—(1 Samuel xi. 5-8)

    ABSALOM AND JOAB—(2 Samuel xiv. 28-33) . .

VIII. MICAH'S MOTHER CURSING—(Judges xvii. 1, 2) . 54

IX. A SINGLE FLEA—(1 Samuel xxiv. 14; xxvi. 20) . 57

X. THE GOING IN THE TOPS OF THE MULBERRY TREES

    (2 Samuel v. 22-25; 1 Chronicles xiv. 13-16) . 64

XI. MINISTERING ANGELS—(Psalm xci. 11, 12; Matthew

    iv. 5, 6; Luke iv. 9-11) 70

XII. The Hammer and the Rock—(Jeremiah xxiii. 29)   77

XIII. The Fig Tree—(Habakkuk iii. 17; Paraphrase
xxxii. 1)   81

XIV. The Cock Crowing Twice—(Matthew xxvi. 34, 74,
75; Mark xiv. 30, 71, 72)   84

XV. Fasting and Taking Nothing—(Acts xxvii. 33-36)   90

XVI. Mode of Treating Natives—(Acts xxvii. 3; xxviii.
7; 1 Peter iii. 8)   94

XVII. Natural History. Coral—Trees: Cocoa-nut,
Bread-fruit, Orange, Sandal-wood . .   109

XVIII. Natural History. Plants: Taro, Yams, Plantains, Arrowroot   120

XIX. Natural History. Animals: Serpents, Shell-
fish, Turtle   135

XX. Manners and Customs: Cooking and Eating;
Drinking Kava   148

XXI. Courtship and Marriage on Aneityum . .   162

XXII. Diseases on Aneityum and their Remedies .   176

XXIII. Civil Government on Aneityum   188

XXIV. Nup-u-tonga or Foreigners   204

XXV. Native Agency—Aneityumese Teachers . .   219

XXVI. Native Agency — Rarotongan and Samoan
Teachers   234

XXVII. Commencement of the Mission on Aneityum .   243

XXVIII. The French on the New Hebrides, 1887-8 .   254

XXIX. Bishop Patteson's First Impressions of
Aneityum   260

XXX. Biographical Sketches, Heathen and Chris-
TIAN—Rangi and his Son Thomas Amos . 268

XXXI. Lasarus and Ester—(with illustration) . . 281

XXXII. Inhalvatimi and Thiganua 291

XXXIII. Williamu 304

XXXIV. Williamu's Letters 320

XXXV. Conclusion 350

BIBLE ILLUSTRATIONS FROM THE NEW HEBRIDES.

—‍+‍+‍—

CHAPTER I.

NAKEDNESS AND CLOTHING.

" And they were both *naked*, the man and his wife, and were not ashamed."—GENESIS ii. 25.

" And the eyes of them both were opened, and they knew that they were *naked;* and they sewed fig leaves together and made themselves aprons " (breeches, *old version*), (things to gird about, *margin*). —GENESIS iii. 7.

" Unto Adam also, and to his wife, did the Lord God make coats of skins, and *clothed* them."—GENESIS iii. 21.

" Now when Simon Peter heard that it was the Lord, he girt his fisher's coat unto him (for he was naked), and did cast himself into the sea."—JOHN xxi. 7.

" NAKED savages ! " This is an expression often used both by missionaries, travellers, and others. Now, in one sense, it is quite correct, but in another sense it is quite incorrect : for the most part it is misleading. In their heathen state all the natives of the New Hebrides, the men at least, are naked, so far as anything they wear can protect them from cold or heat, rain or wind. But, on the other hand, there is no native who goes absolutely naked, or without any covering. They have all some clothing, some conventional dress, however scanty, which secures decency.

A

While Adam and Eve were in a state of innocency they were both naked, and were not ashamed. But after the fall, conscious of shame, they took fig leaves and made themselves girdles. And the natives of the New Hebrides retain, as nearly as may be, this primitive costume. All the world over dress is more or less conventional. A lady's ball-room dress, conventionally proper there, would not be considered proper in a church. In like manner, scanty as the native costume is, so scanty that it cannot be minutely described, the natives feel quite decent and proper while thus dressed; but without this, in a state of complete nudity, they would feel as much ashamed as we should do, if in the same condition.

When God had revealed the first promise to Adam and Eve, He covered them with skins, generally supposed to be the skins of the sheep or goats slain in sacrifice. Now, our natives on Aneityum, while heathen, were not only content with their fig-leaf-like girdles, but they would wear no European clothing of any kind, even had it been given them for nothing. But no sooner did they abandon heathenism and profess Christianity, than they adopted our mode of clothing. Without any special teaching from us, European clothing, more or less full, became the badge of Christianity; and when once they put it on they never gave up its use. On one occasion, shortly after I went to Aneityum, while I was sailing round to the other mission station in my boat, we saw about half a score of natives walking single file along the beach; we were too far from the shore to recognise them individually. But, nevertheless, one of my native boatmen said, "Six of these men are heathen, and four are Christian;" I said to him, "How do you know that, when they are so far off that you do not know who they are?" "Oh," said he, "do you

not see that four of them have on white *lavalavas*, while the
rest have none?" A *lavalava* is a fathom of cloth, which is
wrapped round the loins, and is the smallest portion of
European clothing ever worn by a native man. 'On another
occasion, in the first years of the mission, Nahoat, one of the
principal chiefs, then newly professing himself a Christian,
was ill with a severe cold. Mr. Geddie visited him, and offered
to pray with him. Nohoat gladly accepted his offer. But as
he was lying with nothing on but his native dress, he said to
the missionary, "O, Misi, stop a little till I put on my *lavalava.*" He evidently thought that European clothing was
essential to Christian worship. We had never taught this
doctrine; but seeing the natives had taken up the idea, we
allowed them to retain it; it acted powerfully in promoting
their civilization. Our Sabbath-day clothes have a marvellously
elevating influence on the community; they are an important factor in our Christian culture. No doubt Campbell's
translation of 1 Peter iii. 3, 4 is the correct one, "Whose
adorning let it be not *only* that outward adorning of plaiting
the hair, and of wearing jewels of gold, or of putting on of
apparel; but let it be *also* the hidden man of the heart, in
that which is not corruptible, even the ornament of a meek
and quiet spirit, which is in the sight of God of great price."
This is our rendering in the Aneityumese, sanctioned by the
authority of the late Rev. Mr. Meller, Rector of Woodbridge,
Suffolk, and Editorial Superintendent of the Foreign Versions
published by the British and Foreign Bible Society; one of
the ablest and most exact Biblical scholars of his day. It is
only those of us who have had personal experience in the
training of "naked savages" to the use of decent clothing,
that can fully appreciate the great breadth and exceeding

minuteness of Bible teaching, and how important it is to translate every word with painstaking accuracy. The *verbal* inspiration of Scripture is a doctrine of vastly greater importance than shallow theologians and superficial critics, who talk and write so confidently, would lead us to believe. The Apostle Peter emphasizes the inward adorning; but, in accordance with the whole tenor of Scripture, instead of condemning, he sanctions and encourages elegant female dress, and valuable female ornaments; and we found our hands strengthened by his words in our efforts to civilize the savage.

Adam and Eve, in what might be called their heathen state, before the gospel of Christ was revealed to them, and accepted by them, wore nothing but the fig-leaf girdle; but after they became Christian, so to speak, they accepted and wore a fuller and better costume. The Lord clothed them with skins. True religion led the way in the civilization and history of the human race. The Church became a separate society. Men called themselves by the name of the Lord, by some name equivalent to the name Christian given to the disciples at Antioch. Cain followed his father's profession as a tiller of the soil, but to that he added architecture or house-building, and builded a city. Abel fed his flocks and lived on the produce. Jabal originated the nomadic life, and owned herds of cattle. Lamech cultivated poetry. Jubal invented instruments of music. Tubal-cain (called by the Greeks, with a slight change of the letters from Hebrew to Greek, Vulcan, and made him the god of the Hammer-men) smelted the ores and produced the useful metals. While Noah brought ship-building to such perfection that, even in modern times, his ark became a model, in its proportions, for the Dutch and other shipbuilding nations in Europe.

There is nothing new under the sun. History repeats itself. This same process was observed on Aneityum. The fall of man is everywhere recognized. A sense of shame is universal. I have seen naked children on the islands—naked little boys and girls; but I never saw either a naked man or a naked woman—such may exist, but I never saw any of them, nor never heard of any such in any island of the South Seas. The dress might be very scanty according to our ideas of dress, but it was always in accordance with some conventional standard by which decency and propriety were secured. No sooner was Christianity introduced into Aneityum than the natives began to wear European clothing, as far as the climate required it, and as far as their means enabled them to obtain it. Like the human race after the first promise, they took a new departure both in religion and civilization. The Sabbath was observed; the worship of God, public and private, was set up; a higher standard of family life was adopted; education became general, and the Bible was read; a juster and a gentler type of civil government was established; a steadier industry arose; individual ownership of property began to be more fully recognized; and all traces of the socialistic principle disappeared, and a better knowledge of the mechanical arts was acquired. They could not build ships like Noah, or his son Ham, their great progenitor; but they made larger and better canoes, and before long they were able to handle an oar, to steer a boat, or to harpoon a whale, as skilfully as if they had hailed from Newburyport, Hobart, or Peterhead, or any of the great centres of the whale-fishing industry. In short, in a small way, they began to take their place in the comity of Christian and civilized communities, and year by year they continue to advance in Christianity and culture.

Peter was naked, but not absolutely so; he had on some underclothing, but he threw on his upper garment. In the Aneityumese New Testament we have rendered it, "he had nothing on save a *lavalava*," which is the way a Christian native would dress when fishing. In Scotland we say of a man who is working, that he is stripped to the shirt, when he has thrown off his vest as well as his coat. But we do not mean that he has nothing on but his shirt; and every one understands what is meant, although out of Scotland it would be understood literally. Peter was naked, simply in the sense that we say a savage is naked, when his clothing is sufficient for decency but no more. He was not dressed in his usual apparel. In every language there are brief elliptical expressions, which cannot be taken literally, but which no one misunderstands who knows the idiom of the language; and this word *naked* is one of these, both in the Scriptures and among ourselves.

At the trial of the Bishop of Murray in the General Assembly of 1638, Mr. Andrew Cant, minister of Pitsligo, bore witness "that the Bishop was a pretty dancer; at his daughter's bridal he danced *in his shirt*." Of course this could mean no more than that he had stripped off both his coat and vest.

CHAPTER II.

THE CURSE ON CANAAN.

"And Noah awoke from his wine, and knew what his younger son had done unto him. And he said, Cursèd be Canaan; a servant of servants shall he be unto his brethren. And he said, Blessed be the Lord God of Shem; and Canaan shall be his servant. God shall enlarge Japheth, and he shall dwell in the tents of Shem; and Canaan shall be his servant."—GENESIS ix. 24-27.

THIS prophecy is amazingly distinct, and yet it was very long in being fulfilled. At first, and for many long centuries, it seemed as if a blessing and not a curse rested upon the family of Ham. For nearly 2000 long years the dominant races upon the earth were the descendants of Ham. It was nearly 900 years before the Canaanites, those specially marked out in the curse, were subdued by Joshua. All the first great empires that arose in the world were established by the descendants of Noah's younger son. According to the marginal reading of the Bible, generally recognised as the most correct, Nimrod, the grandson of Ham, by Cush, his eldest son, went out into Assyria, and builded Nineveh. And for ages the city which he built, and the empire which he founded, continued to overshadow all Western Asia. When Layard was carrying on his excavations in Nineveh, and had disinterred a monster statue, the natives, as soon as they saw it, all shouted out, Nimroud! Nimroud! thus adding to the testimony of Scripture a tradition of 4000 years continuance, as to who was the founder of the city. Mizraim, the second son of Ham, founded the Egyptian monarchy and the Philistian commonwealth. Canaan, the fourth son of Ham, settled in Palestine, and his descendants founded first the Canaanitish kingdoms, then Tyre and Sidon, and subsequently Carthage. Also the great empire of the Hittites only now brought to light. These were for many long centuries the leading nations of the world; they possessed its highest civilization, and held all but a monopoly of its commerce.

How slow are God's threatenings in being inflicted! how slow are His promises in being fulfilled! And there can be no doubt that when Isaiah, Jeremiah, Nahum, and others of the Hebrew prophets were respectively warning their fellow-countrymen of their danger, exhorting them to repent of their sins and be obedient to their God, and fearlessly predicting the judgments that were about to descend upon *them*, and upon the *guilty nations* around—the sceptics of those days—the men who had ceased to believe in a personal God and a special providence; in the truth of prophecy and in the efficacy of prayer—the agnostics, the materialists, the rationalists, the pantheists, and the atheists—all the advanced thinkers of those days; the men of professedly high culture and refined taste; the men who had avowedly risen above the superstitions of the times—these all would attempt to turn aside the point and force of those threatening predictions, by referring with a sneer to the prophecy of Noah. "It is now," they would say, "nearly 2000 years since Noah predicted these judgments against the descendants of Ham, and when are they to be fulfilled?" It would be convenient for them to ignore the conquest of Canaan by Joshua, and with great assurance they would proceed to say, "Is not the sea coast still occupied by the five Lords of the Philistines? Are not the kings of the Hittites on the other side of Lebanon as powerful as ever? Does not Tyre sit, as of old, queen of the seas? Is not Egypt, as she has ever been, the chief among the nations? And who, what people on the face of the earth, can stand before the great king, the king of Assyria? Is not Nineveh the metropolis, the mother city, the mistress and ruler of the whole world?" So, no doubt, spoke the scoffer, and the believer in prophecy, inspiration, and Holy Scripture found it very difficult to answer his objections. It required faith like that of Abraham's to enable them to hold on by God's covenant: they had to endure as seeing Him who is invisible.

But the Lord is not slack concerning either His promises or His threatenings, as some men count slackness; a thousand years are with Him as one day. Even then, the believer had not long to wait till Nineveh, Egypt, Tyre, and other Hametic nations fell. But if difficult then, it would be easy now. Let any one take a look at New Zealand, and then accompany us in our mission vessel, the *Dayspring*, and we can show him this prophecy, which was uttered more than 4000 years ago, fulfilled to the very letter. In the South Seas he will find portions of the three races, Shemetic, Hametic, and Japhetic, as distinctly marked off from one another as were the three sons of Noah, when they took their leave of the ark among the mountains of Ararat, or when a century later their speech was confounded at Babel; when the earth was divided, and the three families, each according to their tongues, took possession of their respective portions, when—

"The world was all before them where to choose,
And Providence their guide."

But let us take the prophecy verse by verse. "Cursed be
Canaan ; a servant of servants shall he be unto his brethren."
Ham was cursed in the person of his youngest, probably his
favourite, son. He was cursed in his descendants. Now in
the New Hebrides we see this curse lying in all its crushing
weight. The Papuans, the poor descendants of Ham, are
lying in the lowest state of degradation, trodden down by
the iron heel of every oppressor. Let us take the next verse,
"Blessed be the Lord God of Shem ; and Canaan shall be his
servant." In the fulfilment of this blessing we find that the
whole of the Malay race, descendants of Shem, in the South
Seas, had abandoned heathenism, had embraced Christianity,
and had the Bible translated for them into the six principal
dialects of their language, while the whole, or nearly the
whole, of the Papuan race, the children of Ham, were still
lying in heathen darkness. And wherever these Malays,
these children of Shem, go in the South Seas, these Papuans
are willing to be their servants. Everywhere we see the
Papuans serving the Malays, Canaan being the servant of
Shem ; but nowhere do we see the Malays serving the
Papuans, or Shem being the servant of Canaan. Now let
us take the last verse : "God shall enlarge Japheth, and he
shall dwell in the tents of Shem ; and Canaan shall be his
servant." We, the descendants of Japheth, seem to be specially
called of God at the present day to colonize and evangelize
the world. Our fellow-countrymen in New Zealand, for
example, are dwelling in the tents of Shem—they are dwelling on the land long occupied by the Maories, a tribe of the
Malays ; while the rowdyism of Sydney and of Brisbane are
reviving the slave-trade, kidnapping the poor Papuans, and
carrying them into servitude in Queensland, Fiji, and New

Caledonia. But especially has God enlarged us, and given us the heritage of Shem, by making us the representatives of His visible Church, to dispense its blessings to the heathen ; and these poor Gibeonites are willing to become hewers of wood and drawers of water to us for the house of the Lord. Yes, "Canaan shall be his servant."

CHAPTER III.

BENJAMIN'S MESS.

"And they set on for him by himself, and for them by themselves, and for the Egyptians which did eat with him by themselves: because the Egyptians might not eat with the Hebrews; for that is an abomination unto the Egyptians. And he took and sent messes unto them from before him: but *Benjamin's mess was five times so much as any of theirs.*"
—GENESIS xliii. 32, 34.

THERE is no difficulty in understanding why there were three tables—one for Joseph, one for the Egyptians, and one for the Hebrews. Joseph, either from his rank, or from his being a foreigner, did not eat with the Egyptians; and his brethren would eat by themselves, because to eat with the Hebrews was an abomination to the Egyptians. But that Benjamin should have five times the quantity of food sent to him that was sent to any of his brethren, who, doubtless, after the manner of a feast, had abundance, is contrary to all our customs, and to all our ideas of table etiquette; but to a native of the South Seas Joseph's mode of procedure would cause no difficulty, it is quite in accordance with their own. There is no religious caste among them, as in India; but for nationality and rank they make a difference in the quantity of food supplied at meals. At our feasts we have different courses, one following another; with the natives each guest receives his full share of the food at once. Our custom also is for each one to eat as much as he pleases, and whatever is not eaten of each course is left on the plate, or on the table, or in the house. But this is not the custom in the South Seas. Each guest, having received his share of the food, eats what he thinks proper, and whatever is left he puts into his basket, or ties up in a leaf, and takes it home with him, to eat next day, or divide among his family or his friends. But perhaps I cannot illustrate this better than by giving an account of a little feast that we had on Aneityum, in one of the first years of our mission, at the opening of a new school-house, which was also to be used as a place of worship.

The feast was provided by Amosa, a Samoan teacher, who had charge of the station, and Nemet, the chief of the district. There were four parties of us, composed of three nationalities; viz., a missionary party, a teacher party, and two Aneityumese parties. There were the two mission families; Dr. and Mrs. Geddie and their children being with us at the time. We had also four Rarotongan teachers and their wives and some children, who had been left with us for two months or so by the captain of the *John Williams*, till the vessel went up to Sydney for repairs. A party of Aneityumese also accompanied us. We had a service of singing, prayer, and addresses in the new building. After that the oven, a very large one, was opened, and the contents carefully divided into four parts. A table was set for the missionary party in the teacher's house; and, we being the most important strangers, a mess like that of Benjamin's was brought to us. It consisted of two large baskets of taro, steaming hot from the oven; two fowls, cooked in the same way; a large fish, in shape and size like a goodly 14 lb. salmon, cooked also in the oven; a large bunch of beautiful bananas, fully ripe and yellow, all fit for eating, and a large basket of fresh cocoa-nuts, all husked and ready for drinking. My wife had provided tea and sugar, and other accompaniments; so that we sat down to what, in some places, would be called a high tea, or a knife and fork tea, or a tea with something, and that greatly beyond the ordinary, to it. Mats were spread outside, under banyan and bread-fruit trees, for the other three parties, as Abraham provided for the three celestial visitors under the oak at Mamre. The next largest portion was for the Rarotongan teachers, which, though greatly less than ours, was yet twice as much as they could possibly eat. The third portion was for the Aneityumese who had accompanied us; it was a full meal, but not much more. And the fourth portion was for Amosa and Nemet and their friends who had provided, the feast, and consisted of the smallest of the taro, and the most diminutive of the fishes; it was a scanty meal, and barely allayed the cravings of their hunger. After we had partaken to satisfaction of our sumptuous meal, our Aneityumese servants came and gathered up all that was left, as the disciples did with the remains of the loaves and the fishes, packed it into baskets, and took all home; to have left anything behind us would have been an insult to our entertainers. Enough of what was brought home was set apart to do for our breakfast next morning, the rest was divided among the natives living on our premises, and when they had all had a good meal, whatever was left, if any, was carried forth as a kind of overflow meal to their friends and neighbours outside of the mission household. The Egyptians, like the Papuans, were descendants of Ham. Egypt was Ham's land. We may therefore legitimately infer that the people would do in Egypt then very much as the people do on Aneityum at the present time; and that Benjamin's servants, who would be waiting somewhere outside, in one of the courts of Joseph's palace, would come in when the feast was over, and gather up the remains of his mess, put it into scrips, or bags, or baskets, and carry all home to their lodgings; the servants of the others would do the same, and in that time of famine they, as well as their masters, would feast on those royal dainties till they were finished. Benjamin would have the honour, but his brethren and the servants would enjoy the benefit, and Joseph would be applauded for his princely hospitality. On Aneityum, in heathen times, he was the *great* man who had the most food, and he was the *good* man who dispensed it most liberally. He was the *poor* man who had little food, and he was the *bad* man who was stingy with his food, and gave it grudgingly. Liberality in giving food was the highest virtue, and stinginess with respect to food was the greatest sin.

We hear nothing of servants in the narrative; but we cannot conceive of Jacob's sons going all the way from Canaan to Egypt with a solitary ass, or even more, each, to carry up a supply of corn for their families, amounting to upwards of one hundred persons, exclusive of servants. A few years before, when Jacob returned from Padan-Aram, he had a large number of men-servants and maid-servants, even a great household. We may safely suppose that Jacob's sons had a large number of retainers and servants accompanying them, —that they formed a large caravan, although the historian does not find it necessary to refer to them for the purpose of his narrative; the servants not doing anything that required their presence to be noticed. Brevity being so carefully studied by the sacred writers, everything not essential to their main subject is invariably excluded.

The more natural, beautiful, and truth-like do the Scripture narratives appear, in proportion as we know the manners and customs of the times and the places to which they refer; and from the most remote and obscure corners of the earth, even the tiny and distant isles of the sea, come light and knowledge to illustrate and confirm the truth of sacred history.

CHAPTER IV.

"Thou shalt not suffer a witch to live."—EXODUS xxii. 18.

THIS text may receive some light from our missionary experience. The Hebrew word *mecashepha*, translated witch, wizard, sorcerer, magician, &c., comes from the verb *cashaph*, which signifies to pray, to offer prayers or worship; but is restricted to the worship of idols, hence it signifies to use enchantments, to use magical songs, to mutter. It was the connection of witchcraft with idolatry, and hence with the virtual renouncing of Jehovah, which rendered it a sin so displeasing to God, and made it to be treason under the Theocracy. For a century and a half after the Reformation burning for witchcraft was common in this country. In the early part of last century this practice ceased. The scepticism that afterwards prevailed, as well as the clearer knowledge that was diffused throughout society, banished superstition, and in all intelligent circles destroyed the belief in witchcraft. The belief lingered among the ignorant; but for a century and a half, if any of the laws against witchcraft have remained in the statute-book, they have been a dead letter.

That evil spirits exist the Scriptures amply prove; that men may hold communication with them is possible; that they did so in ancient times the Bible clearly affirms. Satan appeared to Adam and Eve and tempted them; he did the

B

same to our Saviour in the wilderness. Dealing with familiar spirits was common in Old Testament times. Our Saviour spoke to the evil spirits and cast them out. That men should still hold intercourse with evil spirits is certainly possible. But, as the eminently judicious Thomas Scott, the commentator, says: "As by certain degrees of civilization wild beasts are banished or extirpated, so, in some stages of civilization, the practice of witchcraft is nearly excluded." It is so in this country at the present time, and Satan acquiesces; "nor is he any loser by exchanging the practice of witchcraft for the prevalence of scepticism." Witchcraft is generally understood to mean "a compact with evil spirits, by whose agency and assistance, applied for by certain incantations, effects of various kinds may be produced, by which malice, or covetousness, or other corrupt passions may be gratified." A current belief in our times is, that there is no such thing as witchcraft, and that there never was such a thing; that it never was anything but pretence; that in most cases men who were cleverer than their neighbours, or who were better acquainted with the laws of nature than others, either professed themselves or allowed others to believe that certain things were accomplished by supernatural powers that were done simply by superior skill or through a better knowledge of the laws of nature; that sleight-of-hand was passed off for a compact with the devil; and that those persons found it to be for their advantage to allow such delusions to pass uncontradicted. Furthermore, it is also a part of the popular belief still, that, in those times, if an old woman was only very poor and very ugly, it was quite sufficient to raise the suspicion that she was a witch, irrespective of anything connected with her former character or history. We are certain of this, that, whether any person in those remote times was in league with the devil or not, and through the agency of evil and malignant spirits inflicted injuries of various kinds on others, there was among the community at large, whether rightly or wrongly, a fixed and firm belief in the existence of witchcraft, and they acted on this belief.

In reading such books as Sir Walter Scott's "Letters on Demonology and Witchcraft," or the Rev. Walter Scott's "Lectures on the Existence and Agency of Evil Spirits," and learning the history of witchcraft in England, Scotland, and New England, one is led to exclaim, "Oh, poor human nature!" one's blood is apt to boil at the cruelties exercised by the witch-finders and witch-prickers of those times, and we cannot be too thankful that we live in an age of Christian light and knowledge, when witchcraft has disappeared. Still there is another side to this question; and after living three and thirty long years in lands where witchcraft was in the air, so to speak; where "I believe in witchcraft" was the first article in the popular creed; accepted as true as certainly as "I believe in God the Father Almighty" is among us; I am led to be much more charitable towards our forefathers in their prosecutions for witchcraft, than would be sanctioned by the average of public opinion in the present day. Our forefathers had doubtless as much common sense as we have; they were naturally as just and as humane as we are; but they lived under different circumstances, and they are not to be blamed for doing what they did, as we should be blamed were we to do the same. As opportunity makes the thief, so ignorance and superstition produce the witch. Human nature is the same in all ages, and men everywhere are greatly influenced by their surroundings and their environments. Our forefathers were just emerging from the ignorance and superstition of the dark ages; and it was by slow degrees that they emancipated themselves from the errors of the times, from the belief in witchcraft and kindred opinions, and attained to our present standing-ground on these questions. The belief in the supernatural has prevailed in all ages and in all countries; it is co-existent with the human race. Religious belief and feeling, or a belief in the supernatural, is as much an essential part of man's nature as conscience or reason; and it manifests itself either in true religion, or in superstition; either in the worship of God, or the worship of the devil; or it may be partly of both. The existence of superstition is essential to the existence of witchcraft. Where superstition abounds the belief in witchcraft will also abound. In the New Hebrides there is the grossest ignorance, and hence there is the most debasing superstition. The belief in witchcraft is universal and unwavering. Witchcraft is accepted as a reality, as a thing about which there can be no doubt. No death, at least the death of no person of any importance, is ever recognised as resulting from natural causes; the death of such persons is always ascribed to witchcraft; and the question to be answered is, by whom has the death been caused? Of course it is always ascribed to some enemy. On one occasion my fellow-missionary, Dr. Geddie, was over at Port Resolution on Tanna, and was urging Miaki, a principal chief there, to give up heathenism and become a Christian. Miaki said he wished to do so as soon as he had avenged the death of five of his men—of two who had been killed in battle, and of three who had been killed by witchcraft. Dr. Geddie, knowing that the killing by witchcraft was pure imagination, tried his best to reason him out of his belief, and to convince him that the sacred men had no power whatever—that God only has the power of life and death. But, alas! Leviathan was not to be so easily tamed. Miaki remained firm in the belief, that the three men were as certainly killed by witchcraft, as that the two were shot in battle. A new faith must be implanted before the old beliefs can be eradicated. It gives way only before "the expulsive power of a new affection." The belief of the natives in witchcraft is much stronger than was the belief of our forefathers three centuries ago. We are quite safe in assuming that the sacred men in the New Hebrides possess no more supernatural power than did the witches in Scotland two or three hundred years ago. These sacred men, however, possess and exercise a tremendous power; but it is exercised by working on the superstitious fears of their fellow-countrymen. A similar power was possessed and exercised by those who professed to deal in the black arts in the days of our forefathers; and in like manner the secret of their power lay, not in any compact which they had made with the Evil One, but in the strong superstitious fears of the age. This is undoubtedly the case in the New Hebrides. If a native becomes unwell, and if he fancies that he is bewitched, or if it is known that some sacred man has performed some incantation upon him, no European medicine, or no treatment that we can give, will cure him; he believes that it may mitigate the disease, or ward off death for a time, but till the incantation is taken off, either by the person who laid it on, or by some other person equally powerful in spells, the sick person believes that he cannot recover; he has the sentence of death in himself, and he will as certainly die as if he had been mortally wounded by a spear, or a bullet, or

any lethal weapon; hence the sacred man who, by his incantations, works in this way on the superstitious fears of any
of his countrymen, so as to cause his death, is as really a
murderer as the man who shoots him dead with his musket.
To prevent incantation the natives, on some islands at least,
are scrupulously careful, after every meal, to collect every
particle of skin, or rind, or crumb, and either burn them or
cast them into the sea, lest any enemy should get hold of
them, and form some incantation with them, and employ it
to cause sickness or death.   As soon as Christianity was
generally professed on Aneityum, the native belief was, that
the sacred men had no longer any power.   It was astonishing
how rapidly the superstitious fears of the people were dispelled, and their belief in the *natmasses* or spirits was not
only shaken, but completely lost.   The effect was almost the
same as that which the Christian fathers attributed to the
birth of Christ, or as that which Dr. Blair so eloquently
ascribes to the Saviour's death, when he says, "In that hour,
the foundation of every Pagan temple shook—the statue of
every false god tottered on its base—the priest fled from the
falling shrine—and the heathen oracles became dumb for ever."
But by and by we learned that, while they sincerely believed
that the witchcraft of Aneityum was one of the lost arts,
there was still a partial belief that in the heathen islands
around the power of witchcraft remained.   When some of our
adventurous young men went to Tanna or Eromanga, they
sometimes brought home material for witchcraft from those
islands, and threatened or attempted, by such ingredients, to
practise witchcraft.   Navalak and Paulo, two of our principal
chiefs, came to me one day very angry with two of these
young men, who had returned from Tanna, and who were

threatening to bewitch them, and compass their death by this means, in revenge for some punishment which they had inflicted upon them for some offence of which they had been guilty. They evidently believed that the young men possessed some power to do them mischief, and wished to have them punished for their conduct, as being a species of treason-felony. I strongly condemned the conduct of the young men, but counselled forbearance, and comforted the chiefs with the assurance that these threats, or attempts at witchcraft, were utterly powerless; that the devil has no power as against God; that the Lord has said, "There is no enchantment against Jacob, neither is there any divination against Israel;" that Balaam of old had no power to bewitch or curse the children of Israel; and Satan and his servants have as little power now to bewitch God's people. They were two good Christian men, and they believed my words, and went away pacified and satisfied.

Some ten or twelve years ago a young woman was married at my station, and, as often happened on such occasions, one or two young men were greatly disappointed, and hence were very angry. One of these had been at Eromanga during the whaling season, and had brought home with him a quantity of the material used there for incantations, the chief ingredient of which was a species of black lead. With us marriages were usually performed in the church at the Wednesday prayer-meeting. After the service was over the missionary always shook hands with the bride and bridegroom, his wife followed and did the same, and afterwards as many of the congregation as wished to do so. On this occasion one of these disappointed young men went up with the others, and shook hands with them, and left on the bride's

hand some of the incantation matter, without her observing
it. It so happened that on that day my wife and I were
going on board the *Dayspring*, our mission vessel, to visit
some of the other islands, and to be absent for a month.
The vessel was lying in the offing, and we went on board
direct from the church, and knew nothing of what I am
about to relate till our return. The young bride had hardly
left the church, when one of this young man's companions
went up to her, and said, "Did you see what So-and-so did
to you?" She said, "No." "Look at your hand," said he,
"and see how black it is. You are bewitched." She opened
her hand and looked, and lo, there were the marks of the
black pigment! She stood transfixed, as if she had been
shot. She felt that she had been bewitched, and was certain
that she would die. She cried all the way home, more than
three miles; she cried all night, cried all the next day, and
all the next night, would eat nothing, cried till her eyes were
red and her face yellow, till she had all the appearance of one
suffering from jaundice; she was sure she would die, and
most certainly would have died, in spite of all that her friends
could say to make her believe that there was nothing in the
incantation. But it so happened that there was a small party
of Tannese working to a white man, about eight miles distant,
and among these was a sacred man, who was held to be able
to remove the effects of witchcraft. He was sent for, and
when he came, he took a small branch of a tree held to be
sacred on Tanna, dipped it in water, and sprinkled it over
the head of the poor girl, repeating at the same time some
unknown words. The enchantment was held to be taken off,
the young woman's superstitious fears were removed, and in
a short time she was herself again. It has almost invariably

happened in our mission that when any untoward event occurred on the one side of the island, another of the same kind took place on the other side. About three weeks afterwards there was a marriage at the other station, and a disappointed young man practised the very same trick upon the young bride, with essentially the same results, which had to be removed by similar means. We had a good deal of trouble before we eradicated the belief in this importation of foreign witchcraft. The wife of one of our principal chiefs was supposed to be bewitched, and, as it was believed, narrowly escaped with her life; and many of our best and most intelligent natives were greatly staggered in their belief about it. When I spoke to them on the subject, they said, "You know our hearts are weak and dark. We know that Satan has lost all power to work by witchcraft on this island, because we have ceased to believe in him and worship him; but we thought he might still be able to work by the black arts belonging to the heathen islands where he is still worshipped."

There are few subjects on which certain of the wouldbe advanced thinkers of this nineteenth century wax more eloquent than when they are denouncing our forefathers on the subject of witchcraft. No terms are strong enough for decrying the ignorance, the bigotry, and the fanaticism of our ancestors, especially the clergy of those times, on this subject; so much so, that the belief largely prevails, that such was the fanaticism of the times, that if a woman was only poor, and old, and ugly, and perhaps a little better informed than her neighbours, she was sure to be suspected of being a witch, would most likely be tried, and very probably be burned. It may frankly be admitted that the recog-

nised witches and wizards of 200 or 300 years ago had no
more supernatural power than the sacred men of the New
Hebrides of the present day; but the people of those times,
like the savages of our days, were superstitious, and believed
in witchcraft—they believed that certain persons possessed
supernatural power to inflict evil, and to cause sickness, death,
or other calamities; the ancient witchcraft, like the modern,
was always employed for evil, never for good; the true worship
and service of God produces nothing but good, the worship
and service of the devil is always connected with malignant
purposes.   Moreover, certain persons in those times professed
to possess supernatural power, and practised on the superstitious fears of the people, just as the sacred men on the
New Hebrides do at the present day, and no doubt they often
caused the death of superstitious people.   The two young men
on Aneityum who wrought on the superstitious fears of the
two young women, would as certainly have been murderers,
had those two young women died, as they evidently would
have done had the incantations not been, as they believed,
taken away, as if they had shot them; at all events they
would have been chargeable with culpable homicide, and on
the heathen islands such things are of frequent occurrence,
and would still be more frequent, were it not that a salutary
fear is inspired by the threats of the chief, the secret machina-
tions of the avenger of blood, and the counter incantations
that can be brought into play by some other sacred man.
Now assuming, as we may safely do, that the witchcraft of 200
or 300 years ago was essentially the same as the witchcraft of
the New Hebrides at the present day, the witches of those
times were not as a class poor, old, innocent women, of the
type of Mause in Ramsay's "Gentle Shepherd," they were

largely a wicked class of men and women, practising on the superstitious fears of the people for selfish and wicked ends, and through the influence of those fears bringing on sickness, or causing death and other evils, and extorting payments or levying blackmail to avert those calamities; and they are barely extinct even yet. At this very hour, amid all the blazing light of this nineteenth century, with the schoolmaster abroad, science popularised, the penny newspaper in every man's hand, knowledge, scriptural and secular, so universally diffused, that the light of the moon is become as the light of the sun; yet just now, I happen to know of an old, bold, wicked woman, who gives her neighbours to understand that her wishes and her curses are not to be despised, as her words seldom fall to the ground; and hence she levies blackmail over a good part of the district, and she tells her friends that the highest lady in the parish never refuses her anything that she asks from her; and that, not because she loves her, but because she fears her. What would this beldame not have done 200 years ago? Are we therefore to blame very severely the authorities of those times for inflicting punishment, even capital punishment, on persons guilty of such crimes, any more than we should blame the authorities of the present day when they punish men for threatening to shoot the Queen or any other person? These witches or wizards were no doubt often murderers, or at least manslayers, just as the sacred men in the New Hebrides are at the present time, and deserved to be punished as such; not because they were in league with the devil, and possessed power derived from him, but by professing to possess such power, and threatening, or affecting, to exercise it, they were culpable to the extent of the mischief likely to accrue. Hence, in these circumstances, the burning

of witches was not the absurd, outrageous, indefensible crime
that, tried by our light and in our circumstances, it would
undoubtedly be. It was a rude kind of justice, like a great
deal of the justice of those times. It was society protecting
itself against a formidable and peculiar evil. No doubt many
innocent persons suffered, but they did the same in many other
ways, as the laws were then administered. Witchcraft does
not now exist, because the elements out of which it grew, viz.,
ignorance and superstition, are removed. In those times
superstition prevailed among all classes. It was found to be
nearly as strong among the upper ten thousand, as among
servant-maids, cottars' wives, well-to-do tradesmen, and wealthy
farmers. Persons of the highest rank were accused of witchcraft, as well as poor old women. After the death of King
Edward IV. of England, his mistress, the beautiful Jane
Shore, became attached to Lord Hastings. Their known
partiality to the young princes rendered them obnoxious to
the Duke of Gloucester, who accused them of witchcraft.
On this charge Hastings was beheaded, and Jane Shore was
committed to the Tower. After a mock trial she was ordered
to do penance in St. Paul's in a white sheet, and was paraded
through the public streets, the Bishop of London heading the
procession. Be it admitted that, while the ostensible charge
against them was one of witchcraft, the real charge sought to
be made out was one of treason. Nevertheless, such was the
superstition of the time, that it was easier to establish a
charge of witchcraft than a charge of treason, and the most
easily proved charge answered the purpose of the tyrant best;
and the public mind recognised the charge as quite competent.
In Scotland, too, ladies of the highest rank were at times
accused of practising witchcraft, of seeking to compass the

death of royal personages, by incantations and pactions with Satan; and, no doubt, traitors at times sought to accomplish their ends by such means.

The superstition of 200 years ago was almost equal to anything existing in the South Seas at the present time. History informs us that before the Revolution, when so many of the Scottish nobility fled over to Holland, Colin, the young Earl of Balcarres, was engaged to be married to Maritia de Nassau, a charming young Dutch lady, a relation of the Prince of Orange. But when the marriage day came, and the bride and her party arrived in the church, the bridegroom was not there; and when his friends went to seek him, they found him sitting in his morning gown quite oblivious of his engagement. As he went out hastily, he forgot the ring in his writing-case,—a friend in the company gave him one, the ceremony went on, and, without looking at the ring, he placed it on the finger of the fair young bride. When the ceremony was over, the bride happened to look at the ring, and, to her horror, she discovered that it was a mourning one, with a death's-head and cross-bones on it; and the belief then was, that any woman married with a mourning ring would die within a year. On seeing the ring the young lady fainted, being fully impressed with the belief that she would die within a twelvemonth; and in spite of all that could be said or done to her, she pined away and died before the year was out. Imagination kills, and imagination cures. Now, if such was the power of superstition at that time in the most enlightened court in Europe, more than 150 years after the Reformation, what must it have been among the people in general? What ample material must have existed for producing witchcraft!

Under the Mosaic Law witchcraft was regarded as a sin

against God, it was a worshipping of the devil, a breaking of the first, second and third commandments. It was idolatry; and no sin was so heinous, or so displeasing to God, or so severely punished, as idolatry; it was, as I have said, treason under the Theocracy. In the days of our forefathers it was as a crime against man, rather than as a sin against God, that witchcraft was held to be punishable. It was the crime of men in compact with the devil, or using incantations for malignant purposes; it was the use of the black arts for the perpetration of black deeds, for destroying life and property. The persons who professed these arts, or claimed these powers, in those times were regarded by the authorities very much as we at present regard men who are found to have dynamite or other dangerous substances in their possession, and for which they cannot give a satisfactory account. This is the view that is taken of witchcraft by the heathen in the New Hebrides and elsewhere at the present time; it is a crime imperilling the safety of society.

There is this marked difference between the views of our forefathers and those held in modern times. They looked upon the danger as lying in the power possessed by those who had the knowledge of secret incantations, and exercised that knowledge for evil purposes. Modern theology and modern science have successfully proved that the danger lies wholly in the superstitious fears of those against whom these arts are practised. If they have no superstitious fears the incantations are perfectly harmless. If they are possessed with superstitious fears, like the natives of the New Hebrides, the likelihood is that the incantation will be injurious, probably fatal. Incantations are like certain diseases, or certain states of the atmosphere, that have no effect upon healthy constitutions,

but are injurious or fatal to those whose constitutions are
weak; with this important difference, that, in the case of
those diseases, the state of the body is the chief, but not the
sole, cause of their taking effect or not; but in the case of witchcraft it is the imagination alone that kills or saves. Bryant
and May's safety matches will not ignite unless you strike them
against the prepared portion of the box; so those incantations
were powerless, except when they were practised upon people
filled with superstitious fears; but on such the results were
more or less fatal or injurious. They are powerless with us;
because the superstitious fears are awanting. It is Bryant
and May's matches without the prepared box; they will not
ignite. Our forefathers believed that there was a positive,
supernatural, satanic power possessed by the sorcerer, and
exercised by him through his incantations; they took no
account of the superstitious fear. On the other hand we
know that the case is reversed. But, nevertheless, although
they acted ignorantly in punishing those who profess to
practise witchcraft, in order that they might protect society,
the punishments which they inflicted, no doubt, restrained the
evil to a great extent, and tended to the protection of life and
property. But, in these completely altered times of ours, it is
as unjust to blame our forefathers for the burning of witches,
as it would be to blame them for inflicting capital punishment for twenty other crimes, for all of which the penalty
is now removed from the criminal list, and blotted out of the
statute-book.

It is admitted on all hands, that in the ancient systems of
witchcraft, whether in Greece and Rome, in Egypt or in the
far east, as well as among our forefathers, imposture, as well
as superstition, came largely into play. It is so in the New

Hebrides and elsewhere. The sacred men are cunning as
well as superstitious, impostors as well as wizards. I knew a
Maori priest in New Zealand who used to go to the missionary
for medicine for a sick man; this he carefully administered
till the patient was nearly well; he then removed him to a
sacred enclosure, took a branch from a consecrated tree,
dipped it in holy water, and with the water sprinkled the
man's head, pronouncing over him certain cabalistic words.
He then declared him healed, and the man brought him a
large present for the cure.

On some islands in the New Hebrides when a native is
attacked with acute rheumatic or other pains, it is supposed
that an evil spirit has entered into him, and is tormenting
him. A sacred man, whose office it is to exorcise spirits, is
sent for. On his arrival he examines the man, and causes
him to lie down on a mat with his face to the ground; he
performs various incantations over him, sings certain songs,
and repeats certain prayers. He then rubs him, and sham-
poos him, and applies heated stones to the most painful
parts; then he takes a sacred leaf, gesticulates with it, and
calls upon the spirit to come out of the man; then draws his
hand across the man's shoulder, lifts it up, opens it in presence of the assembled people, and there is the spirit in the
form of a live lizard, which had been concealed in the leaf!
If the patient speedily recovers, a large pig is sent as payment for the cure; if no improvement takes place, some
excuse is easily invented to cover the failure.

There is one important difference between the witchcraft
of the Bible, the witchcraft of this country in former times,
and the witchcraft of the New Hebrides. In Bible times
women, as well as men, practised sorcery and used enchant-

ments. In this country it was chiefly women, and those poor old women, who were credited with these supernatural powers. But in the New Hebrides these powers belong exclusively to the men. When we went to Aneityum there was one young woman who was regarded as a kind of vestal virgin, and who performed some ceremonies at feasts, but she was not recognised as having any power to cause sickness or death. There was plenty of dancing on Aneityum in heathen times; they danced nine months in the year; but a "dance o' witches" was a thing that the wildest poetic fancy would never have dreamed of. Of no woman in the New Hebrides could it ever have been said, as of Tam o' Shanter's Nannie—

> " For mony a beast to dead she shot,
> And perished mony a bonnie boat,
> And shook baith meikle corn and bere,
> And kept the country-side in fear."

In the islands it is the men, and the important men only, who are believed to possess supernatural power, and direct supernatural operations : according to the popular belief it is those only who are in league with the devil; who bring on diseases and cause death; who raise epidemics and send forth the pestilence; who shake the earth, convulse the sea, and agitate the air; who cause the thunders to roar, and the forked lightnings to issue from the clouds; who raise the tempests, and command the hurricanes that spread desolation over sea and land. Hence it is some man like Balaam, and not a woman like the Witch of Endor, who is consulted and called in to curse enemies, or tell the fate of battles; it is some man like Manasseh, and not a woman like Jezebel, who uses enchantments, practises witchcraft, and deals with

C

familiar spirits; it is some man like Simon Magus, and not
a woman like the Pythoness of Philippi, who bewitches the
people and secures gain by soothsaying; they are some men
like Jannes and Jambres, and not simply the wise women, who
withstand the missionaries and counteract their efforts; it is
some men like Elymas the Sorcerer, and not some women like
Herodias and Salome, who turn away the deputies or the
chiefs from the faith, and cease not to pervert the right ways
of the Lord. With them men are everything, women are
nothing. It shows the position long assigned to women in
this country, when they are credited with the power of the
supernatural. In those heathen isles they have no such
position assigned to them. There is no woman in those
islands, whether young or old, rich or poor, beautiful or ugly,
that is eligible to be a witch!

With a certain class of people it was believed that the
inhabitants of those islands, at least when the islands were
discovered, were living in a state of Arcadian simplicity; that
those children of nature were the happiest beings on earth;
that their lives were innocent as those of childhood; with few
wants, and those amply supplied by the bounties of providence;
and that they were objects of envy, but not of pity. This is
a very great mistake. Our greatest blessings when perverted
become our greatest curses. True religion is the greatest
blessing that is enjoyed by man, the source of his highest
happiness; but false religion is one of the greatest curses to
which he can be exposed, the source of his greatest misery.
Perhaps the worst element in the heathenism of the New
Hebrides is the system of witchcraft that exists among them.
It is a fearful bondage. It keeps the people under something
like a reign of terror. According to the popular creed, earth,

and air, and ocean, are teeming with spirits, all of them
malignant—they have no beneficent deities,—and the sacred
men are supposed to have full power over all the malignity of
the unseen world, and can direct it against whomsoever they
may think fit. Hence every one lives more or less in terror.
When Christianity was universally accepted on Aneityum, and
the power of the sacred men had ceased, as it certainly did
cease, the change to the people was marvellous. Men breathed
a different atmosphere. They all felt, if not the highest form
of liberty, the truly spiritual, at least a foretaste of this liberty.
In a very palpable sense they were all brought out of darkness
into light; and from the power of Satan unto God; from the
bondage of corruption into the glorious liberty of God's children. On this account Christianity, as drawn directly from
the Bible, is the greatest gift that can be conferred upon them,
the choicest blessing they can possibly receive.

CHAPTER V.

"So he brought down the people unto the water: and the Lord said unto Gideon, Every one that lappeth of the water with his tongue, as a dog lappeth, him shalt thou set by himself; likewise every one that boweth down upon his knees to drink. And the number of them that lapped putting their hand to their mouth were three hundred men: but all the rest of the people bowed down upon their knees to drink water."—JUDGES vii. 5, 6.

I NEVER understood these two verses till I went to Aneityum. In this country we never lap water like a dog; and when we put our hand to our mouth, we make a cup of the palm of our hand, and drink as if it were out of a small cup, in no way resembling the lapping of a dog: but these men lapped not with their tongue like a dog, but putting their hand to their mouth. However, shortly after I went to Aneityum I saw what appeared to me to give a satisfactory solution of the difficulty. I was standing one day by the side of a stream where it was crossed by a path: a native came hurrying along, but he stopped to drink; he did not, however, bow down upon his knees as most people do among us, who wish to drink heartily, nor did he lift the water to his mouth with his hand formed cup-like as we do; but he stooped till his head was within eighteen inches or so of the water; then he began to throw up the water into his mouth with his hand as fast as a dog could lap; and he looked, as near as might be, like a dog lapping. I said at once to myself, that is the way

Gideon's soldiers lapped. I had an opportunity scores of times afterwards, of seeing the natives drink in the same way; and I observed that, as a general rule, it was the strong, the vigorous, and the energetic who drank water in this way; never the feeble, the lazy, or the easy-going; and the inference that I drew respecting God's intentions towards Gideon and his army was this. The Lord wished to select the very best men in that army, and with them to accomplish the deliverance of Israel. Moreover, this selection was to be made in such a way, that those not chosen could have no ground of offence against Gideon, and hence could not be thrown into antagonism. The proclamation to depart before day of all who were fearful and afraid, relieved the army of 22,000 faint-hearted soldiers, leaving 10,000 men, presumably all mighty men of valour. But the Lord said that these were still too many for His purpose, and another test was named. The men were all to be taken to the water, and according to their mode of drinking they were to be divided. The *Well of Harod* was at hand, " gushing from the rocks which form the basis of Mount Gilboa." " It supplies a pool of clear water," says Canon Tristram, " fifty feet in diameter, and at this pool there is room for a large number to drink together." Here, then, Gideon must have tested his men. All the 10,000 except 300 bowed down upon their knees to drink. But the 300 lapped like a dog, putting their hand to their mouth. The Lord promised to Gideon that by those 300 He would deliver Israel. And, judging from what I have seen on Aneityum, I would infer that they were the very *élite* of the whole army, for courage, strength, activity, coolness, and the power of endurance; men who knew not the meaning of fear, and were totally ignorant of faint-heartedness; men who

possessed in the highest degree every soldier-like qualification;
men like the Gadites that joined David when he was in the
hold, who could handle shield and buckler, whose faces were
like the faces of lions, and were as swift as the roes upon the
mountains, and of whom it might be said, as David sung of
Saul and Jonathan, "they were swifter than eagles, they
were stronger than lions."

While God was delivering Israel miraculously, the task He
had appointed for these 300 men required special qualifications; hence there was nothing arbitrary in this apparently
simple mode of selecting the valiant 300; it was a means,
though never employed, so far as we know, either before or
since, that fully secured the end. By a principle of natural
selection, which man would never have thought of, it secured
the survival of the fittest. It was only men after the type
of David's mighties that could have accomplished the work
they were called upon to perform. When the three companies surrounded the camp, broke their pitchers, held
their lamps, blew their trumpets, and cried, "The sword of
the Lord and of Gideon," it was needful that their voices
should be like the voices of lions, to strike terror into the
hearts of their enemies; and when, hungry and weary, they
went up by the way of them that dwelt in tents, on the coast
of Nobah and Jogbehah, and smote the host of 15,000 men
in Karkor, when the host was secure, it was necessary that,
like Asahel, they should be light of foot as a wild roe; hence
their appearance was unexpected and terrific, and their
enemies fled; and when they tore the flesh of the princes
of Succoth with the thorns of the wilderness, and rased to
its foundation the tower of Penuel, in which the nobles
trusted, they were found in all these cases to be men of such

powers, that, according to God's promise, five of them could chase a hundred, and a hundred of them could put ten thousand to flight, for they were God's elect, and filled with His Spirit.

Since writing the above I observe that Dr. Kitto, in his note on this passage in his Pictorial Bible, has observed the same practice in the East. His remarks are so much to the point that I cannot do better than quote them. He says: "These two modes of action have been differently understood, and the first (the lapping) in particular has been the subject of various interpretations. The dog drinks by shaping the end of his long thin tongue into the form of a spoon, which it rapidly introduces into, and withdraws from, the water, throwing each time a spoonful of the fluid into his mouth. The tongue of man is not adapted to this use, and it is physically impossible for a man, therefore, to lap, literally, as a dog laps. The true explanation, probably, is that these men, instead of kneeling down to take a long draught, or successive draughts, from the water, employed their hands as the dog employs its tongue—that is, forming it into a hollow spoon, and dipping water with it from the stream. We have often seen it done, and the comparison to the lapping of a dog spontaneously occurred to our mind. Practice gives a peculiar tact in this mode of drinking, and the interchange of the hand between the water and the mouth is so rapidly managed as to be comparable to that of the dog's tongue in similar circumstances. Besides, the water is not usually sucked out of the hand into the mouth, but, by a peculiar knack, is jerked into the mouth before the hand is brought close to it, so that the hand is approaching with a fresh supply almost before the preceding has been swallowed ; this is another resemblance to the action of a dog's tongue. When travelling with small caravans, we have had opportunities of seeing both processes." He then shows that those knelt down to drink who had plenty of time, but that those to whom time was an object lapped like a dog; and concludes by saying, "This explanation may help to show how the distinction operated, and why those who 'lapped, putting their hand to their mouth,' were considered to evince an alacrity and readiness for action which peculiarly fitted them for the service on which Gideon was engaged."

Thus both the Antipodes and the Orient supply testimony as to the minute accuracy of the Scripture narrative; so that by the mouth of at least *two* witnesses every word of the Bible may be established.

CHAPTER VI.

SHIBBOLETH VERSUS SIBBOLETH.

" And the Gileadites took the passages of Jordan before the Ephraimites : and it was so, that when those Ephraimites which were escaped
said, Let me go over ; that the men of Gilead said unto him, Art thou
an Ephraimite ? If he said, Nay ; then said they unto him, Say now
Shibboleth ; and he said, Sibboleth : for he could not frame to pronounce
it right. Then they took him, and slew him at the passages of Jordan."
—JUDGES xii. 5, 6.

THE Gileadites, a portion of the half-tribe of Manasseh, had
lived for 300 years on the east side of the Jordan, and had
retained, as far as the sound of this word was concerned, the
original Hebrew pronunciation ; but the Ephraimites, living
for the same length of time on the west side of the river, had
lost entirely the old original sound, and had adopted a softer,
smoother pronunciation. In all living languages changes of
this kind are continually going on. The Gileadites were a
pastoral people, inhabiting a mountainous country, and living
remote from cities : hence their language would be the Doric
of Israel, and they would retain the strong primitive pronunciation. The Ephraimites lived in the very centre of
Canaan, and, next to the tribe of Judah, were the leading tribe
in Israel. And up to this time the ark, the one central altar,·
and the tabernacle were at Shiloh, within the boundaries of the
tribe of Ephraim. This city was the residence of the leading
priests ; it was the leading centre of religion, literature, and

civilization: hence the Ephraimites would naturally take a first place for refinement in speech and manners, and thus the stronger and rougher sound would become softer and more mellifluous—*sh* would become *s;* the letter *shin* would become *samech*. This would be the new and fashionable pronunciation; and it had become adopted by the whole tribe. The word *Shibboleth* means, first, an *ear of corn*, and next, a *river*. The crossing of the river would soon lead to the use of the word by the Ephraimites; the Gileadites would soon observe their pronunciation of the word, and thus secure an easy test for discovering their enemies. The Ephraimites, not knowing the Gileadite pronunciation, and not suspecting the use to be made of their answer, would easily fall into the trap thus laid for them. *Sh* is such a common sound with us, we have from 300 to 400 words in the English language commencing with *sh*, to say nothing of its frequent occurrences in the middle and end of words; and with our organs of speech the sound is so easily pronounced that we can hardly understand how any difficulty can be felt in its pronunciation. But I may remark that *sh* is not a common sound. So far as is known to me, the sound of *sh* is found in no language spoken in the South Seas. Certainly it is found in none of the dialects of the Malay-Polynesian language. It is not found in the Maori, the Samoan, the Tongan, the Raro-tongan, the Tahitian, nor the Hawaiian. It is not in the Fijian language, it is not in the Aneityumese; and, so far as I have observed, it is not found in any other of the Papuan languages. Dr. Kitto observes that *sh* is a very difficult sound to acquire by those who have not learned it in childhood; and hence the Ephraimites were unable to pronounce it, and evasion or escape from this test became impossible. We found this the case on Aneityum. The sound of *sh* is not found in the language; and the natives did not seem capable of acquiring the power to pronounce it. They never could pronounce English words containing this sound. The nearest they could come to shirt, ship, sheep, sheet, &c., was sirt, sip, seep, and seet. So that had the Aneityumese been with the Ephraimites on that memorable day, every one of them would have been slain at the fords of the Jordan; for not one of them could have said *Shibboleth*, every one of them would have said *Sibboleth*.

But we have a parallel case among ourselves. No Englishman can pronounce *ch* and *gh* as they are pronounced in Scotland. Ask an Englishman to say *loch*, and he says *lok*. Ask him to say *Waugh*, and he says *Wa;* or ask him to say *Gough*, and he says *Goff*.

But this process of change, such as that which took place among the Ephraimites we see going on daily under our own eyes in the South Sea Islands. As I have said the Malay-Polynesians have not *sh;* but except in one principal group, viz., that of Samoa, and two or three small groups, they have not even *s*. In all the other groups they use *h* instead of *s;* thus *tasi*, one, in Samoan, becomes *tahi*, one, in Maori, and *soa*, a friend, becomes *hoa*. And not only do they use the *h* instead of the *s*, but they cannot pronounce *s;* the nearest that a Maori can come to *sixpence*, is to say *hikapene*. And in the early stages of the New Zealand colony, one of the common jokes played upon the Maories by waggish *pakehas*, or white people, was to offer a native a tempting reward, if he would say, split a sixpence; and then to laugh at him in his hopeless attempts to pronounce the sentence. The Gileadites could not have devised a surer test to discover an Ephraimite than by asking him to say Shibboleth; for it was a physical impossibility for him to do so. The narrative is not a myth or a fiction, it is true to the first principles of language.

For three hundred years we have adopted *Shibboleth* as an English word, equivalent to *test*. And every party, both political and religious, has had its *Shibboleth;* its party test; some word or formula which expressed its distinctive principle, and hence every man who had the courage of his convictions and could not in conscience pronounce this *Shibboleth*, was according to the temper of the times, deprived of office, or place, or emolument, or privilege, or liberty, or life itself. Its operation has been good when it excluded the evil; but the reverse, as has often been the case, when it cut off the good.

CHAPTER VII. -

SAMSON AND THE FOXES AND FIREBRANDS, ETC.

"But it came to pass within a while after, in the time of wheat harvest, that Samson visited his wife with a kid; and he said, I will go in to my wife into the chamber: but her father would not suffer him to go in. And her father said, I verily thought that thou hadst utterly hated her; therefore I gave her to thy companion: is not her younger sister fairer than she? take her, I pray thee, instead of her. And Samson said concerning them, Now shall I be more blameless than the Philistines, though I do them a displeasure. And Samson went and caught three hundred foxes, and took firebrands, and turned tail to tail, and put a firebrand in the midst between two tails. And when he had set the brands on fire, he let them go into the standing corn of the Philistines, and burnt up both the shocks, and also the standing corn, with the vineyards and olives. Then the Philistines said, Who hath done this? And they answered, Samson, the son-in-law of the Timnite, because he had taken his wife, and given her to his companion. And the Philistines came up, and burnt her and her father with fire."—
JUDGES xv. 1-6.

"So Absalom dwelt two full years in Jerusalem, and saw not the king's face. Therefore Absalom sent for Joab, to have sent him to the king; but he would not come to him: and when he sent again the second time, he would not come. Therefore he said unto his servants, See, Joab's field is near mine, and he hath barley there; go and set it on fire. And Absalom's servants set the field on fire. Then Joab arose, and came to Absalom unto his house, and said unto him, Wherefore have thy servants set my field on fire? And Absalom answered Joab, Behold, I sent unto thee, saying, Come hither, that I may send thee to the king, to say, Wherefore am I come from Geshur? it had been good for me to have been there still: now therefore let me see the king's face; and if there be any iniquity in me, let him kill me. So Joab came to the king, and told him."—2 SAMUEL xiv. 28-33.

"And when he (the Levite) was come into his house, he took a knife, and laid hold on his concubine, and divided her, together with her bones, into twelve pieces, and sent her into all the coasts of Israel. And it was so, that all that saw it said, There was no such deed done nor seen from the day that the children of Israel came up out of the land of Egypt unto this day: consider of it, take advice, and speak your minds. Then all the children of Israel went out and gathered as one man unto the Lord in Mizpeh, four hundred thousand footmen. Then said the children of Israel, Tell us, how was this wickedness? And the Levite, the husband of the woman that was slain, answered and said, I came into Gibeah that belongeth to Benjamin, I and my concubine, to lodge. And the men of Gibeah rose against me, and beset the house round about me by night, and thought to have slain me; and my concubine have they forced, that she is dead. And I took my concubine, and cut her in pieces, and sent her throughout all the country of the inheritance of Israel; for they have committed lewdness and folly in Israel. Behold, ye are all the children of Israel; give here your advice and counsel.—JUDGES xix. 29, 30, and xx. 1-7.

" And the Spirit of God came upon Saul when he heard those tidings, and his anger was kindled greatly. And he took a yoke of oxen, and hewed them in pieces, and sent them throughout all the coasts of Israel by the hands of messengers, saying, Whosoever cometh not forth after Saul and after Samuel, so shall it be done unto his oxen. And the fear of the Lord fell upon the people, and they came out with one consent. And when he numbered them in Bezek, the children of Israel were three hundred thousand, and the men of Judah thirty thousand." —I SAMUEL xi. 6-8.

WHEN Samson's father-in-law had taken his wife and given her to another man, Samson did not remonstrate with him, or threaten him with legal proceedings. Neither did he go to the judge at Timnath, and cry, like the importunate widow, Avenge me of mine adversary. Such a course he no doubt regarded as unavailing. Neither did he, like the Strome Ferry rioters of our own time, violate the human law in order to vindicate the divine. In seeking redress he kept strictly within constitutional lines, within use and wont, within the law of the land. Hence when, on a beautiful harvest morning, the Philistines looked out and saw nothing for miles around but one unbroken conflagration, fields of wheat, vineyards, and olive-yards all crackling and blazing, or black, charred, and reduced to ashes, and when to the inquiry, Who hath done this? the answer was returned, Samson, the son-in-law of the Timnite, because he had taken his wife and given her to his companion, the authorities did not do as ours would have done, send out a strong body of police to apprehend and imprison the incendiary, they found no fault with Samson. But when the elders of the land met and took their seats in the gate of Timnath, they agreed unanimously, and at once, that the Timnite and his daughter should suffer for Samson's crime. And the punishment was summary, for before night, after the manner of the Philistines, they were both burned with fire.

A hundred and twenty-five years afterwards we find Absalom acting on the same principle towards Joab. Once and again Absalom sends a messenger to Joab, asking Joab to visit him. But Joab, on the way back from Geshur, had evidently discovered the character, principles, and aims of Absalom, and had therefore no wish to introduce him to the court, that with David's other sons he should be a chief ruler; and hence refused to visit Absalom. Upon this Absalom does not write him a letter of remonstrance, or call upon himself, as we might have done, and reproach him for want of friendship or courtesy; but he at once sends his servants to burn Joab's field of barley; and this brought to him the commander-in-chief, and secured the interview which he so much desired, and Joab accepted his explanation as to the burning of the barley.

Now this is not our way of doing things; but such things as these are common occurrences on Aneityum; they are part of the common law of the land, a necessary part of their criminal and ordinary jurisprudence. If a native finds himself aggrieved, he does not go to the offender and expostulate with him, nor does he go to the chief and lodge an information against the offender, but he goes and commits some injury on some one's property, either on the offender's or on somebody's else, as the case may be, in order to arouse public attention, and to lead people to inquire, Who has done this? and for what purpose has it been done? In this way publicity is given to the grievance, and public sympathy is secured for the aggrieved; the evil is redressed, and the aggrieved man is satisfied. Had the injured man complained to the chief, his complaint might have been neglected. But when public opinion is brought to bear strongly on a grievance, redress is almost sure to follow. The natives resort now and again to this mode of redress in all matters, from the most trifling to the most important. On one occasion I found a fine bunch of bananas cut down in my garden, and left lying on the ground, not stolen. On inquiring who had done this, I found that it had been done by a young lad who had once lived on our premises. When I sent for him he never denied the deed; and when I asked him why he had done this—"I did it," he said, "because So-and-so"—two lads living with us—"had said so-and-so about me, which was not true, and so broke my heart; and I did this that you might ask me about it, and reprove them." But I said, "Why did not you come to me and tell me about it yourself?" "Oh," said he, "*tup netho unyima nigki*"—this is our custom—this is our way of doing things.

On another occasion the proprietor of a whaling establishment sent me a letter, telling me that N——, a native who lived about a mile from my station, had stolen a musket from a white man in his employment, and asking me to assist him in recovering it. I sent for the man, and inquired about the stealing of the musket. He never denied the theft; yea, he seemed rather desirous that publicity should be given to the fact. When I asked him why he had stolen the musket, he frankly said: "You know that last year I had charge of one of the whale-boats; but this year Mr. So-and-so has taken it from me, and given it to another man, which was not fair to me. It broke my heart; I was angry, and I stole the musket, that they might send after me and inquire, and then I could tell how badly I had been used." The musket was returned, but the object was gained. The community were thus made aware of N——'s grievances; public opinion was freely expressed in his favour, and the young man's heart was relieved and comforted.

On another occasion one of our very best natives, who had been living, both he and his wife, for a long time on our premises, supplied another example of this custom. He had been acting as cook, and his wife as housemaid. He had given great satisfaction; but all at once he began to act very strangely. My wife could not comprehend him; her patience became quite worn out with him; and one day she said to me, "I do wish you would speak to So-and-so. I do not know what is come over him of late, he acts so strangely. He never actually refuses to do what I bid him, but he turns his back to me when I speak to him, and scarcely ever gives me a civil answer; and this morning, while his wife was passing the kitchen door, he threw a stone at her, and struck her on the head. It looks to me as if he were going out of his mind." I then took the native into my study, and asked him what the meaning of this conduct was, so different from all his past

D

conduct. "Oh," said he, "I wanted you to ask me. You know that I have been a long time about this house, and I am anxious for a change. I would like if you would appoint me to be a teacher somewhere." I said, "If that is all there will be no difficulty. If you go on with your work here, and wait for three months, till I am changing the teachers, I will then appoint you to a school. But," said I, "why did you not come and tell me that you wanted a change?" "Oh, this is our way of doing things," he said—"*Ek atimi imtita atimi ainyak*"—"I am a very timid man, and I did not like to speak; but I did these things that you might ask me." He resumed his work, and gave us entire satisfaction, and at the end of three months I appointed him to be a teacher.

I have known a man, whose wife had proved unfaithful to him, actually go and live with some worthless woman, not from any love of the woman, but simply to call public attention to the conduct of his own wife, and to evoke public sympathy for himself in connection with his domestic troubles.

After we found out this custom we had no difficulties with the natives about it. In the first years of the mission we were often puzzled with the conduct of natives; they were sullen, and wayward, and troublesome, and we knew not what was the matter with them; but after we discovered the existence of this custom, when any native began to act in any strange sort of way, especially if he was living on or near the mission premises, I at once took him into my study, and asked him, in as kindly a tone as possible, as to who or what had broken his heart. Sometimes he would own to nothing, and then I talked seriously, but not angrily, to him for acting thus, and generally with good results; but if it was owing to something that somebody had said or done, the grievance was inquired into, the injured man was satisfied, and the matter ended.

In a rude or corrupt state of society, where judges have little fear of God, and little regard for man; where the strong arm of the law and the firm hand of justice can be put into motion only with extreme difficulty; when it requires a strong expression of public opinion, and an open display of public sympathy, before the redress of any serious grievance can be obtained, this mode of proceeding has many obvious advantages; and no doubt was resorted to on that account, though not for a moment to be thought of in a country like ours. Had Samson laid his grievance before any one of the Lords of the Philistines, it is doubtful if the slightest attention would have been paid to his complaint. "A family squabble," he would have said; "go and settle it among yourselves." But when a whole country-side rose up burning with anger to inquire into the cause of this incendiarism, the Lords of the Philistines were suddenly aroused to a sense of their danger, and retribution swift and terrible overtook the delinquents. Joab's political sagacity discovered the danger to the state that lurked in the fair face, the smooth tongue, and the comely person of Absalom, and his aim was to keep him from the court as long as possible; hence Absalom might have sent twenty messengers to Joab instead of two, without securing a visit from him. But when all Jerusalem knew that Absalom's servants had burnt Joab's field of barley, it was at once known that Absalom had some serious grievance against Joab, and the cautious statesman found that his Fabian tactics, his masterly inactivity, his do nothing policy, would no longer serve his purpose, that at whatever hazard he must visit the irrepressible and popular

prince. The Levite might have gone to Shiloh and represented his wrong, both to Phinehas and to the whole college
of priests, but no redress would have been given him; the
arm of justice was weak. There was not only no king, but
no judge in Israel at that time. Joshua was dead, and
Othniel had not been called to office. But when the messengers went through all the twelve tribes of Israel, and
exhibited the mangled fragments of the Levite's concubine
to the elders of every city as they sat in the gate, a universal
shudder was felt; they all knew that some terrible crime had
been committed, and the Israelites, from Dan to Beersheba,
came up as one man to Mizpeh. It was on lines of policy
similar to this that Saul acted when he slew the yoke of oxen,
hewed them in pieces, and sent them through all the coasts
of Israel; the people recognised under this action the terrible
danger to which the nation was exposed, and a unanimous
and instant response was given to the summons sent to them in
the name of Samuel and of Saul. The Midlothian Campaign
of Mr. Gladstone, in 1880, which overturned the Beaconsfield
government, was as nothing compared with the action of the
Levite and of the newly anointed king: the oratory of Gladstone, in its effects, was like the striking of a lucifer match;
the actions of these two men, in their results, were like
explosions of dynamite.

But some may say that the cases I have adduced from the
customs on Aneityum are trifling compared with those I have
referred to in the Bible. This is quite true. But then the
same laws, that regulate the form and movements of a drop
of water, operate equally on the whole ocean. Such cases as
those I have selected from the Bible could not occur on
Aneityum; the people are too few, and the time I have

referred to, only a quarter of a century, is too short, whereas from the time of the Levite till that of Joab and Absalom was a period of nearly 500 years. While the cases recorded in the sacred narrative were typical as regarded the customs, they were exceptional in degree, and not of everyday occurrence. It was not every night that the wife of a stranger, a Levite, a minister of the sanctuary, on his way to the house of God, was forcibly taken from him, abused, and murdered, in the public streets of one of the principal cities of Israel while the elders took no notice of the crime. It was not every day that a judge of Israel, of the type of Samson, impulsive and irrepressible, had his newly married wife taken from him and given to another man, while the authorities never once inquired into the case. It was not every day, when a king had been newly anointed over God's people, that the king of Ammon laid siege to one of their principal cities, and through the elders of that city sent a reproachful taunt to all Israel. And it was not every day that there was a rupture between the favourite son of the king and the commander of all the forces of Israel. But it is only such cases as these that are put in record by the sacred writers. The custom, however, was no doubt in constant existence, and minor cases of it would be of daily occurrence. Human nature is the same in all ages; like causes produce like effects; and like states of society will produce similar customs. The Bible is true to the principles of human nature; hence the most unlikely events, and the most incredible-like statements, recorded in sacred history, can be paralleled in the most unexpected quarters at the present day.

CHAPTER VIII.

MICAH'S MOTHER CURSING.

"And there was a man of mount Ephraim, whose name was Micah. And he said unto his mother, The eleven hundred shekels of silver that were taken from thee, about which thou cursedst, and spakest of also in mine ears, behold, the silver is with me ; I took it. And his mother said, Blessed be thou of the Lord, my son."—JUDGES xvii. 1, 2.

THIS case of cursing is unique. So far as we remember no other case of the kind is recorded in the Bible. But yet at the end of 3300 years we find the very same practice existing in the New Hebrides.

On one occasion my wife and I were on a visit to Mr. and Mrs. Copeland, on Futuna, an island fifty miles north-east of Aneityum. One morning at daylight we were awakened by a tremendous shouting noise outside the mission premises, and looking out we saw an elderly woman screaming at the top of her voice, in the most angry tones. As the Futuna language is totally different from the language spoken on Aneityum, we did not understand what the woman was saying; we only heard that she was loud, angry, and terribly in earnest. However, when we met our friends at breakfast, for the sake of health always the first thing attended to in the mission families on the islands, we learned that all this excitement had been caused by some stealing during the night. Some property had been *taken*, as Micah euphoniously expressed it in his mother's case, out of the woman's house during the night, and as soon as she discovered her loss, as the custom is on Futuna, she proclaimed it by cursing. With all the power of voice that she could command, she was cursing the thief; imploring every one of the Futuna gods to pour down their most awful judgments on the head of the poor culprit; that so the offender, fearing the awful curses, might restore the stolen goods. Ignorant and superstitious people fear nothing so much as curses and imprecations of this kind. In former times in this country, it was the fear that their imprecations would be followed by judgments, that gave reputed witches such power in levying blackmail, or in securing good presents. In this case the woman cried loud that they might hear her, and with intense earnestness that they might fear her; and she was successful, for before our breakfast was over the stolen property was restored. The scene was now totally changed, anger gave way to joy; the crime of stealing was entirely overlooked, and the warmest blessings were invoked upon the head of the thief, because the stolen property was returned. We have no such custom as this on Aneityum; but then the Aneityumese are Papuans, descendants of Ham; whereas the Futunese are Malays, descendants of Shem, the same as the Israelites. Micah's mother had evidently acted very much as they do on Futuna. One morning when she rose, she found that the chest containing her treasure had been broken open, and the bags containing her 1100 shekels of silver had been taken away. An old divine says that " outward losses drive good people to their prayers, but bad people to their curses." This is the effect, as we see, among the heathen on Futuna, and Micah's mother had strong heathen proclivities, she was like old clothes tainted with the plague; as good old Bishop Hall says of

her, "After all her airing in the desert, she will still smell
of Egypt." So as soon as she discovers her loss, the curse
and not the prayer rises to her lips. So hastening to the
door, and lifting up her voice to its highest pitch, she awakens
the whole household. Micah starts from his bed, and her
words ring in his ears till both of them tingle, as she pours
forth against the unknown thief a string of maledictions, as
terrible as those contained in the 27th chapter of Deuteronomy.
Micah hearing those dreadful curses, and knowing his guilt,
was struck with more than superstitious fear, for his conscience bore witness against him, and, dreading lest some
terrible judgment from God should overtake him, he went to
his mother and confessed the crime, and told her that the
eleven hundred shekels of silver, about which she had uttered
those dreadful curses, were with him, and that he would
restore them. The poor woman, like her sister on Futuna,
as much overcome with joy as she had been carried away
with anger, pours forth her benedictions upon her son, utterly
forgetful of the theft, and thinking only of the restitution;
and, as if afraid that her curses would take effect, she hastens
to intercept them, and says, "Blessed be thou of Jehovah,
my son." Some commentators think that Micah's mother
adjured her son, or put him to his oath about the money,
and thus extorted the confession from him; but as appears
to us, the custom on Futuna affords a much more natural
explanation. Thus in a rocky islet, "far amid the melan-
choly main," comes forth a witness for the historic truth and
accuracy of the Old Testament Scriptures. Even there "the
tenants of the rock, in accents rude," all unconsciously, bear
testimony to the truth of the inspired Record. Do they not
deserve the Bible in return for such a service?

CHAPTER IX.

A SINGLE FLEA.

"After whom is the king of Israel come out? after whom dost thou pursue? after a dead dog, after a *flea?* "—I SAMUEL xxiv. 14.

" For the king of Israel is come out to seek a *flea*, as when one doth hunt a partridge on the mountains."—I SAMUEL xxvi. 20.

THIS is one of those slight allusions which clearly prove that the Bible was written in the East. In this country one royal personage speaking to another would never have employed the illustration, which David once and again used in speaking to Saul. But there the flea was so well known, that a reference to it was quite natural. In this country its name is unmentionable in the hearing of ears polite. In the East fleas are so plentiful and so well known, that Kitto says even ladies have no delicacy in speaking openly about them in public companies. Canon Tristram says, " Fleas are the great pests both of the inhabitants and of travellers in the Holy Land, and it is impossible to keep free from them. They are the only vermin towards which the natives have a thorough animosity, and which can disturb even Moslem equanimity. Their numbers force the Bedouins to change their camps more frequently than they otherwise would, and if the luckless traveller incautiously pitches upon the site of a camp which has been deserted even for a month, he is soon driven away by the swarms of fleas, which rise from the dust and the refuse stubble on the ground, where they are concealed in myriads."

In New Zealand, New Caledonia, the New Hebrides, and in all the South Sea Islands fleas are one of the greatest pests, so that one chief speaking to another as David did to Saul would excite no surprise. As in the East even ladies can talk about them and not be accused of vulgarity. When we went first to New Zealand, one morning, shortly after our settlement on the Manawatu river, on looking out, I was shocked to see one of the principal chiefs of the district standing with his blanket spread out on a fence before him, and he himself busily engaged catching and killing fleas! But as time went on my sensibilities on this point became very much blunted : such or similar exhibitions were far too common to excite any surprise. These insects breed in the ground, especially in the sand, and during certain months in the year no amount of cleanliness can eradicate them, although it can do much to keep them bearable. On Aneityum, and I suppose it will be the same elsewhere, about the month of November, when the weather becomes warm and dry, it makes the place too hot for the fleas, and they nearly disappear for some months. As in Palestine, deserted houses soon become very much infested with these vermin, and any person who unawares enters one of them, comes out with quite a colony of fleas adhering to him. On the other hand, when a native erects a new house, and gets the floor covered with fresh, clean cocoa-nut mats, every native in the neighbourhood wishes to come and sleep in that house, it is for some weeks so comfortable.

There are two species of fleas on Aneityum ; a native and a European. They are about the same size and the same colour, but quite distinct in appearance. The native flea has long straddling hind-legs, and appears to belong rather to the creeping than the "jumping cattle." The European flea is a comparatively recent importation. It was brought to the island in this way: One of the first vessels that anchored in the harbour of Aneityum had a dog on board. A native stole the dog, and carried it off inland : but unhappily he got more than he bargained for; he got the fleas which it harboured as well as the dog ! and the fleas have remained, multiplied, and increased ever since. It is curious how insect, as well as other forms of life, are extended over the earth. One of the Wesleyan missionaries told me that, when they went to Tonga, there were no mosquitoes there; but on one occasion when the missionaries were assembled at their annual conference, one of them looked out at a window, and there was a cloud of mosquitoes in front of the house. Whence they came no one could tell. They had been wafted no doubt by the wind from some other island or group. But they maintained their footing there ever after.

The existence of fleas in those islands is a fact, as in Palestine, that cannot be ignored; no prudent reserve can conceal the fact that they are one of the household pests of the South Seas. But although, while with native houses and natives living as they do, it is extremely difficult to abate the nuisance, yet in the mission-houses, by care, cleanliness, and great activity, if they cannot be quite extirpated, they can at least be reduced to something like a "vanishing quantity," and kept, something like the Canaanites of old, under tribute; and if still a living, yet not a reigning power, occasionally irritating, but never dangerous neighbours.

But there are no bugs on the islands. If they do chance

to be brought, as they sometimes are, by vessels, they are immediately killed out by the cockroaches, a species of beetle which buzzes but never bites any human being; so that had Mrs. Carlyle lived, not in Chelsea, but in the New Hebrides, she might have had occasion to send out her maids to look the bedclothes on the fences; but she would not have been required to commence those energetic crusades against the bugs in 5 Cheyne Row which she describes so graphically in her letters.

Men of genius have the rare faculty of dignifying not only humble, but even disgusting objects. When Burns proposed publishing his "Address to a Louse, on Seeing one on a Lady's Bonnet at Church," Mrs. Dunlop and all his lady friends strongly opposed his intentions; but genius prevailed over prudence; he published the poem, and criticism and posterity have approved of his resolution. It was only a man of Lord Beaconsfield's genius that could stand up in the House of Lords, and tell that august assembly, that in comparison with the enormous wealth of this country, the National Debt was a mere *flea bite*, and thus convert an expression, otherwise vulgar, to one of classical propriety. So it was the poet in David, and not the prince, that seized this humble, and rather coarse proverb, and, by the unconscious touch of his genius, raised it up to dignity and elegance. He expressed his humility in tones of honest genuine pathos, by comparing himself, in the first instance, to a dead dog and a flea; and in the second to a partridge and a flea; but on both occasions the *flea* stands prominently out, as the object of comparison. David was so harmless, and, in his own estimation, so despicable, that he says: "After whom is the king of Israel come out ?" He is not come out in search of royal game; he is not hunting lions or bears; he is not even deer stalking; he is pursuing a dead dog, hunting a partridge upon the mountains; he is come out to seek a flea, a single flea. "A creature," says Matthew Henry, "which (as some have observed), if it be sought, is not easily found; if it be found, is not easily caught; and if it be caught, is a poor prize, especially for a prince."

It is recorded to the disgrace of one of the late Roman emperors, that he occupied a good part of his time in killing flies with a bodkin, and that on one occasion, when a nobleman asked one of the pages if the Emperor had any company in his room, the page said: "No! not even a single fly."

We smile at the game laws in Tahiti, and the royal hunts as practised there before the introduction of Christianity. In Ellis's "Polynesian Researches" a graphic picture exhibits a view of royalty while enjoying this privilege. There were no horses on the island; but when the king and queen travelled, they were always carried on men's shoulders, with their feet hanging down in front, over the breasts of the men who were carrying them respectively; and they possessed the exclusive privilege of hunting over the heads of the men; their heads were the royal preserves set apart as special hunting ground for the king and queen of Tahiti, and they were privileged to eat all the game that they caught.

The natives of Aneityum can employ low and undignified comparisons, without intending or wishing to be vulgar, and without really being so. One day my wife was giving a little girl a lesson in the letters, and to see that she was not learning them by rote, she began to try her on them crosswise, by pointing to them in different directions. When she pointed to j, as the pencil she was using was not very sharp, the girl evidently was not sure whether she was pointing to j or to k, and

said : " Do you mean the one with the *fly dung* on its head ? "
referring to the dot above the *j.* She afterwards found that
the girl's mother, when teaching her, had employed this
homely illustration to assist her memory; an illustration
original to us, but one of the most obvious to a native,
inasmuch as greatly to the annoyance of both natives and
foreign residents, at least those who have any responsibility
about cleaning, especially the cleaning of windows. Those
troublesome insects, wherever they alight, leave marks without
number, like the dots above the letters *i* and *j*, and which are
especially visible on glass.

Burns is the only poet who has immortalised a *louse*, and
fixed it as a gem in our national literature, "to point a
moral," while the verse, in which that lesson has been incul-
cated, has been perhaps more frequently quoted than any
other verse he ever wrote. Lord Beaconsfield is the only
orator who has immortalised a *flea-bite*, and left it to sparkle
as a classical proverb in all time to come, after having employed it as the most successful argument ever brought forth
in the defence of reckless and extravagant national expendi-
ture. And David was the only sacred writer who selected
the detested *flea* as an illustration, and by skilfully using it
once and again exorcised the evil spirit from the soul of Saul,
gave it a place in the pages of inspiration, and made it to be
a vehicle of spiritual instruction to all generations. Verily
God hath chosen the base things of the world, and things
which are despised, and things which are not, to bring to
nought things that are, that no flesh should glory in His
presence.

The flea seems still to cleave to the lips of Oriental princes.
When Tawhiao, the Maori king, was in this country, he was

interviewed by one of the staff of the *Pall Mall Gazette.*
During the process his majesty fell asleep, much to the
chagrin of the interviewer. When he woke up, and found
his unwelcome visitor still there, Tawhiao said to the offended
journalist, " I say, sir, you are as troublesome as a flea, and
as persevering." " If the Maori monarch had been a fashionable wit of the last century," said a writer to the press, " he
could scarcely have turned out a neater epigram." It is
doubtful, however, if the interviewer, who had perhaps never
seen a flea in his life, would understand the force of the
simile ; he would certainly not do so as clearly as Saul understood David. But this form of speech came easily and
naturally from the lips of Tawhiao ; and to any one who, like
myself, had lived eight years in New Zealand, and a good
part of that time in the interior, and who had slept many
a night in a *Maori whare,* or native hut, and had known by
experience the habits of such bedfellows—to such the illustration, though homely, would seem pat and pithy.

General Gordon too could use the contemptible insect with
good effect. " When Sebastapol fell the Russians," he said,
" carried off everything from the vile place, literally everything, but rubbish and *fleas.*"

CHAPTER X.

"And the Philistines came up yet again, and spread themselves in the valley of Rephaim. And when David inquired of the Lord, he said, Thou shalt not go up; but fetch a compass behind them, and come upon them over against the mulberry-trees. And let it be, when thou hearest the sound of a going in the tops of the mulberry-trees, that then thou shalt bestir thyself: for then shall the Lord go out before thee, to smite the host of the Philistines. And David did as the Lord had commanded him."—2 SAMUEL v. 22-25; and 1 CHRONICLES xiv. 13-16.

THE Hebrew word *becâîm,* translated *mulberry,* is generally understood now to be the same as our poplar or aspen tree. "There is every reason to believe," says Dr. Tristram, "that the mulberry here means the aspen." The eminently sound and sagacious John Brown of Haddington, the first, and, considering his advantages, the greatest of all the Browns, says, "By a sound, made no doubt by angels, on the tops of those trees in the valley of Rephaim, was David warned when to attack the Philistines." This was a natural explanation a hundred and more years ago. But there does not appear to us to be any occasion for calling in angelic agency here; no mention is made of angels in the text, and the sound of a going might, we think, be produced by ordinary agencies. We have no wish to follow in the wake of the so-called higher criticism, and eliminate the supernatural out of nearly every portion of the Biblical narrative; but neither have we any wish to call in the supernatural where the natural appears, as in this case, to be sufficient. God is ever sparing in His putting forth of miraculous or supernatural energy. Although He "is free to work," as the Westminster Confession says, "without, above, and against means, at His pleasure; yet, in His ordinary providence, He maketh use of them." According to the most approved translation, Psalm civ. 4, "Who maketh His angels spirits;" should be rendered, "Who maketh winds His angels or messengers." Now, as appears to us, winds were quite sufficient, under the ordinary providence of God, to cause the sound of a going to be heard in the tops of the trees. I have read somewhere, though I cannot remember in what book, that the mulberry or aspen did not grow near the sea shore, or in the Philistian territory; but in the high table land, and in the valleys in the neighbourhood of Jerusalem. Assuming this to be the case, our explanation is simple and natural. The sound of these leaves, when moved by a light breeze, would be a phenomenon unknown to the Philistian soldiery. The night wind blowing upon the groves of aspen trees, with their tremulous leaves, would produce such a sudden and, to them, unwonted sound as might be easily believed to be the tread of a numerous and powerful enemy. At this moment they were so timid and suspicious, that the sound of a shaken leaf would chase them, and they would flee. Encamped, as the Philistines were, in an enemy's country, and in the very locality where they had formerly been defeated, and that enemy, too, still under the command of David, a man so able and courageous, so noted for skill and prowess—for skill in devising stratagems, and determination in carrying them out; a man who, ever since the day he slew Goliath, had been a terror to the Philistines; a man whose name the Philistian mothers had ever since invoked as a terror with which to frighten their children into quietness, when they could not

E

otherwise still their crying; just as, in ages long after, it is said the Oriental mothers stilled their crying children by threatening them with the name of Richard Cœur de Lion. In these circumstances, when David, by the command of God, who knew the end from the beginning, and knew at what time the wind would blow, had led his men round to the rear of the Philistian host, and was waiting the divinely appointed signal—when the Philistines had newly set the middle watch, and all was again still and quiet, suddenly there springs up a gentle breeze; on a thousand aspen trees the leaves quiver, watchmen are startled; it is like the sound of a multitude; they give the alarm, the half-sleeping soldiers awake. What is this sound on the tops of the trees? They are startled and panic-stricken. In another instant from behind the army, from the quarter least of all expected, a tremendous shout arises. David's seven-and-thirty mighties, at the utmost pitch of their stentorian voices, cry out, "The sword of Jehovah and of David!" and the whole Israelitish host prolong the echo, and rush down with irresistible impetuosity on the Philistines, upon whom the terror of the Lord has now fallen, and they are fleeing down the valleys towards the plain in breathless haste and tumultuous confusion. David and his men pursue them with resistless force and with irrepressible ardour, and smite them down from Gibeon as far as Gazer. The victory was complete, and so thoroughly was the Philistine power broken, that it was many a long day before the five lords durst again lift up their heads, or attempt an attack upon Israel.

On Aneityum there are no aspen trees, but the gentle breeze, in a quiet night, stirring the leaflets of the cocoa-nut palm, produces a sound that would not be unlike the going in the tops of the mulberry trees; it is a sound exactly like that of a heavy shower of rain. To a stranger the illusion is so complete that the rustling is often mistaken for the rain. When I went to Aneityum in 1852, I left Mrs. Inglis at Anelgauhat with Mrs. Geddie, and Mr. Geddie and I went round to Aname to my station, that we might erect two rooms of a weather-boarded house, which I had brought from New Zealand. We had to build a stone foundation before we could erect the frame. Although it was in the beginning of July, and hence the middle of winter there, yet the weather was fine, and the days hot, and working hard all day under a tropical sun, a kind of labour too, to which I had not for a long time been accustomed, when night came I felt very tired. We slept in the house of Amosa, the Samoan teacher, which stood in the midst of a grove of cocoa-nut trees. On the second or third night, when we went to bed, the evening was clear and calm, not a breath of wind was moving the trees. It had been blowing a fresh trade wind during the day, but, as it often happens, it had calmed down before sunset. During the night I happened to awake; and lo! as appeared to me, it was raining heavily; how glad I felt! Now, thought I, the weather is broken; there is heavy rain, I shall get a good rest to-morrow, and I do need it. I turned myself, and fell asleep with pleasing hopes. At daybreak, shortly after six o'clock, I again awoke, and heard Amosa and his household singing their hymn at family worship. When they had finished, I arose and looked out at the window, and there, to my great disappointment, instead of a pouring wet morning and a day's rest, as I had expected, I was forcibly reminded of Thomson's well-known lines—

" But yonder comes the powerful king of day,
    Rejoicing in the east ; "

the earth flooded with his light, and another hard, toilsome
day's work before me, under the rays of this tropical burning
sun.   The supposed rain during the night was only the sound
of the cocoa-nut leaflets moved by a gentle breeze, resembling
the going in the tops of the mulberries.

Twelve years later, in 1864, and about the same season
of the year, the Rev. James D. Gordon, afterwards murdered
by a native of Eromanga, arrived at Aneityum from Nova
Scotia.   He landed at Anelgauhat, and was occupying a bedroom at the end of the printing-office, at a short distance
from the mission-house.   One beautifully clear, calm night,
shortly after his arrival, he went to bed as usual, but some
time during the night he awoke, and heard, as seemed to
him, a heavy rain.   "What a pity it is," he said to himself,
"that that valuable box of goods of mine was left outside,
and not put into the boat-house, where it would have been
kept dry; it will get thoroughly soaked with this rain.   I
must get up at once and see what can be done."   So up
he got in an instant, dressed himself as quickly as possible,
threw on his waterproof, buttoned it up to his chin, got
his umbrella, put his thumb on the spring, ready to put it
up the moment he got out; he then opened the door, and
was about to sally forth, when, lo! to his utter surprise,
there was no rain, nothing was to be seen but a cloudless
sky, the stars shining, and "the moon walking in brightness,"
the island and its inhabitants silent as the grave, and no
sound to be heard but the sea breaking on the reef.   The
supposed rain was nothing but the rustling sound of the

cocoa-nut leaflets, the sound of the midnight breeze playing with the feathery palm. The resemblance is so complete that hundreds of times we have listened to the sound, and if there was any object to be versed by knowing which was which, we had to look out at the window, in order to satisfy ourselves as to whether the sound was caused by the wind or the rain. To me therefore it does not appear in the least necessary to suppose that there was anything supernatural in the sound of the going in the tops of the mulberry trees. In this instance God made the winds His angels or messengers. The supernatural was in God instructing David to make a compass to come in behind the Philistian camp, and await the appointed signal. This, in the exercise of implicit faith, he did, and returned a triumphant conqueror.

CHAPTER XI.

" He shall give His angels charge over thee, to keep thee in all thy ways. They shall bear thee up in their hands, lest thou dash thy foot against a stone."—PSALM xci. 11, 12.

" Then the devil taketh Him up into the holy city, and setteth Him on a pinnacle of the temple, and saith unto Him, If Thou be the Son of God, cast Thyself down; for it is written, He shall give His angels charge concerning Thee; and in their hands they shall bear Thee up, lest at any time Thou dash Thy foot against a stone."—MATTHEW iv. 5, 6.

" And he brought Him to Jerusalem, and set Him on a pinnacle of the temple, and said unto Him, If Thou be the Son of God, cast Thyself down from hence : for it is written, He shall give His angels charge over Thee, to keep Thee : and in their hands they shall bear Thee up, lest at any time Thou dash Thy foot against a stone."—LUKE iv. 9-11.

SATAN can quote Scripture very glibly, but he is a very unsound, and a very unsafe expositor. He wants honesty, truth, and moral principle. He quotes incorrectly, and he then misapplies. He quoted incorrectly, by omitting the words, "in all thy ways," which limits the promise to a condition, and then he makes it an unconditional promise. "In all thy ways" clearly indicates that it was when employed in lawful duty that this help and protection would be afforded ; but not if He had presumptuously, without any call, cast Himself down from the pinnacle of the temple. As Hengstenberg says : "The language in both of the two verses does not apply to dangers which one seeks, but only to such dangers as meet the righteous man unsought, in his course through life."

Abraham's servant said: "I being in the way, the Lord led me." King William, the Prince of Orange, according to Lord Macaulay, recognised this principle very distinctly, when Bishop Walker of Derry was shot as he was needlessly exposing himself. When the King heard of his death, he was very angry, and said: "He had no call to expose himself, and hence no right to expect God's protection. It is totally different with me, my duty calls me to expose myself; and I have a right to trust to the divine protection: it was not so with him." The Bishop accepted the New Theology as taught by Satan, and lost his life: the King held fast by the Old Theology of the Psalmist, honoured God, escaped danger, and saved his country.

I have read an anecdote of one of the Fathers of the Secession Church to the following effect: One Sabbath day he had preached on the ministration of angels, from Hebrews i. 14. After the service was over, his mind became seriously exercised with doubts about the truth of the doctrine, as he had never had any personal experience on the subject. While thus ruminating, he was unexpectedly called to visit a sick person. After he had spoken and prayed, he was leaving the house, and was about to descend by an outside stair, on which there was no railing; he turned to the wrong side of the stair, and instead of going down the steps, as he expected, he was suddenly precipitated on the other side. But before he reached the ground, he felt like a hand catching him, and placing him gently and safely on his feet. From that night till his dying day he firmly believed that the hand that saved him was that of an angel, and he had no longer any doubt about the doctrine he had been preaching, that the angels are "all ministering spirits, sent forth to minister to them who shall be heirs of salvation." Much to the same effect may be found in an interesting book on "The Ministration of Angels," by that good old Puritan, Isaac Ambrose, author of a still better known book, entitled " First, Middle, and Last Things."

But my object in citing this passage is to illustrate it by a practice that prevails on Aneityum, which suggests a simple explanation of the text; and which, I think, it is probable, also existed in Palestine. Most commentators think that the expression, "they shall bear thee up in their hands," refers to the conduct of mothers or nurses holding up children when they are commencing to walk. I rather think it refers to the walking of full grown men, needing help or protection, cases such as our missionary experience can supply. In the first years of our mission, Mr. Geddie and I usually made a visit round the island once a year, taking with us a large party of the most influential Christian natives. We visited every settlement, and held a mission service at each, and the Christian natives distributed themselves and talked to the heathen. These visits occupied the most of a week each time. Sometimes a wet day or a wet night intervened, and then the roads became soft and slippery. In these cases two strong men would come to the help of each of us. One on each side, they would grasp our arms and half carry us up the steep and slippery paths, and sometimes also as we went down on the other side of a ridge ; their object was to hasten our progress and ease our toil; but especially to keep us from falling. This was a common practice with them. But the most notable instance of the kind occurred a short time before I left the Islands. Mr. Annand had been appointed to what was formerly Dr. Geddie's station. It had been vacant for a twelvemonth, during which time I had taken charge of it. I stayed a month

with Mr. Annand, introducing him to the people and to the
work. We visited every school on that side of the island, and
examined every scholar, and as every native was at school, it
involved the examination of every individual on that side of
the island. We were everywhere well received, and kindly
treated, but I shall notice only one special case as illustrative
of our text. We had fixed our headquarters at a place called
Umej, a settlement on the shore. One day we made rather a
long journey inland to a district called Anumej, to visit several
schools in that direction. Our path lay along the banks of
a beautiful stream, which we had frequently to cross. The
valley of Anumej is one of the largest and most beautiful on
Aneityum, and opens up into a most magnificent panorama,
which in the far distant pre-historic, or rather pre-Adamite
times, must have been the crater of some tremendous volcano,
some ten or twelve miles it may be from the one margin to the
other, but the whole interior from the bottom to the topmost
verge was covered with the densest forest, and the trees all
clothed with foliage of the freshest green. Igneous or
aqueous agencies, or both, had forced an opening to the
sea, which now constitutes the valley. As it was nearly
twenty years since I had visited that district with Mr.
Geddie, I had forgotten the distances, and when we had
finished our labours, I found that the day was farther on, and
the road to Umej a good deal longer, than I had calculated
upon. It had also come on a wet day. The road too was only
a narrow native footpath : hence on our return home we had
to hurry along lest we should be benighted. We had a party
of natives with us, who of their own accord had come to accompany us, and to act as guides and assistants. The road became
bad, and travelling was often difficult. As Mr. Annand was

young and active, he tripped along the path with a firm, elastic
step, and it was only on special occasions that he either needed
or would accept of any help. But it was always ready when
he wanted it. It was different with me. With the shadow
of threescore and ten hovering in the near distance, my limbs
were neither so strong nor so nimble as they had been thirty
or forty years before, and the natives instinctively recognised
this; and four of our native teachers, all strong, vigorous
men, spontaneously attached themselves to me, and walked
close behind me, two on my right side and two on my left:
and whenever the road was slippery, or over stones, or among
stumps, or across the stream — whenever there was the
slightest danger that I might fall, or slip, or stumble, that
moment two of those men, sometimes the whole four, two on
each side, seized me by the arms, kept me firmly up, and half
carried me till the danger was over.   In this way we travelled
along for three or_four long hours, till we reached our destina-
tion, the last hour by the aid of torchlight.   This is an exceedingly comfortable mode of walking on such roads.   You walk
with great safety and great ease; being held up firmly, you
have no fear of falling, and being half carried, you walk both
fast and with very little fatigue, and the limbs, being relieved
from the weight of the body, move on with the utmost facility.
Although such attentions on the part of the natives were not
new to me, for they had always assisted me in the same way
when needful, when I was travelling among them, yet as that
was one of the worst and most difficult journeys that I had
made for a long time, I realised more vividly than I had ever
done before, what seemed to me to be the meaning of the
promise made primarily to Christ, but through Him to His
people: "They (the angels) shall bear thee up in their hands,

lest thou dash thy foot against a stone;" for many a time
that night would I have dashed my feet against both stones
and stumps of trees, but for the strong and willing hands that
bore me up on our journey. I have no doubt but that in
Palestine, from the nature of the country, and the character
of the roads, this was a common mode of travelling for aged
or important persons, when the paths were difficult or dangerous. But to Christ were promised angels, not men, to be
His ministering servants, because He was divine; whereas
ministers and missionaries are best served by men, not angels,
at least visibly, because they themselves are human. But
what shall we say of that Gospel which changes heathens
into Christians, and transforms the wildest and most cruel of
cannibal savages into the mildest, and kindest, and gentlest
of ministering angels.

Thirty years before that time, when the natives of that
district were all heathen, a whale-boat was wrecked on the
coast, and one solitary white man escaped ashore with his
life. The natives gathered around him, and took him to the
house of the chief. It was there and then agreed to have
a cannibal feast over the poor man's body on the following
day. Wood was at once collected, and the fire was kindled
for the oven; and before twenty-four hours had elapsed, the
bones of the unhappy man would have been picked, broken,
and the marrow sucked out of them, had it not so happened
that a native was there, who had been at Sydney or somewhere else, and represented strongly to the chief the numbers
and power of the white people, and how most assuredly they
would revenge this man's death. In consequence of this the
chief reluctantly gave orders to save his life; and a party
of natives were told off who conveyed him to the harbour,

and delivered him safely to the master of the sandal wood establishment. Now here were we, thirty years afterwards, two defenceless white men, entirely in their hands, and yet we were as safe, and as kindly and lovingly treated, as if we had been the nearest and dearest of their own flesh and blood. And what made the difference between then and now? Then they were heathen, now they are Christian. Has any other book than the Bible such a transforming power?

CHAPTER XII.

" Is not My Word like a hammer that breaketh the rock in pieces."
—JEREMIAH xxiii. 29.

IN 1844 when I left this country to go out to our Foreign
Mission in New Zealand, I received a set of mason's tools from
my friend the late Mr. Thomas Binnie, builder, one of the
hundred men in Glasgow who were worth remembering.
Among those tools was a good whinstone hammer. During
the eight years I was in New Zealand, although I did require
to use some of the other tools, I did not require to use that
said hammer. But according to the ancient proverb, " Keep
a thing for seven years and you will find use for it : " and
certainly such was my experience. When I went to Aneityum
and had erected my house—it was a wooden frame and the
walls were partly weather-boarded, and partly wattle and
plaster—I found it was necessary to build two stone and
lime chimneys, one for our kitchen, and one for our dining-
room, which served also for our parlour, in wet or cold
weather. Very happily for me I accidentally discovered a
large quantity of stones, among which I found quite enough
very suitable for my purpose. The discovery was made in
this way : one day I was unexpectedly called upon to visit
a native woman, who was dangerously ill. She was the
chief's wife of Nohmunjap, a district about a mile and a half

distant. I went off at once to visit her, I administered some medicine, and my patient soon recovered. On the shore opposite to the settlement there was a great collection of stones, whinstone and basaltic, partly in the sea and partly on the beach, which had all been thrown out of the mountain side by some volcanic eruption, in some long past era in the pre-Adamite period of the island's history. When I began to build my chimneys, I went off to examine those stones, for the recovery of the chief's wife secured my liberty to take whatever I wanted. I took with me a party of my most intelligent natives, to assist me in selecting suitable stones, in carrying them to the landing-place, and in rowing the boat home. They were all deeply interested in my work. I found the stones well suited for my purpose; they were of the proper size and shape and of the very quality that I wanted; they were of a very workable material, they were what Scotch masons would have called good *skelping* stones easily cut into shape. When I had measured their length and breadth, applied rule and square to them, and marked the lines accordingly, and then struck them with my well-tempered, square-faced hammer, along those lines, I could with ease not only break the stones, a thing the natives had never seen done, but cut them along those lines into the very shapes that I had marked on them. When the natives saw this done, they were amazed; they opened their eyes and their mouths, they held up their hands, and shouted aloud till they had exhausted all the exclamations in the language. I never saw them so surprised, except in the case of one man, after the chimneys were erected. He came into our dining-room, and I caused him to look up the chimney; and when he saw daylight and the sky at the top, he was fairly out of himself; he rushed back to the middle of the floor, danced and leaped, crying out, "*Ah! wauho! Kahispin! Kaiheug vai cama! ak Misi! ak Misi Inglis! He aha nitai inigki!*"—"*Oh! wonderful! prodigious! Mercy on us! O Mister! O Mister Inglis! What thing is this?*" A little mechanical as well as medical knowledge often helps to increase the influence, and promote the usefulness, of a missionary. As soon as I could speak intelligibly to them, I made the hammer and the stones a familiar text to them, and spoke to them somewhat in this manner. "You are surprised with the hammer, but God says, 'Is not My Word like a hammer, that breaketh the rock in pieces?' Now you see what a hammer can do with a stone, it not only can break a stone but it can cut it into a particular shape; with the hammer I can cut the stone straight, or square, or round, as I wish; but if I strike the stone with a piece of wood, it has no effect whatever upon it. God says our hearts are stony, they are hard as a stone. Now, as it is only a hammer that can break a stone, and cut it into shape, so it is only God's Word that, like the hammer, can break our stony hearts, and form them into shape. Man's word is like a piece of wood, it has no effect upon the heart of men. Before the missionaries came to this island, many white people came here, and some of them talked a great deal to you, but you remained as you were—your hearts were not changed. And why? because it was only the words of man that they spoke to you, which was like striking the stone with a piece of wood. But when the missionaries came, they brought the hammer, the Word of God, with them, and they struck the stone with this hammer; they applied the Word of God to your hearts. They translated the Word of God into your language, they read it to you; they taught you to read it, you read it yourselves; you committed portions of it to memory, you believed it, you obeyed it, it broke your stony heart, it brought your heart into a new shape, you gave up your heathenism, you accepted Christ as your Saviour, and took God's law as the rule of your lives; and hence wickedness and misery are largely banished from the island, and goodness and happiness are come in their place." This simile the natives never forgot during all the five-and-twenty years that I was on the island. Every now and again those who were leading in prayer might have been heard using such expressions as the following, "O Lord, Thy Word is like a hammer, but our hearts are like a stone. Oh take Thy hammer and with it break our stony hearts, take Thy good and holy Word, and with it make our sinful hearts what Thou wishest them to become, holy and just and good, that we may be blessed and happy, and that Thy name may be praised and glorified for ever and ever. Amen."

CHAPTER XIII.

"What though the fig tree shall not *blossom*."—HABAKKUK iii. 17.
"Although no *flowers* the fig tree *clothe*."—PARAPHRASE xxxii. 1.

THE Hebrew word *Parach*, which is translated blossom in the Authorised and Douay Versions in Habakkuk iii. 17, signifies, according to Gesenius, "To sprout, to flourish, and to bud as a plant; and to put forth buds, leaves, and flowers as a tree." The natural history of the fig tree was evidently not known either to the translators of the Authorised or of the Douay Versions; still less was it known to Randell, the author of that beautiful paraphrase, the 32nd, in the Church of Scotland Version. The error is even continued in the Revised Version. It is well known to those who have lived in fig-growing countries, that the fig tree never blossoms, and is never clothed with flowers. The fruit of the fig tree is simply an undeveloped flower. My lamented friend, the late Hon. Andrew Sinclair, M.D., Colonial Secretary of New Zealand, was the first to point this out to me. And Canon Tristram says, "The fruit of the fig, unlike any other fruit in this country, is an enlarged, succulent, hollow receptacle containing the imperfect flowers in the interior. Hence the flowers of the fig tree are not visible until the receptacle has been cut open." The commentators have all followed our translators,

F

and accepted their rendering as correct. So far as I know, Dr. Adam Clarke is the only commentator, and Dr. Robert Young is the only translator, who has corrected the mistranslation. They both use the word *flourish* instead of *blossom*. Their rendering is, " Although the fig tree shall not flourish." As I have said, there is no such thing as a flower or a blossom ever seen on the fig tree. It flourishes, it puts forth leaves, and produces fruit, but it never flowers or blossoms. The fruit comes first and then the leaves. Hence, in his poem, on the Seasons, Thomson, "that great master of description," as Hervey calls him, says :

" And rich beneath its leaf the luscious fig."

It was the leaves without the fruit that disappointed our Saviour with the barren fig tree. Whether the leaves were abnormal, as some suppose, or normal, as others infer, it did not alter the condition of the tree ; the fruit should have been there before the leaves.

The Bible is not a single book, it is a library, a literature, an encyclopædia; it touches at more or fewer points the whole circle of human knowledge. It is not merely a knowledge of Hebrew, Greek, and some other language, that a translator of the Bible requires to possess; he would require to know almost everything. The translators of our Authorised Version, and also the translators of the Douay Version, although the best scholars of the age in their respective churches, were alike ignorant of botany, and were not aware that the fig tree was an exception to all other fruit-bearing trees, and that it never blossoms or puts forth flowers ; and, hence, for more than two centuries and a half, a glaring mistranslation has disfigured these otherwise matchless translations. Happily for the credit of the translators very few of their readers could detect the error.

On Aneityum there is no specimen of the common fig tree indigenous; but there is a very poor variety of the sycamore fig. The peculiarity of the sycamore is this: the fruit all adheres to the stock of the tree, and not, as in the common fig tree, to the extremities of the branches. But on Tanna there is an excellent species of the common fig; so good, that the missionaries of the London Missionary Society took plants of it in the *John Williams* on to Samoa. However, when I went to Aneityum I took from New Zealand two or three varieties of the common fig tree, which grew and bore fruit; and although they were annually attacked by a worm, which destroyed the old wood, and prevented the plants from reaching the size they would otherwise have attained, they, nevertheless, served to keep me always sorrowfully in mind that, however beautiful the expression, "What though the fig tree shall not *blossom*," and "though no *flowers* the fig tree *clothe*," they were still mistranslations; and also to secure that, whatever other errors might find their way into the Aneityumese translation of the Bible, Habakkuk iii. 17 would, without doubt, be correctly rendered.

CHAPTER XIV.

THE COCK CROWING TWICE.

" Jesus said unto Peter, Verily I say unto thee, That this night, before the cock crow, thou shalt deny Me thrice."—MATTHEW xxvi. 34.

" And Jesus saith unto Peter, Verily I say unto thee, That this day, even in this night, before the cock crow twice, thou shalt deny Me thrice."—MARK xiv. 30.

" Then began he to curse and to swear, saying, I know not the man. And immediately the cock crew. And Peter remembered the word of Jesus, which said unto him, Before the cock crow thou shalt deny Me thrice. And he went out, and wept bitterly."—MATTHEW xxvi. 74, 75.

" But he began to curse and to swear, saying, I know not this man of whom ye speak. And the second time the cock crew. And Peter called to mind the word that Jesus said unto him, Before the cock crow twice, thou shalt deny Me thrice. And when he thought thereon he wept."—MARK xiv. 71, 72.

CRITICS and commentators have been a good deal puzzled how to reconcile the apparently contradictory statements of Mark and the other three Evangelists about the crowing of the cock. This prediction of our Saviour did not refer to the crowing of any particular cock, but to that time in the morning known as cock-crowing, the beginning of the fourth watch. But Mark says, " Before the cock crow twice," which makes two cock-crowings. This has caused the difficulty to the critics. So much has this been felt that, in one very old manuscript, the word *dis*, twice, is found partially erased, as if the copyist wished in this way to reconcile or assimilate Mark with the other three Evangelists. But the rule now recognised by all modern critics, that the reading most difficult to be accounted for is most likely to be the true one, had not been present to the mind of those redactors, nor yet another principle, equally recognised in our times, that conjectural emendations are almost invariably found to be wrong, when all the facts come to be known. I shall be able to show that there is no discrepancy between Mark and the other Evangelists. Natural history does not seem to have been much studied, by some of the commentators at least. One says, the first crowing of the cock was about twelve o'clock. Another says that the first crowing is irregular. A better knowledge of the habits of the bird would have shown that both these statements were wrong. Even Dr. Kitto, so famous as an Orientalist, is as ignorant of the true facts as the ordinary commentators. Since the doctrine of evolution and the transmutation of species has not yet been established, we may safely assume that the cock-crowing has been the same in all countries and in all ages; that it was the same in Jerusalem in the first century of the Christian era as it is on Aneityum in the nineteenth. In ancient times, when clocks and watches were unknown, the cock-crowing was a distinctly marked time of the morning; but since clocks and watches came into common use, and since poultry, as in towns, were not generally kept, the cock-crowing, as a marking of time, ceased to be attended to, and the habits of the bird were no longer noticed : hence the loose writing of the commentators. But in the South Seas, where clocks and watches were unknown, as in Palestine of old, the cock-crowing was the best marked hour of the night. Like the Jews, too, they had two cock-crowings : the first of these between two and three, the other fully an hour later, between three and four : the first called the false cock-crowing, the second called the true cock-crowing. When we first went to Aneityum, we

soon discovered that time was regularly marked by the cock-
crowing ; but it was some time before we discovered that there
were two cock-crowings. It came about in this way. When
Mr. Geddie, who had charge of the printing-press, was
printing our native books, to secure the greatest possible
accuracy he always sent the proof-sheets over to me, that I
might read them over, and make any corrections. For the
sake of being company to one another, two lads generally came
with them, stayed all night to allow me time to look over
the sheets, and then returned in the morning : the distance
was twelve or fourteen miles. They started earlier or later
according to the urgency of the case. One evening I said
to them, "Mr. Geddie says he is in a great hurry for this
sheet, and wishes you back as soon as possible. I want you,
therefore, to rise very early and leave this place by the cock-
crowing." " But which cock-crowing do you mean ? " they said.
" Which ? " I said, " how many are there ? " "Oh, you know,"
they said, "there are two cock-crowings ; the true one and the
false one." " And what is the difference ? " I said. " Oh,"
said they, " the false cock-crowing is the first one, and then
after a while is the true one." This we afterwards found
ample means of verifying. Cocks, if they are disturbed or
awakened, will crow at any hour of the night. But if left
unmolested, these two cock-crowings are as regular in their
occurrence as the rising and setting of the sun. We had the
best means of knowing this fact every morning that we wished
to observe its recurrence. We had always a good supply of
poultry in our own yard ; and every family on the island kept
poultry. There are no villages on Aneityum, and there are no
farm-houses standing a mile or two apart, as in this country,
but the whole island is occupied with a system of cottage

gardening. The system is this : there is one cottage or hut, or perhaps two, each occupied by a family, and surrounded by a neat reed fence of wicker-work, to protect the garden from the pigs ; there are on the island from fifty to sixty lands or districts, each containing, when we went first thither, from half-a-dozen to a score of such cottages and gardens. Our mission station lay between two such lands, and within about a quarter of a mile of us there might be about twenty families. Every family had poultry, which all roosted on the trees standing round about the houses. Hence thirty, forty, or fifty cocks were within hearing. Every morning, therefore, we could hear both crowings. Somewhere about two o'clock one cock would crow, and a few others would follow, all feeble and drowsy-like, as if half asleep ; then all would subside into stillness. This is the *false cock-crowing :* there is no truth, no heart, no reality in it ; it is only, as it were, a pretence. But about an hour or rather more afterwards (Luke says, " About the space of one hour," &c.), somewhere about three o'clock, or a little later, when one cock crows, immediately there is a full ringing chorus, a perfect storm of crowing, every one more fully alive than another. This is the *true cock-crowing*, the *alektorophonia* of the Gospels, which marks the time with an ' unmistakable distinctness, and is enough to awaken the soundest sleeper, or arrest the attention of the most indifferent listener.

It was this, the true cock-crowing, that awoke Burns out of his reverie, when he was composing his poem, " A Winter Night," when he wrote :—

"I heard nae mair, for Chanticleer
  Shook off the powthery snaw,
And hailed the morning wi' a cheer,
  A cottage-rousing craw."

It was the clear, shrill, true crowing of the cock that startled the poet, and recalled him from his moody musing. It was the same true cock-crowing that awoke Mrs. Thomas Carlyle, when she was staying with the Bullers at Troston Rectory, near St. Edmundsbury in Suffolk, as recorded in one of her *letters*, dated Aug. 11, 1842. "Then about four," she says, "commenced never so many cocks challenging each other all over the parish."

Peter must have heard the low, half suppressed, feeble, false crowing, but it had made no impression on his mind. But when the true crowing rang forth loud and clear, he was instantaneously aroused to a consciousness of his cowardice and his guilt : and when the Saviour looked on him, he remembered the warning prophecy, his conscience smote him, he repented, and wept bitterly.

But the point to which I wish to direct special attention is this, that, to natives of Ancityum, the statement in Mark about two cock-crowings, while the other three Evangelists speak only of one, would cause no difficulty whatever, because to them both expressions convey exactly the same meaning. When they speak of *the* cock-crowing, they mean the true cock-crowing ; and when they speak of the two cock-crowings the expression points to the very same time as the other. Hence, before the cock crew and before the cock crew twice, to them mean exactly the same thing ; the same as, before the morning watch, or before three o'clock, thou shalt deny Me thrice. Whether therefore our Saviour warned Peter twice, as some commentators think, and that Mark gives the words used by Christ on the one occasion, and the other three Evangelists give the words used by Him on the other occasion, or whether He warned him only once, and that Mark gives the full form of the words He used, while the other three writers give the shorter abridged form, the meaning to the Jews and to all the ancients, as it is to the natives of Aneityum, would be precisely the same. The doctrine of verbal inspiration does not mean, that two or more of the sacred writers, narrating the same event, or recording the same speech, must all use precisely the same words, but that they must all convey substantially the same meaning when the statements are properly understood, although the meaning may be more or less fully stated, according as it may be required by the object which the writer has in view. It was not till I was on Aneityum and heard the two cock-crowings so distinctly, that I clearly understood how Mark's words, so different from those of the other three Evangelists, were in meaning the very same as theirs. At the same time this difference of statement showed that he was no copyist. His was independent testimony, and on that account doubly valuable; as "In the mouth of two or three witnesses shall every word be established."

CHAPTER XV.

FASTING AND TAKING NOTHING.

"And while the day was coming on, Paul besought them all to take meat, saying, This day is the fourteenth day that ye have tarried and continued fasting, having taken nothing. Wherefore I pray you to take some meat; for this is for your health: for there shall not an hair fall from the head of any of you. And when he had thus spoken, he took bread, and gave thanks to God in presence of them all; and when he had broken it, he began to eat. Then were they all of good cheer, and they also took some meat."—ACTS xxvii. 33-36.

THIS is a strictly Oriental form of speech. "This day is the fourteenth day that ye have tarried and *continued fasting*." But lest the word fasting should be ambiguous, something like Daniel's mourning for three full weeks, during which time he ate no pleasant bread, neither came flesh nor wine into his mouth, it is added, "having *taken nothing*." Words, as we understand them, could not more unequivocally convey the impression, that during those fourteen days they had literally tasted no food whatever. We have no hesitation in admitting that Moses, on three occasions, literally fasted forty days and forty nights; that Elijah and our Saviour did each of them the same. But then we recognise that they were miraculously sustained. In this case, however, Luke gives no intimation that Paul and his 275 companions in suffering experienced any miraculous support. It was an ordinary voyage, and they trusted to nothing but ordinary means for both their safety and their sustenance. But in this form of speech we have a clear proof that this book was written in the East. It is an exact Oriental idiom. No man brought up in Western Europe, at least no English speaking missionary, could, in Paul's circumstances, have used such a loose, vague mode of expression; but it was doubtless quite well understood by his audience. Although this mode of speaking is stumbling to us, it is not in the least so to the natives of Aneityum, as they themselves speak precisely in the same way. We instinctively know that the words cannot be understood literally; but the natives of Aneityum, without any explanation, know as near as may be what the Apostle meant. Their mode of speaking, like his, is Oriental. For example, you ask a native if he has eaten anything to-day. He says, No, he has eaten nothing. You ask him if he ate anything yesterday. He says, No, he ate nothing. You ask him again if he ate anything the day before. He gives you the same answer; and you might go on putting the same questions and receiving the same answers for any length of time; and were he on board a ship, like that in which Paul was sailing, he would say without hesitation that he had eaten nothing for a fortnight. But if you catechise him a little more closely, you will find what he means by these general assertions. If you say, You have told us that you ate nothing to-day: but did you not drink a cocoa-nut or two, and eat the food contained in the inside of it? He will say, Oh yes. You go on and say, But did you not also eat some bananas yesterday? He will again say, Oh yes. And the day before yesterday, did you not chew some sugar cane? He again answers, Oh yes, I chewed a little. And the day before that, did you not roast a bread-fruit and eat it ? and the day before that, did you not roast some horse chestnuts and eat them ? He says, Oh yes, I had a few. And the day before that, did you not roast a few small yams and eat them ? He says again, Oh yes, I had some. In this way you might go on for the whole fortnight, and he would readily admit that he had been eating something every day. But what a native means, when he tells you he has eaten nothing, is simply this, that no oven has been cooked that day; and that the family or the party have sat down to no regular meal. Now this was precisely the case on board of this ship. During the fourteen days in which the vessel was hove to, and drifting under the pressure of this Euroclydon or Levanter, the waves would be constantly breaking over the bulwarks, and washing along the decks; the hatches would all be battened down, and the fires in the ship's galley would remain extinguished. There would be no cooking on board, no rations would be served out, and no meals served up. Both seamen and passengers would take food when and how they could get it; stale bread, or mouldy biscuit, or handfuls of wheat, or anything else they could lay their hands on, but never once a regular meal; hence Paul said truly, as they understood him, "Ye have continued fasting, having taken nothing." But now that the vessel had been brought to anchor, the sea calm, and the ship steady, the hatches were again opened, and all on board came on deck; and although they probably did not wait till the cooks kindled the galley fires, filled the ship's coppers, and cooked provisions for a full meal, yet, evidently at Paul's suggestion, and by the captain's orders, the stewards served out full rations for the whole company, and Paul, now recognised as the accredited chaplain of the ship, delivered to the whole company this hope-inspiring address, and gave thanks to God in presence of them all. He then broke the bread, Matthew Harvey says in a parenthesis, "It was sea-biscuit," and began to eat. What a change the speech, and prayer, and conduct of Paul made on the whole company! For the last fortnight they had been at their wit's end through hunger and despair. Now they were all of good cheer. During that time, as Paul expressed it, they had fasted, having taken nothing. Now they all had a regular full meal; for when it was over, "they had eaten enough," and rose with alacrity to their work.

On Aneityum the natives never had more than one regular meal in the day, generally in the evening, and which might in Scripture phraseology be called either a dinner or a supper. All their other eating, however plentiful, was at odd times; they did this because they cooked, or made a regular oven, only once a day, and not always that. But since they became Christian, although they should not have even one oven during the whole week, they have always one on the Saturday, in which a sufficiency of food is provided for the Sabbath. The Saturday evening oven is an institution over the whole island, hence there is no fasting on Sabbath. There has grown up, what was formerly unknown, even a regular breakfast on Sabbath morning; and having, like Paul's companions, "eaten enough," they are "of good cheer" when they enter the church, and throughout the day; the psalmist's picture of family life is realised through the whole community—

> " In dwellings of the righteous
> Is heard the melody
> Of joy and health."

CHAPTER XVI.

MODE OF TREATING NATIVES.

"Be courteous."—1 PETER iii. 8.
"Julius *courteously* entreated Paul."—ACTS xxvii. 3.
"Publius received us, and lodged us three days *courteously*."
—ACTS xxvii. 7.

THE mode of approaching and of holding intercourse with
natives is a matter of great importance to a missionary for
securing success among them. Many people think that because
they are low, degraded savages, you may speak to them as you
like, and treat them as you may think proper, it will make no
difference. I have heard white men, who ought to have known
better, shout out to a native, "Come along, you lazy black
fellow," or "Go away, you stupid nigger," or "Now, *kanaka*, if
you don't be smart, I'll let you feel the weight of a rope's end."
But this is a great mistake, they are men, and have all the
attributes of humanity, and all the feelings of human beings;
they are specially sensitive to any improper treatment, they
discriminate very quickly and acutely between rudeness and
politeness, between good and bad usage. Many would scarcely
believe it; but true it is and of verity, that there is perhaps
no place where politeness is of more importance than among
savages. I have seen it hundreds of times. When natives
know you thoroughly, there is nothing that is reasonable that
they will not do for you, if you approach them in the right
spirit. They are as human as any of ourselves; they are

actuated by the same motives, animated by the same spirit, and moved by the same influences. I always made a point of reproving them as seldom as possible. If a native, whom I had engaged to do some work for me, disappointed me, without taking any notice of what had happened, I charitably assumed that there had been some oversight or some mismanagement on my part or some misunderstanding on his part, and on the next occasion I tried to be doubly careful that all my arrangements should be as complete as I could possibly make them, and the results were generally satisfactory, or if not so, I had no ground of real complaint against the natives. There was some good reason if they failed. I remember on one occasion that Mrs. Inglis and I were going round in our boat to the other side of the island. I bespoke a boat's crew the night before. We were to go off at ten o'clock in the forenoon, that being the hour that suited best for the tide. The boat was launched, the sail, the oars, and the luggage were all put into the boat, Mrs. Inglis had taken her seat, and everything was ready for us to proceed on our voyage, when we discovered that one of our crew was awanting, without whom we could not proceed, as I had no odd boatman that morning. I liked always to have a good strong boat's crew, hence I often enengaged an extra man, and not unfrequently, especially when they had any object of their own to serve, we had one or more volunteers, and as it was always well to have the boat well manned, I never discouraged a little volunteering. This morning, however, we had no spare hands. The missing boatman was again and again called aloud by his name, but there was no response. Messengers were then sent out to inquire after him, but with no better results. At this juncture we saw the lad coming along slowly towards the boat, but instead of

hastening along, and jumping into the boat, as I expected him
to do, he deliberately passed us, and went into the bush. This
looked so much like a desire to add insult to injury that I
was quite nonplussed. It was now clear that another boatman must be sought for. We had already lost half an hour;
the case was urgent, and also beset with difficulty. There was
only a limited number of natives who could handle an oar.
In Samoa none of the natives could pull: all the missionaries
got their boats propelled by paddles. This required double
the number of boatmen. It was the same on Aneityum at
the beginning of the mission; not one of them could pull an
oar, or manage a boat, till Mr. Geddie and I had taught them.
Afterwards when the whaling commenced, and they had
acquired practice in boating, they became expert oarsmen.
But at that hour of the day all the natives, boatmen and non-
boatmen, were away at their plantations, a good distance off.
However, messengers were sent off, and at the end of another
half hour the services of two boatmen were secured, and we
set off on our voyage. When we had got fairly under way
my wife, whose patience by this time was all but exhausted,
said to me in a tone of unmistakable earnestness, " I do hope
when we get home that you will take that lad and give him
a thorough talking to. I have sat for an hour in the boat, in
this burning sun, I have four or five hours to sit in the same
condition, before we get to the end of our voyage, and you
know that I lost four hours' sleep last night with fever and
ague. Now see that you don't miss him. We shall soon not
be able to trust to one of them." A few mornings afterwards
I had again to go round to the other station, but I took care
to have all my arrangements made perfectly secure the night
before, but on going down to the beach I was agreeably surprised

to find that my defaulting friend of the former day had been the first to enter the boat and the first to lay hold of an oar. On inquiring at him about his former conduct I found that he had taken ill of a complaint of which he felt a delicacy in speaking about in public, and hence he acted as he did. " But," I said, " why did not you tell me, and then I should have known, and it would have been all right?" " Oh," said he, " I was ashamed, and could not speak about it." Further reproof was unnecessary. I have repeatedly found that, when the conduct of a native seemed to be very ambiguous, and looked from our standpoint to be very bad, the most charitable view of the case was generally found to be the right one. The conduct was better than it seemed to be.

By taking a native privately, and speaking to him quietly, you can do almost anything with him; but speak to him publicly about his conduct, or reprove him openly before the other natives, and you at once throw him into antagonism and make him your decided enemy. He feels, like Jonah, that he does well to be angry. On one occasion a young man living on the premises had been behaving very badly, neglecting his work, and showing a great amount of wilful disobedience. I saw that this could not be allowed to go on, so I took him quietly one evening into my study by himself, and had a long friendly talk with him. I said, " What is this that you have been doing? What kind of conduct is this that you have been carrying on of late? This is not like your former conduct. This is not at all like the conduct of your father and mother. You know how well your father always behaved towards me; he was always kind, and obliging, and helpful; and your mother was always the same to Mrs. Inglis. You, too, used always to be a good boy," (here I enumerated all the good things he had ever done that I could remember). "You came regularly to school, and were diligent in learning to read. I remember, too, when your mother was dying, how attentive you were to her; how, day after day, you waited on her, how you sought all kinds of food for her that you thought she would like, how you went to the sea every day and fished for her, how you went daily to the spring and filled her bottle with fresh water and laid it at her head, how you gathered sticks and kept a nice fire burning beside her every night, how you made worship with her night and morning, sang the 'Happy Land' and the 'Rock of Ages,' and often read the Bible to her during the day. Everybody remarked what a good boy you were, and how kind you were to your mother. Now, as boys who are good to their parents almost always turn out well, the Lord blesses them and keeps them, how is it that you are now behaving in this way?" By this time he had completely broken down, and was crying. "Oh," said he, "So-and-so said so-and-so to me, and broke my heart. I was very weak, my heart was dark, Satan tempted me, and I forgot myself, and did as you saw." I said to him, "Oh, I see you understand; I shall not speak about this again. You go away. You pray to the Lord to keep you, and see that you watch carefully over your heart; and to-morrow I want you to do so-and-so," naming some work for him to do. He went away, and I had no further trouble with him. In dealing with natives, it is of the utmost importance to lead them to cherish feelings of self-respect, to make them feel that they have a character to maintain. While you can lay down no hard and fast lines by which to act towards them, it is always safe to praise them for what is good in their conduct, rather than blame them for what is bad. Among a people like the South Sea Islanders, especially the Papuans, who are so little amenable to authority of any kind, where every man is accustomed to do very much what is right in his own eyes, it is extremely difficult to establish anything like rule or discipline. The missionary must trust to his personal influence, to the attachment which the natives form for himself. John Williams, John Hunt, and all the most outstanding missionaries in the South Seas, exercised a magnetic personal influence over the natives; the natives became so attached to the missionaries that they would have risked their lives for them, as David's three mighties broke through the host of the Philistines and drew water out of the well of Bethlehem, not to save his life, but simply to quench his thirst. Human nature is the same everywhere. During the American War of Independence, an old lady, who had a store in Philadelphia, used to say that the most profitable thing she kept in her shop was politeness, it drew the very children to her even better than sweeties. What was it that gave Miss Nightingale such powerful control over the soldiers and seamen in the hospitals during the Crimean war, so that they would have done anything for her in their power; and in her presence they would not have uttered a single coarse, vulgar, profane, or improper word? It was, no doubt, largely owing to her refined, cultured, polite manner, dominated by a truly Christian spirit. It is by approaching heathen natives in this manner that missionaries may expect to be successful among them.

For politeness the Samoans are said to be the French of the Pacific. They are at least very formal and ceremonious in their intercourse one with another. Our brethren, the missionaries there, met them on their own ground, and added a Christ-like spirit to their court-like forms of social intercourse. The word *alofa*, to love or pity, is, in one form or another, used in all modes of salutation; and, like oil to machinery, softens and smoothes all their social intercourse. Mr. Geddie stayed some time in Samoa, on his way to the New Hebrides, and brought on to Aneityum some of their forms of politeness. *Aiheug*, to love or pity, has the same meaning as *alofa;* and he introduced the salutation, *Kaiheug vai eug,* "My love to thee." The Aneityumese had no form of salutation in their heathen state; they passed each other in heathenism without any recognition; but in imitation of the missionaries, the Christian natives saluted each other; and as Christianity spread, so did the salutation, "My love to you," or, "I wish you well," till the minor virtue of politeness, as far at least as salutations went, had permeated the whole community. Many people think that you may speak as you like to savages. This is quite a mistake. As I have said, you cannot speak too politely to natives. The sovereign of the realm, and the captain of a ship always command—the Queen her subjects, the captain his crew. But in spite of the adage, "The Court is the standard of good breeding," we did not find that commanding was the most successful way of getting on well with savages; but, following the example of our Samoan brethren, and, I suppose, of most of the successful missionaries, we found that the surest and most pleasant way of getting along with natives was, not by commanding or ordering, but by politely requesting them. Even when we were paying a native for working, we invariably said to him, *Aiheug vai nyak,* "Have compassion on me," and do so-and-so; but which in reality amounts very much to the phrase, "Please do so-and-so," or "Please give me so-and-so," among ourselves. But doubtless among natives, whether savage or Christian,

politeness, genuine Christian politeness, is one of the most
certain guarantees for success.   We had on the islands a
trader's wife, who was not recognised as a model for all the
virtues, but who was certainly a model for suavity and
blandness of manner towards the natives.   She had, when
a girl, been boarded and educated in the family of a retired
missionary.   She was naturally kind, and possessed great
tact; and had she been imbued with higher religious principles,
and been placed in more favourable circumstances, she would
have been a power for good among the islands.   When she
wished any special favour, or any important service, from a
native, she would clap him gently on the shoulder, and say,
Ak inhal unyak, ak inhal unyak, aiheug vai nyak, "O my child,
O my child, have compassion on me," and do so-and-so for me,
or give me so-and-so; and the request was never refused.
When she died, one of our natives said to my wife about her:
"She was a kind woman to us when we were working for her;
she did not think much about our souls, but she was always
good in thinking about our bodies."

It is matter of great importance to consider in what manner
the Gospel is to be presented to the heathen, so as to make it
attractive and not repulsive.   As a general rule the heathen
are averse to the receiving of the Gospel.   If they have had
little or no intercourse with white men they are anxious to have
a missionary to live among them, for the sake of the temporal
benefits they expect to receive by him or from him,—for the
fish-hooks, the knives, the hatchets, or any other articles of
European manufacture for which they may have taken a
fancy; but if they can get these from a trader they would
prefer him.   It is not for any religious instruction they desire
to receive.   As a general rule the natives, in their heathen

state, are afraid of the new religion and of the missionaries. Their own religion is a burdensome and expensive system. Their own priests lay on them heavy burdens, and grievous to be borne, and keep them in constant terror, by professing to possess supernatural power to bring upon them sickness and death, and all other calamities; and they think that missionaries are only a class of priests stronger and more powerful than their own, and if they receive the new religion, they will be only adding a load to a burden; if the old religion scourged them with whips the new religion would scourge them with scorpions. Hence they keep as shy as possible both of the missionary and of the new religion. Some young missionaries too, with the very best intentions, present the gospel, not simply as good news, but rather as a system of restrictions. Shocked by the cruelties and abominations of heathenism, they begin and forbid and denounce these, before they can make them understand anything about the blessings of the Gospel. It has been said that a young missionary does very well, if, at the end of the first year, he has done no ill. Let him live very quietly, interfere with nobody, but observe carefully, learn the language as fast as he can, acquire as much knowledge about the people as possible, write down their names, find out the relations of one tribe to another, and do good as he finds opportunity; but never force his services. Let him bide his time, and his time will come, perhaps sooner than he may think it will; but he will then be able to utilise opportunities when they occur. We tried to act upon these principles, to hurry nothing. We trusted for success to "the expulsive power of a new affection." We forbade nothing. We never said, "You must cease smoking, you must not drink kava, you must give over your night-dances and your great

feasts, you must put away all your wives but one, you must
not beat your wife, you must not fight with the neighbouring
tribes, you must not bewitch any one, you must not avenge
yourselves upon your enemies, you must not paint your faces
with black or red or yellow pigments, you must not indulge
in any heathen practices. Some may think that this was
very doubtful teaching, a very loose kind of preaching. But
no; our Saviour began His sermon on the mount, not by
inculcating the tithing of mint and cummin, not by pronouncing woes on the Pharisees, but by the Beatitudes.
" Blessed are the poor, blessed are the meek, blessed are the
merciful, happy are ye," &c. We endeavoured both by our
preaching and our practice, to represent Christianity as something great, and something good ; as something very attractive,
but never in the least repulsive. As I have said we offered
them the Sabbath as a day of rest, a day also with abundance
of food, a day not of amusement and frivolity, but a day of joy
and gladness in the worship of God. We took nothing away,
we deprived them of no enjoyment. But when they came to
know and understand and embrace what was good, the evil
was given up without a grudge. They embraced the Sabbath
and soon rejoiced in its privileges. When they came to understand that Christ was the only Saviour of sinners, and professed their faith in Him as such, they gave up all their
heathen worship and never went back to it. When they came
to understand that the marriage of one man with one woman
was the best and happiest kind of marriage, bigamy and polygamy disappeared without an effort. By our teaching and by
our example we tried to show what a good thing Christianity
is. "Accept of the Gospel," we said, "and see how happy
you will be." They were sufficiently miserable in heathenism,

and our object was to show them that godliness is profitable
unto all things having promise of the life that now is and of
that which is to come. I have often been struck in reading
Dr. Chalmers's sermons, with the way in which he approaches
the unconverted, in order to convince them of sin. He never
assails them on the worst side of their character. He
approaches them on the best. He never begins by telling
them of all the evil that is in their lives and in their conduct,
but by enumerating all their good qualities. He never takes
up the attitude of a pessimist, and sets forth all the evils of
the time, and all the wickedness of the people, and charges
these home upon his hearers or his readers, and says to each
of them, "Thou art the man, therefore repent in sackcloth
and ashes." No, he took a different path in approaching
them. He took them as it were into his confidence, made
them his friends, and made them feel that he was their
friend. He said in effect to them, "There is very much
in you that is commendable; you are industrious, you are
temperate, your character is blameless and irreproachable;
you are honest, you are honourable in all your business transactions; you are just, you are generous, you are kind, you
are genial; you are good husbands, you are excellent fathers,
you are quiet and obliging neighbours; touching the righteousness that is by the law you are blameless. But, nevertheless, although man has nothing against you, yet you know
what your own heart in the sight of God testifies against you.
You are conscious that the love of God is not in you, that
love to God is not the highest and overruling motive in all
your actions—that the heart is deceitful above all things, and
desperately, incurably wicked. The old heart cannot be made
better, it must be made anew, renewed." The charge was

thus made against the race, not against the individual, against what the man's heart said, not against what the world knew, and hence there was no quarrel with the preacher. It was on such lines as these that we endeavoured to approach the natives. We knew that God communicates to men the benefits of redemption chiefly by the ordinary means of grace, the Word, sacraments, and prayer. We strove to bring them under the influence of those means. We translated the Scriptures for them, read them to them, explained them to them, and taught them to read them. We urged the natives to come to the house of God, and take part, as they were able, in all the ordinances of divine grace; and as there is a special fitness in the means of grace for effecting a change of heart, we did our best to bring the natives, and to keep them constantly under these influences. And knowing that human power was totally unable to change their hearts and save their souls, we did all in our power to place them in such relations to the means of grace—the Word, sacraments, and prayer—that those means would most effectually operate to secure their salvation. We endeavoured to place their souls in such a relation to these heaven-appointed means and to the Spirit of God, that we could rest with confidence on the divine promise rendering these means effectual. And we were not disappointed. In twelve years after the arrival of Messrs. Powell and Geddie and their wives, and eight years after our arrival, the whole population of 3500 had abandoned heathenism, professed Christianity, and placed themselves under Christian instruction. We made all our converts missionaries. For a long time, every Sabbath afternoon we sent out two or three parties to visit heathen districts, hold little services of praise and prayer with the natives, and to

talk with them about Christianity. If we knew that the
people of the district to which they were going were not
friendly to the Christian party, we sent with them a strong
body of men, headed by some persons of importance, not to
compel them to become Christian, but to remove from them
all temptation to attack the evangelistic party, which they
might have had, if the evangelists had been weak. On one
occasion this was attempted, and a Christian chief was
severely wounded; but we took such precautions afterwards,
that the attempt was never again repeated. As the work
went on we had to change our modes of operation, but never
to abandon the spirit of politeness; it being one form of that
charity which never faileth.

It has been said, that he who spits against the wind spits
in his own face; and that if men will speak soft words they
will hear sweet echoes. These axioms we found specially true
in our dealings with the natives. We found it always, as I
have said, better to praise them for what they did well, than
to blame them for what they did ill. They were intensely
human. It has been said, that no man can be a successful
teacher who has not studied moral philosophy, that he may
understand human nature, and know how to manage human
beings, that he may know the principles by which men are
actuated. If this is so necessary in this country for a teacher,
it is greatly more necessary for a missionary labouring among
savages. A great many people make mistakes of this kind.
They expect, on the one hand, that the poor and the ignorant
should always be humble and grateful, ready to accept of any
place, and to submit to any treatment; and on the other hand,
that the rich and the great only are likely to be proud. The
reverse of this is usually the case. Other things being equal, it

is among the poor and the ignorant that the proud are chiefly found, so is it among savages. Our heathen natives were at first all proud, and many of them extremely touchy. If one native reproved or admonished another, no matter however justly, the native reproved was very likely to get quite angry, and say to his friends, " What right had So-and-so to speak to me in that way ? Had the missionary reproved me, or had the chief spoken to me, or the teacher, I should have heard them and done as they said. But for that creature—a mere nobody, for him to speak that way to me is quite unbearable." With such feelings among the natives, the politeness of a missionary and his wife comes upon them with an agreeable surprise. They do not expect it. But others have had similar surprises. A few years ago the Synod of the Presbyterian Church of England met in Manchester, when a committee of the friends in that city made arrangements to have the members of the Synod accommodated in private families, both with the view of saving expense, and of creating an interest in the ministers especially, among the leading members of the Church. Two of the ministers were lodged with a family of our acquaintance, excellent people, but who had not happened to come much in contact with ministers. One day during the meeting of the Synod, the lady of the house met with a lady friend, and told her how delighted they were that the committee had sent two of the ministers to them. They were such nice men. They were so cheerful, so agreeable, so sensible, so pleasant in conversation ; they never thought that ministers were such nice men. The Christian culture and politeness of these two ministers had left on the minds of the family a favourable impression on behalf of the whole Christian ministry. But it is not only savages, and well-to-do, but unobtrusive and retiring Christians, who meet with these gratifying incidents, sometimes eminent men are singularly ignorant of things out of their own circle. The late Dean Stanley, when he was visiting his wife's relations, the Earl of Elgin's family, at Dunfermline, made the acquaintance of the late Rev. Dr. Johnstone of Limekilns, and became very much attached to him; and he was wont to say, that if all Presbyterian ministers were as intelligent, as tolerant, and as charitable in their sentiments as Dr. Johnstone, it would be a pleasure to associate with them. Now, there can be no doubt that, without in the least depreciating Dr. Johnstone's reputation, if the learned Dean had possessed a wider acquaintance with Presbyterian ministers, he would have found that a large proportion of them were as intelligent, as liberal in spirit, and as charitable in their feelings and sentiments as Dr. Johnstone himself. But like our natives with the missionaries he was ignorant of the class; and, hence, those characteristics which indicated the rule were looked upon by him as being the exception. Like the Presbyterian lady in Manchester, he required a larger induction of facts to remove his doubts, a greater amount of Christian intercourse to convince him than was needed by the good hostess of these country ministers. But the principle is the same, and human nature is the same through all grades of society. Christian culture is everywhere a power; the minor grace of politeness exerts an influence for good on the rude savage, on the gentle lady, and on the learned dignitary; it is an influence in the same direction, if not in the same degree, on those who squat in huts, on those who live in houses, on those who dwell in deaneries, or on those who inhabit palaces.

CHAPTER XVII

A FEW of the islands are of coral formation, and most of them are surrounded by coral reefs. Specimens of the coral, both white and red, may be often seen as curiosities in houses in this country, but no one would think of comparing any of the coral in those seas with that which Job refers to (chap. xxviii. 18) when he says, " No mention shall be made of *coral*, or of pearls, for the price of wisdom is above rubies." We have all heard of the coral insect, of the millions of those tiny masons that have been toiling on, year after year, and age after age, building up gigantic structures, compared with which the tower of Babel, the wall of China, and the pyramids of Egypt were like the toys and the playthings of children. Now there is a great popular delusion abroad in connection with these so-called coral insects. Most people think of them as plodding away with the instinctive wisdom and the persevering industry of bees building up their combs: or, like ants, raising their hills, and filling their garners with food for the coming winter; but this is not the case. The so-called insect is a kind of polypus, more like a plant than an animal. It cannot move from place to place, it is a fixture. The coral is a mass of lime; it is porous like a sponge; every crevice, every pore is filled with a gelatinous matter: this is all

covered with a very thin skin.   At the outer extremity of
every pore, there is a small orifice or mouth, which is continually sucking in, or secreting the lime, which is held in
solution in the sea-water, and depositing it in the block
below, and in this way the lump of coral continues to grow;
but it grows like a plant, not like the work of an insect.
When sailing in a boat over these coral reefs you seem, at
times, to be sailing over a coral garden.   Many species, and
innumerable varieties, and of various colours, are seen growing
beneath the water, and yet, so far as I have observed, they all
belong to two classes, the branch coral and the brain coral,
—the former like small branches without leaves, the latter in
shape and appearance like a human brain with the bone
removed, but of all sizes, from that of an egg to blocks of
many tons weight.   Coral is found both dead and alive.
The dead coral is in masses and mountains of solid rock, but
containing, so far as I know, no organic remains.   The live
coral is growing on the top of these dead rocks, near the
surface of the water.   To prepare those beautiful specimens
that are exhibited as curiosities, you have to boil the piece
of live coral in fresh water with carbonate of soda, to loosen
the gelatinous matter, then wash it again and again in fresh
water, to remove all this matter, and finally expose it to the
sun to dry it.   It then contains nothing but the skeleton of
this plant-like organism, and is in reality nothing but a lump
of limestone, but so exquisitely wrought, so marvellously
beautiful, that Solomon in all his glory could produce nothing
to equal it.   Hiram with all his highly skilled workmen
could produce no castings, could execute no carvings, half so
cunning or half so curious as these.   Coral thus prepared is "a
thing of beauty and a joy for ever."   The live coral is the only

lime we have on the islands. We collect it out of the sea, burn it with wood in large pits, and build, or plaster, or white wash our houses with it as required.

Trees: the Cocoa-nut.

Among the trees the cocoa-nut, the *Coccos nucifera*, is one of the most beautiful and valuable trees on Aneityum. It is found on all the South Sea Islands. It belongs to the family of the palms, and grows most luxuriantly, especially near the shore. It is an evergreen; hence the Psalmist employs it as an emblem of the spiritual condition of the righteous.

> " But like the *palm tree* flourishing
>   Shall be the righteous one."

> " He shall be fat, and full of sap,
>   And aye be flourishing."

I have the names of twelve species, or distinct varieties, of palms that grow on Aneityum. I may here remark that many people pronounce this word as if it were written *ko-kó-a*, in three syllables, with the accent on the second. But so far as I have ever heard it named in the South Seas, it is pronounced, as if within *kó-ko*, in two syllables, with the accent on the first. The cocoa-nut is a beautiful tree. The trunk grows up straight, without a branch or a twist, till it reaches a height of fifty or sixty feet, with a fine spreading crown of leaves, or rather branches, though usually called leaves, interspersed with large clusters of fruit in all stages of progress. It is always shedding its old leaves on branches, as well as its fruit, and is always producing fresh ones; hence the whole year round you can stand, or sit, " 'neath the shade of the feathery palm," although it is not safe to do either, lest a hard cocoa-nut should strike you on the head. Another peculiarity of the cocoa-nut is, that it is, as all the palms are, *endogenous*, it increases from within, and not from without. It also carries the whole thickness of the trunk up with it from the root. At the end of the first year's growth, the trunk is as thick as it ever becomes. In all cold countries the trees are *exogenous*—they grow from without, their addition of growth are all on the outside, as are seen in the concentric rings, when a tree is sawn across; hence if you bark a tree you kill it, but in tropical climates, a portion of the trees are *endogenous*—the new life, the new matter that supplies growth, goes all up the centre; and you may cut the outside of a cocoa-nut as much as you choose, if you leave the centre untouched, you do not kill the tree; but if you injure the centre, or the top, it dies at once. The easiest way to destroy a cocoa-nut tree, is to kill the central growth at the top. On some islands in the South Seas, if a man wishes to avenge himself secretly on his neighbour, he climbs up one of his cocoa-nut trees, and places a dead snake, or some dead animal, on the central growth of the tree. The decaying animal matter kills this vital part of the tree, and the whole tree dies, while, as in the case of the enemy, who sowed the tares while men were asleep, the author of the mischief is not discovered. In the case of every new leaf or branch, when it comes out, it shoots directly up to its full length, like a round spear ; when it reaches its full length, the fibre that holds it together bursts, and the branch expands. The branches are usually from about twelve to fifteen feet long, with a row of leaflets on each side of the stem, about two feet long each. Every part of the cocoa-nut is useful—its leaves, its wood, and its fruit. Its leaves are made into mats for floors, and they are also employed as a thatch for houses ; its wood is not durable, but it is employed usefully in various ways.   I have seen a boat made out of some species.   On Aneityum one species of palm is split up and used as small rafters for the roof of our churches, mission, and other houses ; but it is its fruit—the cocoa-nut—which constitutes its great value.   Every part of the nut is valuable ; its husk is made into cordage by the natives, and into door mats and brushes by Europeans.   It is also used like horse-hair for stuffing mattresses.   When green the husk of one species is of a sweet taste, and is greatly prized by the natives when they are unwell : they chew the husk and swallow the juice, and seem to be soothed by the operation. The shell is made into cups and water-bottles.   The liquor which the nut contains when full grown and half ripe, which is enough generally to fill one or two tumblers, is one of the most delicious and refreshing drinks that is anywhere known : it is of a slightly sweet and a slightly acid taste, something like lemonade, but much finer.   It is all but equal to the juice of the grape, such as it must have been when pressed into Pharaoh's cup by the chief butler.   It is palm wine ; and by most of the missionaries in the South Seas is used at the Lord's Supper as a legitimate substitute for the fruit of the vine, and greatly to be preferred to the brandified wine of commerce.   It is a wine that cheers but not inebriates. The kernel is no less valuable ; as an article of diet it is to the natives a substitute for both butter and meat, and as an article of commerce it supplies the well-known cocoa-nut oil, which is extensively used for so many purposes, in supply-ing both the necessaries and luxuries of life.   The kernel is now generally dried, and is the *cobra* of commerce.   Two

hundred years ago the quaint but pious Herbert, as quoted by
Ellis in his valuable Polynesian Researches, sang :

> "The Indian's nut alone
> Is clothing, meat and trencher, drink and can,
> Boat and cable, sail and needle, all in one."

What the reindeer is to the Greenlander, the cocoa-nut is to
the natives of the South Seas.

THE BREAD-FRUIT TREE.

The next of the most important trees on these islands is
the bread-fruit tree, *artocarpus*. It is also a beautiful tree;
not unlike an ash tree in shape, except in the foliage. It
has large digitated leaves, every one spreading out like the
open hand of a mighty giant; but hands, in comparison with
which, the hands of Goliath of Gath would have been like
that of an infant. The wood of the tree is of great use to
the natives. It is a soft wood and easily worked; but it is
durable; it is long before it rots. It is valuable for house-
building; but it is chiefly prized by the natives for supplying
them with wood for making their canoes. On Aneityum the
canoes are all hollowed out of single trees; and the bread-
fruit tree, being soft and easily worked, and at the same time
durable, is preferred to all others for that purpose. The chief
value of the tree, however, is its fruit. It is the staple
article of food for two, three, or four months in the year,
according as the crop is plentiful or otherwise, or as the
hurricanes may spare the fruit. There are two crops in the
year, a winter one and a summer one. The winter crop is
ripe about the months of July and August, and is a small
crop. The summer crop, which is a large one, comes on in
December or January, the latter being the month near the

end of which hurricanes most frequently occur, and which sometimes destroy the crop. The fruit is generally round or oval, averaging about six inches in diameter, but there is a considerable diversity in the size. It is called bread-fruit by Europeans, because, in appearance and in consistency, it has a considerable resemblance to fine wheaten bread. It is very easily cooked ; it may be either boiled, steamed in the native oven, or roasted on the embers. In heathen times the natives of Aneityum and the Southern islands of the group had no vessels in which to boil anything. Now they are procuring pots, saucepans, kettles, &c. At Port Resolution on Tanna, the natives cooked their food by immersing it in the boiling springs till it was fit for being eaten. The natives frequently lay their bread-fruit on the hot embers, and keep turning it for fifteen or twenty minutes, or longer, according to cir- cumstances. It is then perfectly cooked. They afterwards scrape off the skin very gently, and you have then the finest hot rolls either for breakfast or any other meal. You have bread nearly pure white, only very slightly yellow, but unadulterated, soft, delicious to the taste, wholesome and nourishing. I have the names of thirty-two varieties of bread-fruit growing on Aneityum. The fruit requires to be eaten as fast as it ripens, as it cannot be kept fresh more than a day or two after it is pulled. The fact that it has to be eaten so soon, as well as its abundance, and its nutritious qualities, has a good deal to do with the improved appearance of the natives during the bread-fruit season ; for they get quite fat, plump, and vigorous, especially during the con tinuance of the summer crop. But they have a mode of preserving the bread-fruit, either when the crop is very plentiful and they cannot eat it all, or when the ripe fruit is blown down by a hurricane; they dig pits about three or four feet deep, and three feet in diameter, line them with cocoa-nut leaves, cut up each bread-fruit into four pieces each, and then cast them into these pits, cover the fruit with leaves and earth. The fruit undergoes a kind of fermentation; by and by they take it out, work it up, and put it back again into the pits and cover it up. When thus prepared it will keep good for some months, and in the "hungry season," when food is scarce, they take it out as they require it, knead it up into little loaves, and cook it in the native oven. The taste is strong, and the smell still more so, but when better food is not plentiful, it supplies a want, and proves a good stand by; it ekes out a scanty allowance, and serves as a substitute till something better can be found. Providence is kind to those simple islanders in supplying their many wants. Paley's famous law of compensation comes often into operation in their behalf, many are the resources on which they can fall back, so that anything like a severe famine is but seldom known; hence they love their islands, enjoy their bread-fruit, bask in the glowing sunshine, and bless the giver of all good.

THE ORANGE.

Of the fruit trees introduced the orange family is that which appears to thrive best. There is a native orange which grows well, but which is so bitter that it cannot be eaten; but on all the islands the ordinary introduced oranges, of different kinds, grow remarkably well. For several years the trees in my garden produced from 20,000 to 30,000 oranges annually, and the quality of the fruit was as excellent as the quantity was large. On one occasion a gentleman from Victoria paid a visit to the New Hebrides, and stayed with us on Aneityum for a couple of months or so, during the time the orange crop was in season. He greatly relished our oranges; but some time afterwards he wrote me, that he had never been able to relish an orange since, the Australian oranges were so poor and insipid after those he had got on Aneityum. Now, if the principles of Christianity were brought to bear with sufficient power on the population of the New Hebrides, the orange groves would soon become so extensive, that the commerce of New Zealand would find it profitable to send down its smartest running steamers to our islands; we should fill them, and flood that colony with the finest oranges, and drive the inferior products of Australia completely out of that market.

THE SANDAL-WOOD.

The only other tree to which I shall advert at this time is the *sandal-wood* tree, which at one time grew extensively on the New Hebrides, especially on Eromanga and Espiritu Santo, but which is now nearly all cut down. It is a scented wood, a hard, knotty, and crooked tree, of slow growth, and does not attain a large size, seldom more than ten or twelve inches in diameter. It is a valuable article of commerce. It used to bring from £30 to £45 a ton in China. It was estimated that one or two firms in Sydney realised as much as £70,000 for the sandal-wood which they obtained on Eromanga alone. The Chinese manufacture the most workable part of the wood into dressing-cases, work-boxes, and various articles of curious workmanship, while the shavings, parings, and other odds and ends are collected, mixed with gums, and burned as incense before their idols in their sacred temples. Referring to the use of sandal-wood in this way for upholding idolatry, the wife of a trader in the islands, who had been long engaged in this business, a very clever, intelligent woman, remarked, on one occasion, to the captain of the *Dayspring*, that she thought, although it appeared to be a very paying business, it was, after all, a very unlucky occupation to be employed in, gathering firewood for the devil; they had made three or four fortunes, but they had as often lost them, and she believed they would at last die in beggary. The sandal-wood tree, according to Biblical botanists, is the same, or at least belongs to the same family, as the algum or almug trees mentioned in 1 Kings x. 11, and 2 Chronicles ii. 8, ix. 10, 11, which Hiram's ships brought to Solomon from Ophir, and with which the king made rails for the house of the Lord, and for the king's house, harps also, and psalteries for singers. The sandal-wood trade was a lucky business in those days. So far as we learn, none of Hiram's ships were lost, and none of those engaged in the trade became bankrupt, or died in beggary; and why? because instead of gathering firewood for the devil, they brought the finest specimens of wood which the regions of the East could supply, to furnish materials out of which to prepare the ornamental work for the temple of the Lord and the palace of the king, and to make those instruments of music with which they sounded the praises of Jehovah. The devil is a bad paymaster; but the Lord keeps and rewards those who serve Him. In connection with the sandal-wood there is a beautiful saying, or proverb, in the East Indies, where this scented tree grows. They say, " A good man is like the sandal-wood tree—as the sandal-wood tree leaves a part of its fragrance on the axe that cuts it down, so the good man leaves his blessing on the head of the man that does him an injury."

In the New Hebrides there are no cereals—no wheat, no barley, no oats; none of these will grow there. Indian corn or maize, however, has been introduced and grows well. But notwithstanding this there is no lack of food; there is an abundance of yams, taro, sweet potatoes, bananas, sugar cane, and other productions. If the natives were Christianised those islands would become the West Indies to Australia and New Zealand. But the commercial value of those islands depends almost entirely upon the natives being Christianised. Where the natives are heathen there is no security for life and property, and no reliable labour to be obtained; but in so far as Christianity is embraced by the natives, life and property become secure, and reliable labour can be obtained on the spot. European capital and native labour combined would develop the resources of the islands.

CHAPTER XVIII.

NATURAL HISTORY: TARO.

I am often asked, What is *taro?* what is it like? how does it grow? is it indigenous on the islands, or has it been introduced? is it good food? how is it cooked? and a great many other questions about it. Taro is the *Arum esculentum* of botanists. It is the most highly prized food on Aneityum. On some other islands the yam is the staple article of food, but on Aneityum the taro holds the chief place. The natives could not hold a feast without taro. They might have yams, bread-fruit, bananas, plantains, horse-chestnuts, sweet potatoes, sugar-cane, and every vegetable that is eaten, but without taro the feast would not be complete. On one occasion I was urging on a marriage, but the parties connected with it pleaded for delay, for which I could see no reason. At last one of the leading men took me aside, and said to me that the taro was not ripe, and would not be ripe for two or three months. "But," I said, "you have plenty of other food." "Yes," he said, "but we could not have a marriage feast without taro: it would never do." In the estimation of the natives, it would have been as much out of place to have a feast without taro, as for us to have a tea-party without bread of any kind. Taro is a remarkably fine root. It grows like a carrot or parsnip, but much larger, and it does not taper at the lower end: it looks as if the point of the taro were cut off straight across. A large taro is about the size and shape of a man's arm from the elbow to the wrist. The top leaves are not unlike those of a turnip, but they project higher up; while in colour they more resemble rhubarb, but are smoother on the upper surface. The skin or rind is black or brownish. The taro is an agreeable and nutritious article of food, mealy or farinaceous like the best potatoes; in taste slightly different from the potato, but equally as pleasant as the potato. In colour the body of the taro is white or slightly yellow. It is indigenous both on Aneityum and everywhere in the South Seas. Dr. Thomson, an eminent army surgeon, while stationed in Auckland, wrote a book on New Zealand, in which he said that taro contained twice as much nutriment as the potato, pound for pound. If New Zealand taro was so much superior to the potato, I feel certain that Aneityum taro will contain three times as much nourishment as the potato, weight for weight. Taro grows both on dry ground and on marshy. It is of all sizes, from three inches to twelve or fifteen, and is proportionate in thickness, from one to three or four inches in diameter. It grows best on marshy ground, but it must be surrounded with running not stagnant water. It needs constant irrigation, hence the common or public canals have to be kept in constant repair. Taro is a slow growing plant. It takes nearly a twelvemonth to come to maturity; when taken out of the ground it can be kept fresh, and good for eating, for little more than a week; but then it grows all the year round. The natives are always taking it up, and always planting it anew; but it grows much faster in summer than in winter. It is propagated in two ways: either by planting the shoots or small tubers that grow around the principal roots, or by

planting the stalk or top of the plant when the root has been
cut off.   The latter is the method which the natives generally
prefer.   The taro can be cooked either by boiling it in a pot,
steaming it in the native oven, or by roasting on the embers.
When cold, it is best heated by cutting it into slices, and
heating it in the frying-pan.   In my lexicon I have seventy
different names for the varieties of taro, and probably the
natives have more than those.

The Yam.

The yam, the *Dioscoria alata* of botanists, is not much cultivated on Aneityum, but on parts of Tanna it is the staple
food.   As a general rule the yam is cultivated as a staple
article of food on the low flat coral islands where water is
scarce, and the taro on the high volcanic islands where water
is plentiful.   The yam, like the taro, is of all sizes; but the
larger roots are three or four times larger than the largest
taro.   Some species or varieties are farinaceous or mealy,
resembling taro; but, as a general rule, the yam is much
softer in texture and more watery than the taro.   In its
substance the yam is granular, which the taro is not.   The
yam, however, is in one respect quite different from the taro,
it does not ripen all the year round; there is only one crop
in the year, but then the yams can be kept good for several
months.   The skin of the yam is very tender, and is easily
injured, and if the skin is broken, the yam soon begins to rot
and decay; the natives, therefore, handle them with great
care; they handle them as tenderly as they would do eggs, if
they mean to keep them.   Yams are cooked in the same way
as taro, but they contain only about half the nourishment of

taro, weight for weight. They are cultivated quite differently from taro. Taro grows best on land over which water is running, yams grow best on light, dry, sandy, or volcanic soil. The natives on Aneityum form a mound from six to ten feet in diameter, and about three feet high in the centre, the earth being first thoroughly pulverised. They plant the seed yam around the mound, the eye of the seed being slightly exposed. The tops of the yams are long slender vines with small leaves. When the vines begin to grow, the natives prepare a frame or a lattice-work of reeds, about a foot high or so above the ground, and stretching away on one side of the mound to a distance of from twelve to twenty feet, which in due time is densely covered with foliage.

When I was in New Zealand, and was contemplating going to the New Hebrides, my much respected and highly esteemed friend, the Rev. James Watkin of the Wesleyan Mission, who had lived several years as a missionary on the Tongan group —islands famous for fine yams—in the way of giving me information and encouragement about the New Hebrides, and what the advantages of the field would be, said, " In the matter of native food you will get so-and-so," enumerating a few of the most important and attractive items, and then said finally, with great emphasis, " And you will get *yams !* " Some of the missionaries, on the yam-growing islands on the New Hebrides and on the Loyalty Islands, used also to speak in glowing terms of the yams on their respective islands, and no doubt truthfully, as they felt. But as I lived on a taro-growing, not on a yam-producing island, and as the taste for yams is to some extent an acquired taste, whereas the taste for taro, like that for potatoes, is to most people a natural taste, I never acquired the taste for yams, and always preferred the taro to the yam.

But the old Latins said: *De gustibus non disputandum*, and we continue to say, as if it were an English proverb, "There is no disputing about tastes;" but be that as it may, one thing is undisputable, that the yam is a most valuable esculent root.

The Banana.

The banana, *Musa sapientum*, is a herbaceous plant which grows luxuriantly everywhere throughout the South Sea Islands. It is propagated from shoots or suckers, and most of the species or varieties attain a height of from twelve to fifteen feet or more. The stock or stem is from six to nine inches in diameter. The banana is not a tree, but the stem or body of the plant is formed of a number of soft concentric layers, about half an inch in thickness, somewhat resembling a thick-necked onion. The leaves are long and pendent, from four to six feet long, and about two feet broad. When slightly heated over the fire they are soft, tough, and flexible as cloth, and are employed by the natives in wrapping up puddings and other articles of food, to preserve the juice from being lost, when cooked in the native ovens. There is only one bunch of fruit on each plant, but it contains about a hundred bananas, more or fewer, from six to nine inches in length, somewhat like a cucumber: the fruit, as well as the leaves, when growing, is of a beautiful pea-green colour, and when ripe a rich bright yellow. The bunch is cut as soon as one or two of the bananas begin to change colour; it is hung up in the house for a week or so, and by that time the whole bunch is yellow and fit for use. When ripe they may be eaten either raw, or baked as a pudding in a dish, and eaten with milk. The taste is delicious, something like a very fine ripe pear, but in substance softer.   Everybody likes it from the very first.   In my lexicon I have the native names for forty-five different species or varieties of bananas.   In Samoa they have more than fifty.   The banana, it is said, produces more nutritious substance in the same space than any other plant.   In Mexico, Humboldt calculated that an acre of ground planted with bananas was sufficient to support fifty men, whilst the same extent of land in wheat would barely supply the wants of three, or if planted with potatoes to support nine.   On Aneityum, as far as we could judge, we found that the banana was as prolific as Humboldt found it to be in Mexico.   Our garden of about half an acre, planted with bananas, went far to feed from twenty to thirty young people living on our premises.   We had, on an average, two bunches a day, or about seven hundred bunches in the year; and most certainly nothing else that we could have cultivated would have been anything like so productive.

There is one banana known by the name of the " Chinese banana," "most probably," says Mr. Mills, "the *Musa cavendishii*, the origin of which is said to be the Isle of France," which was introduced into the South Seas half a century ago, which has been a great boon to the natives, which has been highly appreciated, and has spread over the islands with great rapidity.   When the apostolic John Williams left England in the *Camden* in 1838, an English nobleman, the Duke of Devonshire, presented him with some boxes of plants for the benefit of the mission.   These were landed in Samoa till Mr. Williams should have time to dispose of them.   They remained unopened till after his martyrdom on Eromanga, when they were opened by the Rev. W. Mills, a man of eminent scientific tastes ; but every plant was dead except one shoot of the Chinese banana ;

but this proved to be a priceless treasure. Mr. Mills planted
it out, and tended it with great care. At the end of a year it
produced a bunch weighing nearly a hundred pounds. When
its value was discovered, every chief in Samoa, and every
missionary on the group, was eager to obtain shoots, and in
a short time this new banana was known in every part of
Samoa; and thenceforth every teacher that was sent forth
to any heathen island carried with him a small basket with
a few shoots of this banana as part of his outfit, till they
were introduced into every group from the Society Islands on
the east to the New Hebrides and the Loyalty Islands on the
west; from Savage Islands on the south to the groups of
islands on the line, and I have no doubt that by this time
they are to be found along the whole of the south-west coast
of New Guinea. The Chinese bananas possess two advantages over the native bananas. They are of a finer quality,
and they grow to little more than half the height of the
native banana, and hence are not so easily blown down and
destroyed by hurricanes.

When we went to Aneityum, and were settled on our
station of Aname, Amosa, the Samoan teacher, had a fine
bunch of Chinese bananas in his garden. As soon as it was
fully ripe he brought it in a present to us as an offering of
welcome. We were afraid to accept of it, not knowing how
we should be able to repay the good man for such a rare and
valuable present. When our garden, a small one at first,
was prepared, Amosa, Tavita, Williamu and others, gathered
up among them thirteen small shoots of the Chinese banana
and planted them. Eleven months after this we cut the first
ripe bunch of our own. We never planted any kind but the
Chinese. By the end of a year the suckers numbered sixty

or seventy, and from that time forward we began and gave them away right and left till there was not a native on the island who had not Chinese bananas, *Nohos Saina*, as they called them.

But our bananas were made to serve another and a higher purpose in connection with the mission.   Towards the end of the first decade of missionary operations on the island, a party of Tannese came over to Ancityum in the *John Knox* on a visit.   Our chiefs and teachers were very attentive to them, and showed them everything that was worth being seen, our garden among the rest.   "Look here," said one of the chiefs, "see what bananas the missionary has.   You on Tanna think that if you take the Gospel you will have no food, but look at the missionary's garden; you all know that in three years our gardens are grown out, and will bear no more, but the missionary's garden has been growing for seven years, and it is still as good as ever, and why? because of his Christianity: the Gospel does not keep the food from growing, as your sacred men tell you.   The chief overlooked the fact that, like the dresser of the vineyard in the parable, we had been digging about them and dunging them, that every day we had buried around their roots all the dung produced by our cows and our goats, and in this way pre-served the fertility of the soil.   The argument from the bananas, ill applied though it had been, was, however, more convincing to the Tannese than a whole volume on the evidences.   Taura the chief went home, and went over all his ten lands, publishing what he had seen on Aneityum; and, according to the native accounts that came back to us, from the south of Tanna to the west, from Kwamera to Black Beach, Taura's words shook the whole land.   And had the

disposition to receive the truth on the part of the Tannese
been as strong as the demonstration was clear, all that part
of Tanna had become Christian; but alas! it was then as it
had been of old, no mighty work was done because of their
unbelief.

THE PLANTAIN.

The plantain, *Musa paradisiaca*, grows only to a limited
extent on Aneityum. I have the names of only six species
or varieties. The plantain grows only in the inland districts,
I never saw it growing near the shore. The fruit grows in
quite a different manner from that of the banana. The bunch
of fruit on the banana after it comes out, turns over and
hangs down from the top towards the ground, but the bunch
of fruit on the plantain projects straight up. "The plan
tain or banana," says the *Encyclopædia Britannica*, "belongs
botanically to the same family as Manilla hemp, but its fibre
is not so fine. By adequate preparation, however, it may
be made into fabrics of elegant appearance, as well as more
coarse and strong ones. Hitherto, it would seem, little care
has been bestowed on the preparation and assortment of the
fibres. The extraordinary productiveness of this plant as
a food-producer has been the sole reason of its cultivation,
but every plant yields from three to four pounds of fibre, the
utilising of which needs only labour and care." Our practice
has been this: when we cut the fruit, we immediately cut
down the stem also, and throw it into a pit to be converted
into manure; but had we utilised the fibre, my garden,
assuming Humboldt's calculations to be correct, would not
only have fed twenty-five natives, but produced from a ton
to a ton and a half of fibre equal to Manilla hemp. And if

the French would only let us alone, and if the Labour Traffic would only cease, we might have a hemp manufactory on every island, as well as twenty other industries. The commercial value of the islands, were they first christianised, and life and property secure, and labour obtainable, have never yet been calculated; but it would be immense.

ARROWROOT.

Arrowroot, or more properly, as some say *Arree* root, is indigenous in the New Hebrides, and in most of the islands of the South Seas. The bulbs are very like those of potatoes, but the stalks and leaves are different : they grow up in a bunch to the height of about two feet. Arrowroot cannot be reckoned as a food for people in health; but for infants and invalids it is valuable. Its medicinal properties are great; as a diffusive stimulant for removing chills, and restoring heat to the body, it acts as speedily and as powerfully as brandy, without any of its reactionary and injurious effects. Dr. Seeman, in his very able work on Fiji, says "it is invaluable in cases of dysentery and diarrhœa, the bane of the South Seas," (he should have said of Fiji only), but—"it is necessary to have it genuine." There are two kinds of arrowroot in Fiji, there are the same in the New Hebrides, but in neither group do the natives make any difference in preparing the bulbs for flour, any more than we should in this country between two kinds of potatoes in the making of potato starch. The Bermuda arrowroot is universally recognised as the best that comes to this country, and is sold at three shillings and sixpence a pound if not more. When we were living in London in 1877 we were introduced by our friend Canon

I

Tristram to the widow and daughter of a missionary, who
had laboured along with him in Bermuda under the Church
Missionary Society, and who annually received from their
friends a small quantity of the genuine Bermuda arrowroot.
My wife and they made an exchange between the Bermuda
and Aneityum arrowroot, that they might both compare them
respectively. They did so, but each of them preferred their
own. Both kinds were genuine, both were good; and they
concluded that each preferred that to which they had been
most accustomed. But the Bermuda and the Aneityum were
evidently different species of the same plant. The Aneityum
contained the most starch, which renders it so valuable in
bowel complaints : but the Bermuda must possess some other
properties which enhance its general value so much. The
supply of Bermuda arrowroot is very limited. It is said that
there is more port wine drunk in London than all that is
produced in Portugal; so it is affirmed that there is more
Bermuda arrowroot used in London than all that is made
in Bermuda, and it can be bought cheaper in some places
in London than it can be bought in Bermuda itself. Such
are some of the achievements of commerce! The Aneityum
and Fiji arrowroot is the *Tacca pinnatifida* of the botanists.
The Bermuda, I presume, is the *Maranta arundinacea,*
"which," it is said, "comes to us from the warmer regions
of the New World."

For more than a quarter of a century the natives of
Aneityum have prepared arrowroot and made a contribution
of it, first for the payment of their Bibles, and next to assist
in sending the Gospel to the heathen on the other islands.
During the three years that my station was vacant, the
natives made the average quantity of arrowroot, and prepared

it with as much care as when we were living among them.
It is true the Rev. Joseph Annand was living on the other
side of the island, and exercised very efficiently a general
superintendence over them, weighed the arrowroot, and put
it carefully up in casks; but the chief responsibility fell upon
the natives themselves. To the friends and supporters of the
mission, the history of the arrowroot movement, even had
there been nothing else, would have been accepted as a satisfactory proof that the Christianity of the natives was genuine.
I have been told by those who ought to know, that there is
no foreign mission station belonging to the Free Church,
where the contributions for the extension of the Gospel are
proportionately so liberal, as those made by the natives of
Aneityum; and these are all made in arrowroot. I have
elsewhere stated how Mrs. Inglis learned to make the arrowroot from Tutau, the wife of a Rarotongan teacher; how she
taught the natives on the following year; and how the process went on till it became a settled industry, a standing
institution, and a part of the mission. It is now made on
every island where Christianity has got a firm footing. It is
made like potato starch. I had twenty-eight schools, and
every teacher and his people made a contribution. It was
done in this way. At the proper time they made a plantation
of arrowroot; when it was ripe they dug it up, and prepared
it at the rate of four or five schools each week. The natives
provided the raw material and I provided zinc tubs, buckets,
graters, sheets, bags, tables, and casks, and what might be
called the plant of the manufactory. The Teachers' Institution
was utilised for three months during the vacation for drying
the arrowroot. In order that it might be made properly,
I provided everything that the natives did not themselves

possess. Being thus assisted they went to the work with a will. I also appointed two of the most active and trustworthy of the natives to attend to the drying, sifting, weighing, and packing of the arrowroot. The process was as follows. I shall describe it as it was done at my station. On Monday morning the natives collected all the ripe arrowroot. Then so many of them were told off to collect food and make an oven for the whole party, that they might be strong for the work; another party, mostly of women and girls, were appointed to wash the tubers, and scrape the skin off, and then grate them to a pulp; a third party of strong men and boys undertook to strain the grated matter through a thin cloth into tubs. It was night before the work was done. This was the great day. The tubs were all left full. On the Tuesday morning the men returned and found the arrowroot all sunk to the bottom of the tubs, and the water almost pure. This they poured off, and filled the tubs again with fresh water, and stirred up the sediment till it was all mixed with the water. This process was repeated two or three times during the course of the day; at night it was again all strained through the thin cloth, so that no mote or impurity of any kind should be found in the arrowroot. On Wednesday morning the water was again poured off, and the pure arrowroot was ready for being dried. When first strained the arrowroot is bitter and poisonous, at least fowls eating it die; but when the water has been changed on it five or six times it is sweet, or tasteless, and perfectly wholesome. In the backyard of our Teachers' Institution tables had been erected; first rough frames had been fixed up, about three feet high. These were covered with old reed fencing, being a wicker work about four feet broad; large fresh banana leaves were

spread on these tables, and the lumps of wet but still solid
arrowroot were laid on the leaves, and exposed to the sun,
and before night it was so far dried that it could be removed
from the leaves, broken up by the hands, and spread out on
cotton sheets, which my wife had prepared for the purpose.
Meanwhile, we had the Teachers' Institution prepared with
tables, by placing the forms across the floor, and covering
them with boards on which the sheets and the arrowroot could
be spread out at night, or on wet days; the windows were
all opened; and hence it could be put out or in as required in
the shortest time.   On the Thursday morning the two men
appointed to watch it had it all spread out on the tables, and
exposed to the sun; and, if the weather was good, by Saturday it was fit for being sifted, and could be rolled up during
the Sabbath, without being injured.   If rolled up wet it soon
became heated and discoloured; but if the weather was unfavourable, and it was still damp, it was spread out on the
sheets, on those tables in the house, and covered with other
sheets to prevent dust falling on it.   If the weather was
good it was fit for being put into casks by the end of a fortnight; but if the weather was wet or showery, it was three
weeks or a month before it was quite dry.   The same process
was gone through in all the twenty-eight schools.   The
teachers and the natives got the arrowroot all made and
washed at their respective lands, but it was all brought to
the mission station to be dried and finished up.   The planting
and the making was all done by the general public; the two
or three men whom I appointed to watch it, and whom I
paid for their work, did all the rest.   The time required for
the whole process was fully two months.   The time that each
person gave to the work was in general three or four days.

They had little or no money, but they gave their labour without grudging. In all that we got them to do for the mission, we tried to spread the labour as widely as possible, that it might touch the whole community, but touch each person as lightly as might be—touch them so lightly that it was never felt to be oppressive; and thus what they did for the Gospel was felt to be a privilege and not a burden. If wise arrangements are made, it is astonishing how much help may be cheerfully obtained to advance the kingdom of Christ.

CHAPTER XIX.

HAD the Rev. Gilbert White, M.A., the eminent naturalist of last century, lived on our island, he would no doubt have made the Natural History of Aneityum as interesting and as well known as the Natural History of Selbourne; and Sir William Jardine, Bart., of Jardine Hall, would have brought out a new edition of the book, with additions, and have interested scientific observers with his many important facts. But as I am writing only a chapter on this subject, and not a book, and as I have not had time to make any extensive observations, I shall confine myself to a very few specimens. Mr. White regretted that he lived in an inland locality, far from the sea or any large river, and hence had to confine his observations to land animals, and could give no account of those inhabiting the waters. On the other hand, as I resided always on the sea-shore, I shall say little of land animals, but confine myself chiefly to denizens of the sea. The only indigenous quadrupeds on the island are a small rat, and perhaps the pig. The British or Norway rat has, however, made good his residence on the island. There is no tradition as to the origin of the pig on Aneityum, but as its name is *pigath*, which may be a corruption of *pig* or *piggy*, it looks very like as if English were its origin. Among the Malays the name for pig is everywhere *puaka*, which some regard as a corruption of *pork*, although other derivations have been suggested. There are four kinds of lizards on the island; the smallest, which is very beautiful, is about six inches long; the largest is from a foot to eighteen inches. There are three species of bats, one smaller than our common bat, a second called the stinking bat, and the third a large species, generally called the flying fox. When flying it seems larger than a common crow. It is fat and good eating, much prized by the natives, but has a very offensive smell. There are two species of swallows, both smaller than the swallows in this country; they never migrate, but remain on the island all the year round. There are four species of pigeons, one a small species, but remarkably beautiful, fully realising the description of the psalmist—

" Whose wings with silver, and with gold
Whose feathers covered are "—

these colours being laid on a ground of the loveliest green. There are two species of hawks, about the ordinary size of hawks in this country. There is no hawk on Tanna, though only forty miles distant. Hence hawk feathers are a standing article of export from Aneityum to Tanna; they are in great demand for making plumes with which to adorn the heads of the Tannese chiefs. There are two species of owls, one larger and one smaller; there is one or more species of paroquet, a heron, gulls and other sea-birds, and several species of small birds resembling the robin or the linnet, but rather smaller. There is also a very small bird just like a wren. There is a bird called the *Lau-aing*, resembling a water-hen; its feathers are black and its legs yellow, its beak like that of a common fowl. Like the ostrich, " she layeth her eggs in the earth, and warmeth them in the dust." When hatched, the young ones seek food for themselves, but only a few of them live. The habits of this bird furnish the basis for a proverb : the natives say of a mother who neglects her children, *" Et ithivaing lau-aing aien,"* She is just like a *Lau-aing.* I have the native names of more than forty species of birds, of more than seventy species of sea-fish, of more than thirty species of fresh-water fish, and over seventy species of shell-fish. The natives are great fishers; around all the island, twice a day, at low water, in good weather, they are out on the reef—especially the women—gathering shell-fish; these are a standing and much-prized article of food.

There are no poisonous reptiles on the island. There are two species of serpents. The one, called the *Nimyeuv,* is found in the woods, chiefly on the mountains; in colour it is brown on the back and yellow on the belly; the other, called the *Nispeuv,* is found on the shore, chiefly among rocks, and is to some extent amphibious in its habits; its colour is formed by a succession of alternate black and grey bands round the body of an elegant appearance. Both of them, when full-grown, are found from two and a half to four feet in length, but the bite of neither of them is poisonous. There is, however, a small shell-fish called the *Inhaag,* which contains a virulent poison. This fish is a gasteropod, and inhabits a univalve, cone-shaped, spiral shell, about two inches in length. It does not bite, or inflict any wound; but when disturbed, it blows out its poison, which seems to be a vapour rather than a liquid. It is generally the hand that comes in contact with the poisonous matter. In a short time the hand becomes painful and swells; then the swelling extends up the arm, and finally the whole body becomes affected, and, unless prompt measures are adopted, death follows in a few hours. In the year 1855, from January 1st till April 1st, out of thirteen deaths four were occasioned by the poisoning of the *Inhaag*. In three of these cases the persons were dead in less than twelve hours. In the case of the fourth, a strong man, he lingered for a fortnight, and then died. The native treatment was to bandage the arm and to make incisions. I used oil copiously, both internally and externally, and often with good effect. But I wrote to my friend, the late Dr. Logan of Wellington, New Zealand, a retired navy surgeon, asking his advice. He advised me to try the remedy employed in Africa for the bite of the rattlesnake, which is to dig a hole in soft earth, place the arm in the hole up to the shoulder, then fill up with earth, and let the arm remain buried for four or five hours. This was like applying a large poultice, and it seemed to act accordingly and draw the virus out of the part affected. I instructed the natives in the application of this remedy, and for many long years before we left the island I never heard of a death caused by the *Inhaag*. Accidents generally occurred in this way. Around the whole island, the natives, as I have said, at low tide, by night or by day, or both, as it may happen, go out in great numbers in search of shell-fish. The *Inhaag*, like the other shell-fish, lies generally in the sand or among the stones; and when searching for other fish, they occasionally disturb it. If they see it, they are in no danger; they can catch it with impunity at the spiral or closed end of the shell, as it then squirts out its poison in the opposite direction; and after the ejection of the poison it is harmless, and the natives even cook them and eat them without any danger. The *Inhaag* is not plentiful; otherwise nobody would

be safe ; and as it is, I have reason to think that carelessness
is often the cause of accidents with this fish. The number
of cases of poisoning in 1855 was unusually great. The sea
had frequently receded very far at low tide, and the natives
at those times went far out into new ground, where, like
other shell-fish, the *Inhaag* was more numerous than in the
old fishing-ground, and the danger in the same proportion
greater.

At certain times different kinds of fish appear to be more
or less poisonous, though quite wholesome at other times,
apparently as they are in or out of season. After eating
them, at these times, the natives become very sick, and soon
after the sickness is over their hands and feet are daily
affected with sharp pains, and are rendered more or less
powerless. Some fish are recognised as always poisonous,
others as always good, and a third class as poisonous at times
only. Mrs. Paton of Aniwa and some of her children were
nearly killed on one occasion by eating a poisonous fish which
they understood to be a good one. After the severe sickness
was over a rash came out on their skin, and for a long time
they felt now and again cramps and a prickly sensation in
their hands and feet. There seems to be a perfect infatuation
among some natives to eat fish, even when they know them
to be poisonous. Even Ester, one of the most sensible women
on Aneityum, nearly poisoned herself in this way. For many
a day her hands and feet were occasionally benumbed. Mrs.
Inglis said to her, " O Ester, did you not know that that fish
was poisonous?" "Oh yes," she said, " I knew." " What, then,
made you eat it ?" " Oh," she said, " I cannot tell ; I was so
eager to eat fish that I could not keep myself from it, though
I knew the danger." On one occasion I knew of a native

who caught a decidedly poisonous fish, and knew it to be so, and yet he cooked it and ate it, though every native in the place remonstrated with him; and he was dead in twelve hours. On Aneityum the liver of the shark is very poisonous. It makes excellent lamp oil, is purer and burns better than train-oil; but after melting the liver and making the oil, the natives are so afraid of the poison, lest it should injure their food, when they touch their food with their hands, that they not only wash their hands thoroughly, but they hold them over the smoke of a fire for a considerable time to remove the last taint of the poison. On one occasion, Pita, one of our Samoan teachers, got the liver of a shark, had it cooked, and ate it. All the natives protested, and remonstrated with him to the utmost. His poor wife wept and cried. "O Pita," she said, "if you eat that fish, and poison yourself, and die, what is to become of me and these poor children in this strange land?" "Oh," said Pita, "the sharks are not poisonous in Samoa, and why should they be poisonous here?" In the face of all this opposition, eat it he would, and eat it he did. We, in our different circumstances, cannot understand the fish-crave that dominates those ichthyophagists, those fish-eating islanders. We knew nothing of all this, but shortly after midnight we heard a rap at our bedroom window. It was Pita's wife. "O Misi," she said in the most plaintive tones, "Pita is dying; do come and pray with us." I rose at once and went with her. Pita had all the appearance of a dying man, and I prayed with him as such, and administered such medicines as seemed most suitable. He was a strong, powerful, healthy man, in the prime of life; he survived and recovered; he escaped, as it were, with the skin of his teeth. His pulse had come down to about fifty, and continued at that for some time. Among my medicines I had a bottle of brandy, which had remained there for some years unopened. Acting on the authority of medical books, I administered small doses of this stimulant several times daily, till the contents of the bottle were nearly exhausted, and the pulse had risen to something approaching its normal condition. Pita lived many years after this, and finally returned to Samoa; but he never became quite his former self—he carried the effects of that poisoning with him to his grave.

In the stream that runs past the mission station at Aname a flood, on one occasion, by carrying away quantities of mud, laid bare two enormous shells, which, when the water subsided, I got the natives to carry out, and place one on each side of the garden-walk in front of the mission-house. Unless I am very much astray in my conchology, these shells were specimens of the *chama gigas*, or *gigantic cockle*, the largest and heaviest shell yet discovered. They appear to have been first seen by Captain Flinders in the Indian Ocean, although before that time Captain Cook found shells of the same kind on the Great Barrier reef on the east of Australia. They were so large and so strong, that when his seamen placed a piece of a ship's cable in the opening or mouth of the shell, the animal snapped it in two as easily as Samson did the green withes with which the Philistines bound him. "We have seen," says Maunder in his "Treasury of Natural History," "an immense pair in the church of St. Sulspice in Paris, where they serve to hold holy water." This shell, he says, is also called *Tridacna*. Why this name was applied to it is not to me at all obvious. According to Ainsworth, *Tridacna*, or *Ostrea tridacna*, means shells that can be eaten at three bites; but if the animal that lives in the *chamas gigas* was ever eaten at three bites, it must have been by some of the giants who warred against Jupiter, and who heaved up Ossa on the top of Pelion, and compared to whom Goliath must have been a pigmy; or by some of the less fabulous *megatheria*, which basked in the sun and disported themselves in the deltas during the far remote palæozoic ages recorded in the chronicles of geology. Those two shells, which were not mates, were each four feet long, two feet seven inches broad, and nine inches thick at the umbo. I had not the means of weighing them, but each of them was as much as two men could with some difficulty lift up from the ground. Some time afterwards I found single shells apparently of the same species, but not quite so large; and there were others which I did not see, but of whose existence the natives informed me, and which were imbedded in the sands or adhering to the reefs. Small bivalves—that is, small compared with these—either of the same or of a similar species, from six to twelve or fifteen inches long, are found alive, adhering to the reefs in great numbers; but no live specimens of this large size were ever seen on the island, even by the oldest natives. Being so large, they could not be numerous, and hence the natives would easily kill them out. "A number of those cockles," says Captain Flinders, "were taken on board the ship, and stewed in the coppers, but they were too rank to be agreeable food, and were eaten by few." But on Aneityum, where the natives pick the bones of a whale as neatly as they do the bones of a herring, a *Tridacna* would not stand them long. The native name of those shells is *nipjineri;* but the two which I obtained were worshipped as *natmases*, or gods, in the days of heathenism, by the name of *Nethuing*. From time immemorial the upper part of those shells had been seen above the stones and mud in the channel of the stream; and when the natives were feeding pigs for feasts, before giving the food to the animals, they laid it upon these shells, in the belief that, by doing so, virtue would proceed from the *natmases* to make the pigs large and fat. When they were about to plant taro they laid their *niraks*—the sticks with which they dig the ground—on the shells, in the belief that, by doing so, they would secure an excellent crop of taro. Every undertaking on the island was preceded by an act of homage to some *natmas*. In their own way, the Aneityumese, like the Athenians, were (δεισιδαιμονεστεροι) "very religious," and there, as in Athens, it was easier to find a god than a man. How those shells came to be in such a place, and how long they had remained there no one knew. But time's destroying fingers, by the agency of the elements and the help of accidents, had left their impress on them both; the edges were chipped, and the enamel was corroded, and they had not that smooth and white appearance which they must have had when the animals were alive, and had not yet enjoyed the honours of an apotheosis or rites divine?

Aneityum, as is well known, is a fertile island; if it were fully and skilfully cultivated, it would soon be a little earthly paradise, like the garden of Eden itself. Food of all varieties, and to almost any amount, could easily be raised. But the *sea* there is nearly as rich in its supplies of food as the *land*, from the whale that tumbles about with his enormous bulk, to the flying-fish that rise from the crest of the waves on their finny wings, and skim along for fifty or a hundred yards, and then sink into their native element. Many of the fish in those seas are coarse and hard; but some of them at least are soft, and very delicate eating, equal to trout, herring, or salmon at home, or any of the fish mentioned in good old Izaak Walton's "Angler," yea, as tender as anything to be found either in the still waters of Lochfyne or in the rapid currents of the Pentland Firth, each of which is so famous for its matchless herrings.

THE TURTLE.

But the most highly prized denizen of the sea there is the edible or green turtle (*Chelonia midas*). As we are on the edge of the tropics, they are not so large as in lower latitudes nearer the line, nor are they so plentiful; nevertheless, they are sufficiently numerous to supply a fair amount of sport in the catching of them, and sufficiently large to supply a fair amount of food in the eating of them. They are amphibious, although they live in the sea, and feed on a kind of sea grass; but at the breeding season, the female comes ashore, digs a deep hole in the sand above high-water mark, and lays her eggs, to the number of one or two hundred, covers them up, and, like the ostrich, leaves them to be hatched by the heat of the sun. When the chicks come out of the shell, they make direct for the sea, and are never seen again till they return something like full-grown. A friend of mine, an eminent naturalist, the late John MacGillivray, Esq., F.R.S., told me that he was once encamped on a sandy beach on the northern coast of Australia; he was lying awake on his couch one night, and a fire was burning before him. By and by he saw the sand being upheaved near the fire, and then a tiny turtle, about the size of a dollar, emerged from the earth, and waddled off direct

for the sea, then another, and another, and another, and
finally a whole troop of them followed, and all made direct
for the ocean. His tent had been pitched on the top of a
turtle's nest, and probably the heat of the fire had has-
tened the departure of this orphan-like family, for whose
preservation and support God had otherwise made ample
provision.

The natives generally catch the turtles at night, but sometimes during the day. They have various modes of catching
them, but the most effectual is by means of nets furnished
with floats and sinks : the floats are not corks, however, but
cocoa-nuts, and the sinks are not leads but round stones.
When they catch the turtles, or entangle them, the first
thing to be done is to turn them over on their back; they
are then quite helpless, as they cannot turn themselves over
again. The natives seldom catch more than one or two at
a time, but occasionally they are more successful. One morning in 1875, a little fleet of canoes went out with two large
nets, and secured no fewer than six, out of a small shoal of
turtles which they had descried. They went out at daybreak,
and in less than two hours the whole six were hauled ashore,
and were lying on their backs on the beach within two
hundred yards of my door, but all of them alive. I weighed
one of them and found it to be 324 lbs. The six would
average 300 lbs. each, or 1800 lbs. in all.

Now only think of nearly a ton of genuine turtle ! What
an amount of pure, green fat must have been there ! that
transcendental delicacy, sacred to the festive boards of wor-
shipful aldermen ! What oceans of soup, pure, unadulterated
and genuine, could have been manufactured from such a large
supply of the real material fresh from the ocean ! none of

your mock turtle; none even of those lean skinny animals, closed in water-casks, and half starved on the passage from the Island of Ascension or elsewhere to England, and more dead than alive when they reach the Thames, and on which all the skill of London cooks is exercised in preparing that most admired and highly prized of all decoctions—*turtle-soup* —on occasions such as when our friends the·Lord Mayor, such as Sir Andrew Lusk, M.P., or the late Sir William McArthur, M.P., were wont to entertain their Majesty's Ministers to dinner, and dispense with such dignified courtesy the hospitalities of the Mansion House. Think again, moreover, of all these six fine turtles being eaten by savages and missionaries! The natives very generally, if they catch but one, give the mission family the head, which is the choicest portion. In the days of heathenism it was given to the chief, but now he foregoes his claim in favour of the missionary, but the missionary on his part recognises the obligation, and when he kills a pig he sends a roast of it to the chief, remembering the proverb about *giff-gaff*. On this occasion they brought us the finest head of the six. Brother and sister Murray and their little boy from Anelgauhat happened to be with us on a visit. But only fancy two mission families taking a holiday and luxuriously dining on a delicacy that would not only have graced a civic banquet, but would have been prized on the table of royalty itself.

This, I am aware, is a hazardous revelation to make, for the sake of our poor missionaries; pity for them is almost certain to be changed into envy, everybody's teeth will be set a watering, tears of sympathy for them will cease to be shed, and missionary contributions may perhaps dwindle down to driblets. "What!" they will say, "show pity, compassion, sympathy, for whom ? for people living better than aldermen, and dining on green turtle! Verily that man told us the truth who said, that some of those missionaries get into a very good way of doing."

CHAPTER XX.

COOKING—EATING—DRINKING KAVA.

THE principal mode of cooking on Aneityum and in the New
Hebrides, as it was in New Zealand, and in the South Seas
generally, was the native oven. On Aneityum, and in the
southern islands of the group, they had no means of boiling
anything; they had no vessels that could stand the fire. The
process of cooking was this:—In the first place a round pit
was dug, from nine inches to two feet deep, according to the
width; and from eighteen inches to three or four feet in
diameter. If it was a permanent oven, it was paved in the
bottom. Every family had a collection of fire stones, that
could be made red-hot without breaking; these stones were
from the size of a hen's egg to that of one's fist. The next
thing to be done was to collect a quantity of dry, generally
soft, wood, mostly branches of trees; if it was a large oven,
larger pieces were used. I shall describe a Saturday's oven,
being generally one of their largest, and also one of their best.
Often two or three families united to make one oven. In the
morning the men went away to the plantation for taro, or to
the woods for bread-fruit, or horse chestnuts—a much larger
and better fruit than ours that goes by that name; another
would go for a bunch of bananas, &c. If some fish happened
to be caught, they would be forthcoming; or if a pig had been
killed in the district, a leg or a shoulder of it would also be

there. They never salt their pork; but when a pig is killed it is at once divided among friends, and then cooked by them, but to be repaid at some future time, which is never forgotten. Some ripe cocoa-nuts are also stripped of the husk, the kernels grated down into a small wooden trough. This they strain through a cloth; in former times through a piece of native cloth that grows round the butt-end of the cocoa-nut branches; it is not unlike cheese-cloth in texture. The juice thus strained out is the true cocoa-nut milk, which can be used for coffee. With this milk they mix taro, or yams, or bananas, or occasionally arrowroot, from which to make puddings. This milk serves the purpose of lard, or suet, or butter. These puddings are wrapped up in banana leaves, which have been heated over the fire, and tied firmly by the neck with some cord-like fibre, made from the inner bark of some bush. While the men are away for wood, the women are away for leaves in which to wrap up the food. The taro or yams are carefully scraped, and, when washed quite clean, are wrapped up in banana, or other wholesome leaves; the fish, or pork, or fruit, as well as the puddings, are the same. The natives have a plant which they call *nasieij*, a small bush, the leaves of which grow in little clusters, which, when baked, or steamed, along with meat or fish, are uncommonly tender and palatable, more so than cabbage, kail, savoys, broccoli, cauliflower, brussels sprouts, or any of that family. They generally plant it among their bananas, and near their cottages. They usually wrap it up along with pork, or fowl, or fish, to absorb the juice. The dry wood is put into the pit, and then heaped up as high as it will lie; the stones are placed on the wood, fire is applied to it, and it is soon all ablaze. It continues to burn till all the wood is a mass of glowing embers, and the

stones are red hot. When burned out the whole falls to the
bottom. The stones are all taken quickly out by means of
sticks, or by a pair of native tongs, made of a long stick split
up at the one end. The embers are spread out over the
bottom of the pit; these are covered with a layer of leaves,
and the food—taro, yams, bread-fruit, chestnuts, pork, fish, &c.,
all previously wrapped up, is placed in a row on these leaves,.
and red stones scattered over the top; a second row of leaves,
and a second row of food, and a second covering of hot stones
follow, and if it is a large oven a third row will be laid on, a
quantity of old dried leaves is then added, and the whole is
covered with earth to the thickness of six inches or so. The
oven is now completed, and the process of steaming begins.
It is left for two or three hours, longer or shorter, according
to circumstances. If, for example, it is a turtle that they are
cooking, they will not open it till the morning. Meanwhile,
between sweat and smoke, stones, leaves, and earth, they are
completely begrimed and dirty; and they are all off to the
stream to bathe, the men to one pool and the women to
another, and thus make themselves clean and comfortable for
the Sabbath. At the same time some of the young men are
sent off to pull a quantity of fresh or green cocoa-nuts for the
Lord's day. They select the younger and lower trees, as being
the most easily climbed, and as having also the best nuts for
drinking. It is astonishing to see how easily they can climb
the trees; their toes are nearly as nimble in climbing as their
fingers. Most of the trees lean slightly to the one side, and,
as a matter of course, they take the nearest side, and they
often seem just to walk up the tree on all fours. John
Williams says that when the natives on Tahiti or elsewhere
saw English seamen try to climb cocoa-nut trees, they laughed

at them for their awkwardness, and when they wished to disparage one another, they would say, "Why, you are as stupid as an Englishman!" The fruit is all hanging in clusters among the branches. The natives knap the husk with the nail of one of their fingers, and thereby ascertain the nuts that are just sufficiently ripe for being drunk; these they twist off and throw down to the ground. They then fixed a sharp-pointed stick in the earth, and by striking the rind of the nut against the point they tore off the husk, and the nuts were ready to be opened for drinking. The nuts, thus stripped of their husk, were thrown into a basket, and put away for the Sabbath. When the oven was considered fully cooked, and generally they guessed very correctly, the earth was removed and the oven opened, and taro, yams, fish, pork, &c., came out piping hot, nicely cooked, and as tempting as if they had been taken out of the best cooked baker's oven in our land. The food was then distributed in the following manner. The party sat in a circle, each with his food basket beside him. The person or persons dividing the food went round, and gave to each a taro or two; they went round a second time and gave each a yam, then a fish, or a piece of pork, or a piece of a fowl, a cocoa-nut, or a piece of sugar-cane, till everything was divided. A blessing was then asked, and they ate their supper, as much as they wished. After this every one gathered up all that he had left, and put it into his basket for the Sabbath day; and there was always as much left as would serve them comfortably till the Monday evening. In cold weather they often sliced down their taro on the Sabbath, and warmed it in the frying-pan. On Efate, where the staple food is yams, they often, on the Sabbath afternoon, either roasted small yams, or made an oven, the wood and other requisites being provided on the Saturday, because it was believed that the cold watery yams had a tendency to produce bowel complaints; and the missionaries never thought of enjoining anything that was found to be incompatible with health. The cooking in the native oven is a slow and laborious process, and must evidently in time give way to pots, saucepans, kettles, frying-pans, and American or other stoves, but it cooks food remarkably well; we liked our taro better when it was cooked in the native oven than when done in any other way. To those holding the principles of the Sunday Society, a missionary Sabbath will no doubt be the reverse of attractive; but to the natives, who regularly worked 365 days every year, who, in anticipation of some great heathen feast, when the sacred men had made every kind of common food *tapu*, had fasted or fared very very scantily not only for days but for weeks, and even for months, till the bones of their back and shoulders were far more prominent than the muscles—to people who had passed through this experience, it was no difficult matter to make them believe that 52 days' rest in the year, the first day in every seven, with three plentiful, well-cooked meals on each one of those days, was anything but a repulsive mode of life, even though accompanied by public and private religious exercises—two sermons and a Sabbath-school, and family prayers morning, noon, and night. But very likely the time may come when those who had never known the wars of Canaan, who had been ignorant of the bondage of Egypt, the brick kiln, and the iron furnace, will look upon the manna as light food, will prefer an æsthetic to a spiritual religion, will say of the Lord's service, "What a weariness is it!" "When will the new moon be gone, that we may sell corn?

and the Sabbath that we may set forth wheat?" When a feeble piety will be followed by a low morality, when they shall make the ephah small and the shekel great, give small measure, and charge a high price, and falsify the balances by deceit. When they shall shun self-denial and seek after self-indulgence; when they shall plead for doubtful amuse- ments, and practise the pleasant vices, till they shall be drinking with the sons of Belial, and dancing with the daughters of Midian. Should such things happen again, as they have happened before, and have happened elsewhere, no trial will have happened but what is common to man, and common to missions; but to every temptation, and to every trial, God will provide a way of escape, that His servants may be able to bear it. He will watch over His own work, while His Word shall endure for ever.

KAVA AND KAVA- DRINKING.

The kava plant is found, I believe, in all the South Sea Islands, within the tropics as far west as the Solomon group, and is converted into an intoxicating beverage. From the Solomon group westward the betel-root, the chewing of which renders the teeth of the natives quite black, grows plentifully and is commonly used as a narcotic. The root of the kava plant, and the extreme base of the stem, are the parts from which the drink is prepared. These being washed and dried are chewed; in some groups this operation is performed by young men, in other groups it is done by young women, good clean teeth being the qualification for this office. When the root is sufficiently chewed, the masticated fibres, in the form of round, dry balls, are deposited in a common bowl;

these are then diluted with water, and strained through a piece of native cloth, or through fern leaves. When the beverage is ready, the priest, or any head man, pronounces a toast or prayer over it, after which the first cup—the cup is made from the lower half of a cocoa-nut shell—is handed to the person of highest rank in the company. It is not given to women or to the common people; it is kept exclusively for chiefs and principal men. This description applies to all heathen islands, and to Aneityum in its heathen state. It is no longer drunk on Aneityum. It has long been prohibited. To prevent the injurious consequences that flowed from its use, the natives, once and again, rooted the kava all out, not by the instigation of the missionaries, but by an edict of the chiefs, supreme and subordinate; but of course the roots were not so completely eradicated, but that in time they again sprouted, and the plants grew up anew. The drinking of kava, therefore, on Aneityum is not now carried on with that dignity and eclat with which it was done in former times; kava is now a sort of smuggled article, and is obtained and drunk very much in the same way as alcoholic liquors are obtained and drunk in the state of Maine, and in the other prohibitory states in America. When the Rev. James Cosh, now of Balmain, Sydney, was our missionary on Efate, he found that the leading men in the village met every evening, after the toils of the day, to drink kava; and though at first he thought the practice was harmless, there being no bad language, no quarrelling, and no fighting—all was good feeling and innocent hilarity, but erelong he found that, when they left the banqueting-house and went to their own homes, they were all so dead and stupid that scarcely one of them was able to conduct family worship. They were no longer Christians, they were in reality, on this point, all back again to heathenism. Mr. Cosh took them and talked seriously to them, and, by a powerful exhibition of moral suasion, he led them to abstain from the stupefying liquor, so that they could conduct their evening as well as their morning devotions with clear and unclouded intellect.

Speaking of kava, Dr. Seeman, in his able work on Fiji, says, "The beverage has the look of coffee with plenty of milk in it, and an aromatic, slightly pungent taste, which, when once acquired, must, like all acquired tastes, be perfectly irresistible. It tastes like soapsuds, jalap, and magnesia. Drunk in moderation it has probably no bad effect, and acts upon the system something like betel-nut, but taken to excess it generates all kinds of skin diseases, and weakens the eyesight. Fortunately, kava, unlike distilled spirits, does not make people quarrelsome ; it has rather, like tobacco, a calming effect, and when Fijians extol the virtues of their national beverage, they often and justly make this observation. Nearly all the lower class of whites in Fiji are kava drinkers, some regular drunkards. And what has always surprised me is that, considering the Fijian to be a tropical climate, most of these drunkards enjoy such a long life."

It is not true, however, that these men as a general rule enjoy long life. I know on reliable authority that throughout the South Seas the class referred to in general do "not live out half their days :" few of them live past the age of forty. Where this is the exception it is easily accounted for. They are generally men of vigorous constitutions, and they live, not in consequence of drinking, but in spite of it. In most cases, this drinking especially of alcohol, though excessive, is only occasional, not habitual; it is not daily

tippling, but occasional outbursts of violent drunkenness.
For months at a time they are, from necessity, abstainers at
least from spirits.   Many of those captains, engaged in what
is called the Island trade, sail their vessels on teetotal
principles; they adopt it from necessity, as the only means
of safely prosecuting this business with the class of men they
have generally to do with.   The men are paid at the end of
the voyage, or once in six months, as the case may be; the
liquor store is then opened, and drink is then sold to them
till every portion of their wages is expended, and abstinence
is reluctantly forced upon them, a new outfit must be provided on credit, and they must undertake another voyage of
the same kind to redeem themselves from their debts.   "The
poor Indian," says Dr. Beecher, "who, once a month, drinks
himself dead to all but simple breathing, will outlive for years
the man who drinks daily, though he drinks moderately."
In the one case, it is constant war against nature; in the
other case, the system is allowed to throw off the injurious
effects of these debauches, and recruit for a while its impaired
energies.   Those men, too, are almost constantly working or
living in the open air, and in other circumstances favourable
to longevity.

Some twenty years ago or so it was reported, although I
cannot vouch for the accuracy of the report, that one of the
first British governors of Fiji was in the habit, occasionally
at least, of leaving Government house of an evening, and
stepping across to the kava-drinking hall of the chiefs, and,
in order to ingratiate himself with the native aristocracy,
joined them in quaffing off a cup of the soothing, saponaceous
mixture, prepared for the company by the chief butler of
Fiji.

A rather formidable objection against Nephalism is presented to some minds by the supposed fact that stimulants or narcotics are in use among all nations—wine, beer, ardent spirits, kava, opium, tobacco, &c.—and hence they infer that the desire for stimulants and sedatives is a natural appetite, universal as the species, and is to be regulated, but not extinguished, and that, in this light, total abstainers, with the best of aims, are nevertheless fighting, as it were, against God and nature. There is a certain amount of plausibility about this objection. Nothing is more certain than this, that every attempt to benefit mankind in a way contrary to the established order of God's providence must end in disappointment. But it has always appeared to me that a fallacy lurks in this objection. It assumes what requires to be proved. No one will deny that the taste for stimulants and sedatives is easily acquired, and when acquired is far stronger than our natural appetites; but it is equally certain that these desires sleep till they are awakened or created. The objection assumes that these tastes or desires are always awake or alive. This requires to be proved, which it never has been. They cause no uneasiness till acquired. Let the drink be prohibited, and the customs be abolished that awaken those appetites, and misery only, not happiness, will be removed. If the principle of this objection proves anything, it proves the universal depravity of man, but nothing more; his disposition to abuse the bounties of providence, and by converting medicines into luxuries, to seek higher and more exquisite enjoyments than is compatible with sound and permanent health, and the laws of our earthly existence. Man is prone to pervert every one of God's blessings. In consequence of this perversion the greatest good has always become the greatest evil; religion

is perverted into superstition ; civil government into tyranny ;
means of self-defence into weapons of unjust and aggressive
warfare ; the strong social feelings into the "social evil;"
and the most valuable medicines into the most destructive
luxuries. The love of stimulants, the desire for pleasurable
excitement must be regulated, like every other desire, by
higher considerations than mere temporary gratification.
Scientific knowledge, and higher Christian principle, will lead
men to deny themselves a present enjoyment, for the sake
of averting a future evil, and securing a higher future advantage, and will urge them to endeavour, both by example and
persuasion, that their less enlightened brethren may follow
the same course. We wish to bring back those stimulants
and sedatives from the category of pleasant but perilous
luxuries, and confine them again to the list of valuable and
powerful medicines.

"The medicinal value of the kava plant," says Seeman,
"has of late claimed some attention. In the French translation of Golding Bird's work on calculous affections, Dr.
O'Rorke has inserted among others the following remarks :—
'The kava plant is the most powerful sudorific in existence,
and its stimulant qualities render it applicable in those cases
where colchicum is prescribed. The intoxication it produces
is not like that caused by spirituous liquors, but it rather
induces a placid tranquillity, accompanied by incoherent
dreams. Kava is as powerful in its therapeutic action as
lignum vitæ, or guiacum, sarsaparilla, &c., and the islanders
use it as a specific against the diseases brought over to them
by foreign vessels. On the other hand, this drug, used to
excess as an intoxicating agent, over-excites the skin by its
sudorific effects, and eventually even causes elephantiasis.' "

Throughout those groups the most common forms of disease are fever and ague, as in the New Hebrides, and diarrhœa and dysentery as in Fiji. It is well known that these diseases are most frequently caused by some checking of the insensible perspiration; and consequently those medicines that act promptly and powerfully on the skin are of the highest value in such maladies. Here we see a benevolent Providence beforehand with man; side by side with the bane rises up the antidote. The poor ignorant savages have not discovered this. They found in the kava a fascinating luxury, with present enjoyment, and only a remote penalty; but of its medicinal properties their knowledge was limited in the extreme. Hence, by using a powerful medicine as a daily luxury, the blessing was perverted more or less into a curse. God has here provided the materials, it rests with scientific skill and Christian principle to rectify the evils and secure the advantages. In New Zealand, where neither ague nor dysentery prevail, the kava, the *piper methysticum*, is not found; there is a *piper* there, it is true, but it is the *piper excelsum*, and is not used for making kava; and hence the New Zealanders never had this liquor; so far as I am aware, they had no intoxicating drink till they were supplied with it by foreigners. It is not true, therefore, that the use of stimulants is universal, as our objectors allege; here was a whole people without them; and even in the kava-drinking groups, not a tithe of the people partook of the indulgence. Its use was confined almost exclusively to the chiefs, the same class who contracted a morbid craving for human flesh, which in many cases became as irresistible as the longing for kava. But in both cases, those who abstained were the happy, those who indulged were finally the sufferers.

I am not aware that any of our missionaries, or any of the
white residents on those islands, have used kava medicinally;
but assuming the above opinions respecting its medicinal
properties to be correct, it might be worth while to try it in
this way.   Quinine has hitherto been the great sheet-anchor
in fever and ague, and diaphoretics in dysentery; but if
kava were found effectual in that formidable disease, ague, or
in that still more fatal malady, dysentery, it would be an
important addition to the pharmacopœia for the South Seas.
But whatever uncertainty may remain for some time as to
its therapeutic value, it is clear as day that its use as a
luxury—mild and gentle as its effects may seem to be—is
highly perilous to health; a headache next morning is its
first admonition.   Those gentlemen who complacently drink
their wine, or sip their toddy, aiming at exemplary moderation as the acme of a model life in the use of stimulants, and
who think that in this way they are obeying God and following nature, copying, at a safe distance, the example set by
saints, sages, and savages—Noah and Lot, Belshazzar and
Alexander, Pomaré and Thakombau—let them for their comfort and encouragement pass an evening in imagination in
the public hall of some town or district in Fiji or in the New
Hebrides, and while they see these cheerful kava-quaffing
Bacchanals entering their elysium on the confines of Dream-
land, let them look up to those rafters where the skulls of
enemies are suspended as trophies; and, dancing among these,
or glaring through those empty sockets, they may see gnomes,
and goblins, and spectres, the personifications of such diseases
as *lepra*, *ophthalmia*, and *elephantiasis*, eyeing with compla-
cency the joyous group beneath, and deliberately choosing
this, that, or the other, as their future victims.   Let them

return when years have passed away, and, instead of that noble savage, with eagle eye, and agile step, and prince-like bearing, they will see a feeble man, prematurely old, with eyes inflamed, skin diseased, and legs thick and rugose as that of an elephant.   Let them then gaze on the wine sparkling before them, and perhaps the utterances of the ancient oracle may be clearer to their apprehension, as it sounds forth these words, " Look not thou upon the wine when it is red, when it giveth his colour in the cup, when it moveth itself aright ; at the last it biteth like a serpent and stingeth like an adder."

CHAPTER XXI.

COURTSHIP AND MARRIAGE ON ANEITYUM.

OF the two ordinances that survived the fall and were taken out of Eden, namely, the Sabbath and Marriage, the former was utterly unknown on Aneityum, and the latter, though distinctly recognised, was but a feeble institution. The strangulation of every wife on the death of her husband, and the frequency with which female infants were killed, had reduced the female population of the island to 65 per cent. of the male, as we found to be the case when we were able first to take a census of the population. Only sixty-five females for every hundred males was a very gloomy outlook; but we did our best to save female life and promote suitable marriages. In heathenism every girl was betrothed, often as soon as she was born. The parents, or the relatives, or the chief, as one or other happened to be the most powerful, had the full disposal of the girl; she was allowed no say in the matter at all. There was no such thing as Narayin Sheshadri would have called good honest courtship. Marriages were generally celebrated when the girl was about sixteen or seventeen years of age. The husband was generally much older than the wife. As a general rule she lived quietly with him, through fear, for five or six years, till she reached the full vigour of woman-hood, when she showed that she had a will and a power of her own. She then began to cast her eyes on some vigorous

young man of her own age, of that class who could more than
hold his own with her husband, or one who, with the help of
his friends, could more than hold his own with her husband
and his friends; they then eloped; a quarrel and sometimes
a war ensued, if peace was not secured by a large present
being given to the injured husband and his friends. After a
year or two, longer or shorter as the case might be, the
woman would quarrel with her new husband or he with her,
and she would leave him and become the wife of a third
husband. This was not an exceptional case; it was the
normal state of society. When we came to know the people,
we found, in the district where we lived, that among the
thirty or forty families nearest to us, there was scarcely a
woman who had reached middle life, to whom it might not
have been said, as our Saviour said to the woman of Samaria,
"Thou hast had five husbands, and he whom thou now hast is
not thy husband." I knew one or two women who had had
as many as ten husbands. There was a good deal of formality
and feasting about the first marriage of a young woman,
especially if she were a chief's daughter, subsequent marriages
were informal enough. I may give one example. Shortly
before our arrival on the island, Jane, the daughter of Tavita,
the chief of our district, was affianced to Williamu, a sketch
of whom I have given elsewhere. Williamu did not wish her,
but the father was determined that the marriage should take
place, and so preparations were pushed on. At the court of
Ahasuerus, when Esther became one of the brides-elect, she
was kept twelve months in the house of the women under
Hegai before her marriage. Comparing small things with
great, a similar practice existed on Aneityum, and Jane,
Williamu's bride-elect, was, according to native custom, shut

up in a house adjoining her father's, preparatory to her marriage, and an old trustworthy woman was appointed as nurse or guardian, to supply her with food, and guarantee her seclusion. At that time there was living with Williamu one Manura, a native of Tahiti, a Christian; one day Manura, no doubt with Williamu's approval, went and broke open the house in which Jane was shut up, brought her out, and set her at liberty, saying that he would not allow her or any young woman to be shut up like a pig that was being fed for a feast; and thus ended the purposed marriage, and the example of Esther was never again repeated. Had any native of Aneityum done what the Tahitian did his temerity would have cost him his life; but Manura was a Malay, a descendant of Shem, and Tavita was only a Papuan, a descendant of Ham, and was quite willing to submit; for of Shem it was said, "And Canaan shall be his servant."

Our mode of proceeding in connection with marriage was this. We remarried nobody; we recognised all native marriages as valid. When natives gave up heathenism and placed themselves under Christian instruction, we recognised as husbands and wives all who professed themselves to be such, and were recognised as such by the general public, and I enrolled them as married in my catalogue. In New Zealand the Church of England missionaries married none who were not baptized. They allowed them to live together, but they would not marry them. On the other hand, they remarried all couples whom they baptized, although they had been recognised as husband and wife for many years. This always appeared to me as an unscriptural mode of proceeding, and I have never seen anything in the standards of the Church of England that seemed to require it; but there may be some connection between Baptism and " Holy Matrimony" of which I am ignorant.

When an application was made for marriage, the parties were proclaimed on the Sabbath, and the marriage was solemnised in the church at the weekly prayer meeting on the Wednesday following.   In our circumstances we considered one proclamation quite sufficient to secure all needed publicity. At the commencement of the prayer meeting the parties to be married sat down side by side on a clean new mat in front of the pulpit platform.   When the marriage was about to be performed they rose up.   In every country certain phrases come into use that were never intended to become current in that sense.   In England the proclamation of the banns is called the *asking ;* in Scotland it is called the *crying ;* they were *cried* on such and such a day; on Aneityum the marriage is called the *rising,* because the parties *rise* when the marriage is celebrated.   *Erau atithai arau,* the two are rising. We recognised about 700 native marriages, and on my side of the island, between Mr. Copeland and myself, there were enrolled up to the time I left the island 475 Christian marriages ; and on Dr. Geddie's side of the island about the same number.   God signally owned His own ordinance.   Out of these 950 marriages, or thereabouts, during the twenty-five years that I was on the island, there was only one or two cases of final separation.   As might have been supposed, there were many cases of conjugal infidelity, but far fewer than could have been reasonably expected ; and I feel certain that nothing but the Word and Spirit of God could have wrought such a revolution in the moral condition of a community of the lowest savages, all steeped to the very lips in the foulest abominations of heathenism.   We had no legal or civil securities to guarantee the safety of the marriage contract. Public opinion and the fear of God were all that we had to rely upon. We had to trust to moral influences alone. The marriages were nearly all celebrated at our central stations, and at the prayer meetings on the Wednesday, when one-half and often two-thirds of our ordinary congregations were present; for in addition to the ordinary worshippers, there were generally present a large bridal party, so that the sacredness of the place, and the publicity of the occasion, the fear of God and the regard for man, rendered the moral influences as strong as they could be made, and they largely supplied the lack of legal obligations. After the service was over I shook hands with the newly married pair and wished them much happiness, my wife followed and did the same. Then came their friends, and subsequently the bulk of the congregation. But all our married friends, whether united by native or Christian rites, required to be very carefully looked after. I kept a list of every man, woman, and child on my side of the island, and Mr. Geddie did the same. This I corrected annually, and if I heard of any family quarrel, or of any doubtful conduct in either husband or wife, I sent two or three of the wisest of our elders, or teachers, or chiefs, if practicable, friends of the accused or suspected, to visit them, to take them by themselves, and inquire into the reports, to talk quietly to them, and give them such advice as they might think needful. My wife was generally the first, through the women, to learn when anything was going wrong. She heard this, not as a piece of gossip, for she put her foot firmly down to stop all mere gossip; but the teachers' wives, and other trustworthy women, supplied her with the necessary information, which she communicated to me.   And then the session and I took counsel together as to what should be done, and the result of our measures was generally successful.   And by promoting the peace of families, we promoted largely the peace of the island.

The clothing of the bride and bridegroom was at first a matter for serious consideration.   Every professed Christian wore some portion of European clothing, especially at church. And if clothing was deemed indispensable for ordinary worship, it seemed still more necessary for a marriage.   And our Samoan teachers fostered the idea, and lent portions of their own clothing to bedeck the bride and the bridegroom; my wife, too, always made a small bridal present.   There was always a small marriage feast provided by the friends.   After the manner of the Scotch, there was no marriage fee, but a present from the feast was brought to the missionary, consisting of a basket or two of taro, a fowl or two, and sometimes a pig.   This implied a small present of clothing in return.   As time wore on clothing and other property became more plentiful on the islands, marriage presents on both sides became larger; marriage dresses became more stylish, and civilization kept pace with Christianity, and we began to be afraid lest there, as elsewhere, the secular might overlay the spiritual.   In heathen times there was little or no family life on Aneityum—the men of a district slept all in one common house, and all the women in another.   When we began to celebrate Christian marriages, we strove hard to get every new married couple to have a house of their own, and, if possible, to get the house prepared and all ready before the marriage, and this arrangement wrought well; although the bridegroom was often eager to leave the preparing of the house till after the marriage, but I was always strong for him to have the house before the wife; and by speaking to the friends beforehand to help the young man I generally succeeded; and in this way every marriage not only added a new family to the community, but also a new house to the settlement; and the young wife realised the truth of what was said by the Scotchwoman, "It's aye a nice thing to hae a bit house o' yin's ain."

We never interfered in match-making, though often urged to do so. We did what we could by advice to prevent unsuitable matches; but we forced nothing. We left the responsibility always with the parties interested. The notions of the natives on this subject were often very absurd. The bride and bridegroom behooved to belong to the same or contiguous districts; and as women were scarce, if one was married into any particular tribe, another woman, sooner or later, must be married back out of that tribe in return. All old heathen ideas on that subject were tenacious of life, they died hard. My truthfulness, on one occasion, was severely and unexpectedly tried. In meeting an objection that the bride was taken too far away from her people, some eight or ten miles, I said that before I was married, my wife and I lived as far from one another as between Ancityum and Eromanga. When Williamu accompanied us to this country in 1860, he first saw Mrs. Inglis' native place, and then he saw mine; and he told me afterwards that he remembered what I had said about how far we had lived from one another before we were married; and now he saw that what I had said was quite true. How important it is at all times to speak the exact truth. Who could have imagined that my casual utterances were to be thus tested. If they had been found to be incorrect, Williamu's confidence in me would have been rudely shaken.

One day the chiefs came to me to proclaim a marriage. As I have said, we took nothing to do with match-making, though often importuned to espouse the interest of some party, but I tried to improve all such opportunities to explain to the people the Scriptural principles on which marriages ought to be contracted, and to point out to them the evils of ill-assorted marriages, leaving them to carry out these principles themselves, and throwing all the responsibilities on the parties promoting the marriage. In this case I was calling their attention to the fact that the man was much older than the woman, and had been anything but an exemplary man in his general conduct, and that I was afraid she might not like him, but was simply yielding to a strong pressure brought to bear upon her by her friends, for there, as elsewhere, the course of true love seldom runs smooth. The bride proposed was a particularly interesting young woman. I had known her from a child; she had attended all my classes; she was an excellent scholar, good-looking, and well conducted, and was, at the time, a candidate for church membership; and I felt that she deserved one of the best young men on the island. As for the proposed bridegroom, poor fellow, I had a good deal of sympathy for him; he was a man of great force of character, impulsive, often unselfish, and one of those generous natures whom people generally like. He had been ill-used about three years before; he wished to marry a widow, and she wished to marry him; but strong family influences were brought to bear on the widow, and she had to give him up and take his rival. But, there, as much as in more civilised lands, public sympathy comes out at length on behalf of right and justice, and in behalf of the injured; and public feeling was all on the man's side in this case. One chief said to me, "Misi, I have a parable I sometimes speak. If I had a big wild pig that was going about and breaking into plantations, eating people's food, and doing all sorts of mischief, the people would say, Let this pig be killed; we cannot get living for it; but I would say, No, spare my pig, and help me to make an enclosure for him. We set to, we make the enclosure, we put in the pig, and feed him, and he becomes a quiet, tame pig. Now, there was Ratonga. The people said, O don't give him a wife; see what a wild young man he is; he hears nobody's words, neither the chiefs, nor the teachers. But I stood up for him. I spoke my parable. He was married. I talked to him; he has been a well-conducted man ever since; he has two children, and is now a member of the church." I said, "Yes, that is all true, but Ratonga and his wife were both one age. What about Lenia and her?" This was a young man belonging to the same district, and also a candidate for church membership. "O yes," they said, "he is a very good young man, but all the people of her land are against him getting her." "But what about Kula?" I said, naming another young man, "the people said she wanted him." "O yes," they said, "that was some time ago; but when they spoke to him he said, No, she was a distant relation of his own, and he would not have her." "Yes," said another, "and when she went up to Ivanipek to stay with the teacher, the chief there wished her for his son Ketipup (also a likely young man), but when she heard this she was unwilling, and came off home immediately. They have talked about this marriage between her and Injap a great deal, and she thinks of nobody else now." "Yes," said the chief who had spoken the parable, "I spoke to her last Monday, and she said the words about Injap and her were to stand." I said to them, "Well, you go home and search her heart honestly, and see if these words be true, and not said through fear of her friends, and come to me before church time on Sabbath morning, and, if it is good for her, I will proclaim them;" and so ended their interview. On the Sabbath morning the elder came back and said that he had searched the young woman's heart, and that she had said that their words were good for her; because that if Ketipup, the chief's son, and she were married, as they were both young and thoughtless, they would live in idleness, and have no food, and then they would be quarrelling and fighting, and living an unhappy life; but if Injap and she were married, he would be thoughtful, and strong to work, and she would work with him, and they would have plenty of food and live happily together. Whether these were actually her own sentiments, or whether they were the words suggested to her, by a kind of process akin to the leading of evidence, and to which she merely gave her assent, I was not able to say, but I was shut up to proclaim them; and they were married on the following Wednesday. But with all the drawbacks to marriage in such a state of society as we found there, it was an unspeakable blessing to the Aneityumese.

The question of bigamy and polygamy came up for solution in our mission, as in most heathen missions; a question of casuistry more difficult perhaps than any found in Pike and Hayward's Cases of Conscience, and which has exercised the casuistic skill of missionaries, missionary societies, and missionary churches, and on which they have not yet reached unanimity of opinion. The arguments on both or on all sides have been clearly and very fairly stated in a pamphlet

by my excellent and learned friend Dr. Cust, of the Indian
Civil Service. It refers chiefly to the missions in India and
Africa, and gives a list of twenty-five publications on that
subject, mostly pamphlets, seven of the writers being bishops.
Three solutions are offered to the question—(1) That Christian
polygamists be baptized, but not admitted to office; (2) that
no polygamist be baptized till he have put away all his wives
but one; (3) that he be admitted as a catechumen, but not
baptized. Dr. Cust holds to this latter view, especially for
the sake of the wives, that their rights may all be conserved.
He holds that the wives may all be baptized if otherwise
qualified. Our circumstances were quite different from those
that obtained either in India or in Africa. On Aneityum
the marriage bond was so slender, that in general it caused
no painful wrench to separate a wife from her husband, and
there were plenty of eligible men ready to marry the repudiated wives. We had no polygamist literally; we had a few
trigamists, but before these became practical questions the
third wife had become the wife of some other man, so that
we had only bigamy to deal with. We never pushed any
delicate or difficult question, so we allowed this question to
stand over till it was ripe for solution; and when it had
to be practically disposed of, we found it less difficult than
we expected. In the first place, we allowed the husband to
keep either of the wives that he preferred, and before the
day appointed for the separation we had provided a suitable
husband for the repudiated wife, a man who was willing to
marry the woman, and a man whom the woman was willing
to accept as her husband. In this way there was no difficulty;
the women were better pleased, each to have a husband of her
own, than only to be one of the inmates of a harem. Our

first case was a very notable one; it was in July 1854, at the opening of Mr. Geddie's new church. On that occasion Mr. Geddie had no fewer than eleven couples to marry. Among these were four principal chiefs, who had formerly had two wives each, but who had repudiated one of them for some time. However, to give all due publicity to their conduct, they wished to be publicly married to the one, and to declare publicly that they had renounced all claim upon the other. Among the other seven brides were two repudiated wives; one of them formerly belonged to one of those chiefs, and the other had belonged to another chief, who had put her away some two years before that time. It was only chiefs and important men that could secure more than one wife where women were so scarce. A marriage on Aneityum, as in other parts of the world, was then an exciting occasion. As the natives were mostly assembled for the opening of the new church, and as so many marriages were to be celebrated, it was naturally to be expected that there would be a large meeting, and most certainly so it was; the church, which held from 800 to 900, was completely filled; a good many heathen were there; within and without there must have been nearly 1000 assembled. All, however, was order and decorum. After devotional exercises Mr. Geddie gave an address on marriage and the social position of woman. He showed them that God created only one man and one woman at first, and not many women for one man; that the souls of women are as precious in the sight of God as the souls of men; that women are not to be treated as beasts; that wives are not to be treated even as the mere servants of their husbands, but are to be regarded as their equals and companions. After he had married the eleven couples, I de-

livered a short address both to them and to the audience, and
gave them in their own tongue, somewhat amplified, Matthew
Henry's celebrated commentary on Genesis ii. 21, 22 : "The
woman was made of a rib out of Adam's side ; not made out
of his *head* to rule over him, nor out of his *feet* to be trampled
on by him, but out of his *side* to be equal with him, from
under his *arm* to be protected by him, and near his *heart* to be
beloved." I then concluded the meeting with prayer and praise.

At that time every great movement on the one side of the
island reacted powerfully on the other. So about four months
afterwards we had a similar display at my station. In one
day at our weekly prayer-meeting I married no fewer than
thirteen couples. Four of the men had formerly had two
wives each, but had put away one of them, and the four wives
thus put away were also all married at the same time to other
husbands. On the previous Sabbath I preached on the nature
and duties of marriage ; and, on that occasion, notwithstanding
a very unfavourable day, we had a large attendance, especially
of women. I read and briefly expounded the last twenty-two
verses of the Book of Proverbs, which I had translated for the
occasion—a passage which a venerable puritan divine calls a
"looking-glass for ladies, which they are desired to open and
dress themselves by, and if they do so, their adorning will
be found unto praise, and honour, and glory, at the appearing
of Jesus Christ." The thirteen couples were arranged before
the pulpit in three rows, the first row consisted of the four
men who were putting away their wives, and the wives whom
they were keeping. They stood up, and I required each of the
four men to declare publicly that he gave up all claim upon
the wife he had put away, and then I married each of them to
the wife he had retained. The first row sat down, and the

second row, containing the four wives just put away, stood up. These I married with equal distinctness. After this they sat down, and the third row stood up, consisting of five couples who had not been married before. These I also married; and thus concluded an interesting and important service. We had still three more professing Christianity who had two wives each; one of these was a chief who had recently joined us; another was the chief of the district in which we lived, a man by whom the mission had been much benefited. It was under his protection that the Rev. A. W. Murray left the first Samoan teachers, and he was one of the first to make a profession of Christianity, and he had been always true to the teachers and the missionaries. The natives at that time were very fond of new names, and the teachers had gratified them largely in this direction till they had nearly exhausted the more common names in the Bible, as expressed in the Samoan version. To this man and his principal wife they had given the names of Tavita and Patisepa (David and Bathsheba). But though in most other matters his conduct had been very satisfactory, yet about the putting away of his wife he displayed a great amount of duplicity and obstinacy. He was far from being happy. He had two settlements. The one wife lived in the one, and the other in the other. He lived a week or two with the one wife in the one place, then quarrelled with her, left her, and went and lived a similar length of time with the other. But at length good influences prevailed. He and Patisepa were married, and Yauth, his other wife, was married on the same day to a suitable man, and thus Tavita's domestic troubles were happily brought to an end. He was not the highest in rank, but he was the most influential chief on my side of the island. ·

CHAPTER XXII.

THE chief cause of disease on Aneityum is *malaria.* Perhaps the gravest difficulty with which the New Hebrides Mission has to contend is the climate. It is, so far as we know, the least healthy of any group of islands in those seas on which missions have been established. If the laws of life are very carefully attended to, a fair average measure of health may be enjoyed, but these laws cannot be trifled with as they may be elsewhere. There is in general nothing specially deadly in the climate—it kills by inches, rather than suddenly; malaria, more or less virulent, continually infests all the low districts of most of the islands, and is most injurious in warm dry seasons. The presence of this malaria has never once been discovered by any one of the five senses. It walks the earth as invisible as the Evil One himself. It cleaves to the ground: it cannot live on the ocean; hence men are safe till they touch those shores. It requires the four primal elements of the ancients—earth, air, heat, and moisture—for its production; yet it cannot be detected by the most skilfully conducted chemical analysis, although from its effects—various forms of well-marked diseases, chiefly fever and ague, and milder forms of intermittent fever—its existence is as certainly known as the existence of moral depravity is ascertained by the degrading heathenism which prevails on every one of those non-christianised islands. When new missionaries arrived among us, our warnings to them were like the prophecies of Cassandra to the Trojans; when we told them of the danger of walking out after the sun went down, they thought we were merely joking; and when they saw that we were in sober earnest, they began to doubt if we were quite sane, and if there was not some twist about our minds, some mental hallucination on this point. "Surely," they said, "there can be no danger in a climate like this; there is no cold whatever; see how soft, and mild, and balmy the air is." They had still to learn that fever and ague gives no warning; it comes galloping, but goes away creeping. It is not till men are in its iron grasp that they realise their danger, and it is then too late to secure their escape.

There is good reason for believing that sixty years ago the population on Aneityum was at least 12,000. Some have estimated it as high as 20,000; but two terribly alarming epidemics reduced it to less than a third of that number. Samoan teachers were first placed on Aneityum in 1841. It was a few years before the settlement of those teachers that the first epidemic appeared, probably about 1837 or 1838; and it was some time after their settlement, probably 1844 or 1845, that the second epidemic broke out. Both epidemics seem to have been of the nature of cholera. We never could learn anything as to their origin or cause. The mortality was so great that the living could not dispose of the dead, which they did at that time by tying stones to their feet and casting the bodies into the sea. No doubt the epidemic was aggravated by the putrefying corpses. We arrived at our conclusions respecting the extent of the mortality in these epidemics in this way. In the first years of the mission, Mr.

M

Geddie and I made a circuit of the island annually; in each of these visits we spent about a week. We were always accompanied by a party of at least twenty or thirty of the principal Christian natives. At every school-house we held a religious service, at which the natives, as well as the missionaries, gave addresses. We also sent deputations to the heathen to speak to them at their own homes. Both at the two principal stations, and at four other important stations, as we had with us the most intelligent and best informed men on the island, we took down the names of all the men who had died at these places respectively during both the first and second epidemics; and making allowance for a fair proportion of women and children, we calculated that fully 4000 people must have died during each of the epidemics. No doubt those fearful scourges so affected the general health as largely to account for the subsequent decrease of the population; a large proportion of the land was thrown out of cultivation, and a large amount of swamp land, instead of being finely cultivated food-producing gardens, fell into stagnant marshes, largely increasing the fever-producing malaria. What purpose the Lord had to serve by that awfully startling dispensation of His providence is a question not easily answered, only it was not a chance that happened to the people.

The lessons taught through the losses sustained by the Free Church of Scotland last year, in South Arabia and in Livingstonia, ought to be deeply pondered by all the members of that Church, especially by her medical missionaries. These evils I believe to be remediable. As I have shown elsewhere, much will always depend upon the site and structure of mission houses; and the whole question of malaria must be carefully studied. Dr. Gunn, I understand, is projecting a Sanitorium on Futuna. This cannot be too soon gone about. When Mrs. Charles Murray died, I felt extremely thankful that she had a fully qualified medical man at her bedside, and that no reflections could be made, to the effect that the result might have been different if the requisite skill had been available. But when she had not only the most careful nursing, but also the best medical skill, there was no room for any regrets. It was the Lord's will, and not man's unskilfulness, to which her death was due. It was for the sake of the mission families, more than for the natives, that I was so anxious to secure the services of a medical missionary on the group. Such an arrangement not only gives confidence to the mission families on the field, but it eases the minds of friends, especially parents, at home, to think that in perilous junctures, their daughters especially, have the benefit of the best skill which the medical schools of Edinburgh or Scotland can supply. It is true that a medical missionary cannot be everywhere at once, cannot attend to every case at the same time; but whenever danger is apprehended, arrangements can be made to secure his presence and his help. And he can at all times be watching the laws of health; he can have every member of the mission making observations for him; then he can generalise, and then, in consequence of this knowledge, supply every missionary with instructions what he is to avoid, and what he is to do in order to escape the most likely dangers, and to secure the highest degree of attainable health.

The most common disease on Aneityum and in the New Hebrides, generally, is fever and ague. In different groups on the South Seas malaria has different developments. In the New Hebrides it takes the form of fever and ague, from a very mild to a very severe form of the disease. In Fiji it develops into diarrhœa, often of a very troublesome type. In Samoa it produces painful and chronic swellings in the legs and arms, sometimes, if I mistake not, ending in a form of elephantiasis. Of remedies, the great sheet anchor for fever and ague and the other diseases is quinine, and it is matter for thankfulness that it is now become so cheap. The other specific is arsenic; the most convenient form of administering it we found to be Fowler's Solution of Arsenic. This, however, required to be administered with caution. An aperient is generally administered two or three times a week with these remedies. On our way home from the islands, I met a gentleman in the steamer between Sydney and Melbourne, who told me that in Queensland, to which he belonged, they mixed quinine and Epsom salts, and found this mixture more efficacious than when taken separately, enough of the salts being used to act as an aperient.

A common complaint among children I found to be worms; the stomach swelled and became painful, especially after eating, and the child often became much emaciated. For this I found no medicine so effectual as a strong mixture of salt and water; a spoonful administered every morning half-an-hour before any food was taken. This, continued for ten days or a fortnight, generally effected a complete cure; some of the cures were very striking. The medicine seemed to operate in this way. On the fasting stomach the worms were hungry, and greedily swallowed the salt and water, which acted as a poison to the worms, but as a tonic to the child; but whatever the *modus operandi* might be, the remedy was in general effectual.

Ulceration and skin diseases were common; and the most effectual remedy that I found was carbolic acid. It was not, however, till the last year that I was on the island that I became acquainted with this medicine, and that through the Rev. J. Annand, after he came to the station on Aneityum formerly occupied by Dr. Geddie; and the occasion was this. A young lad from my station had been engaged for some two years as cook on Eromanga for Mrs. Robertson, and was coming home; but he had cut the upper part of his foot very badly with an axe. Afterwards some lime fell on it while he was plastering; the foot had been neglected; and finally it became a very bad ulcerated wound. My wife and I were on a visit to the other stations in the *Dayspring*, and arranged to call and bring the lad home. Mr. Robertson had done his utmost, but with very little success. We landed at Mr. Annand's station, and took the lad ashore with us. The smell of the wound was so offensive that he could not stay in the same house with Mr. Annand's natives. I got Mr. Annand to examine the wound; after doing so, he recommended the application of carbolic acid. It was a new medicine to me; I had never heard of it before, so far as I remember; but Mr. Annand was not long from home, and he had brought a supply of the medicine with him. I asked him to dress the wound, which he did, with a preparation of one part of the acid to ten of water, and in two days the offensive smell was all gone. We took the lad home with us. I dressed the foot twice a day as suggested by Mr. Annand, and in less than a month the wound was quite healed, and the lad was in every way perfectly well.

Another case was that of a middle-aged woman, whose skin was all covered with an ulcerous rash, which I never expected to see cured. I gave her a quart bottle, filled with a weak solution of the acid, one part of the acid to about twenty of water. I gave her also a piece of old soft linen. I told her to go home, get a piece of a clean cocoa-nut shell, pour a little of the liquid into it, and twice a-day dip the cloth in the liquid, and wet all her skin with the cloth, and to come back when the contents of the bottle were done. What was my surprise, when, in three weeks, she was present at the weekly prayer-meeting, perfectly cured, her skin as fresh as that of a weaned child, or if one might speak it with reverence, comparing small things with great, the natural with the miraculous, the human with the divine; her skin was as fresh as one might suppose Naaman's to have been when he stood before Elisha, after he had dipped himself seven times in the Jordan.

Female complaints were common, especially *menorrhagia.* I had a copy of Graham on "Diseases of Females," which I often consulted with advantage. In page 91 he strongly re-commends cream of tartar for this ailment and internal passive hæmorrhage. "The value," he says, "of this admirable medi-cine is but little known in such cases; it will, however, be soon ascertained on trial, for where it is suitable, it is equally prompt and successful in its effects." This remedy I often adminis-tered, and with very beneficial, often with very striking, effects. Dr. Graham says it is very effectual in creating red blood.

I was in general very successful with children. Their diseases were mostly acute and of short standing, and one or two, or at most a few doses of medicine generally effected a cure. When a child was brought with disordered stomach, and a very white tongue, a few doses of rhubarb and calomel almost invariably effected a complete cure. Inflammation of the eyes was a common complaint, but a solution of sugar of lead, or of sulphate of zinc, with a few drops of laudanum or liquid morphia, made a very effective lotion.

In their heathen state the natives had no knowledge of medicine : all their cures were effected, or were supposed to be effected, by incantations, and they were all performed by the sacred men ; and it was believed that the sacred men could produce diseases as well as cure them. They did not, however, look upon the sacred men as we do upon the medical profession, as a benevolent class of men, or public benefactors, employed always in curing, but never in causing diseases. They looked upon them very much as our forefathers, in former times, looked upon wizards and witches, as exercising their power to cause pain and suffering, not to produce health and happiness, except when largely paid to remove some malady which they themselves had inflicted. They looked upon them very much as Mohammed did upon women, as an evil, a necessary evil it might be, but still as an evil. Their sacred men they felt to be a public burden. At first they looked upon us missionaries as belonging to the same class as their sacred men, and they thought that if they accepted the new religion, they would be adding a load to a burden. When they became better acquainted with us, and found that we could cure them, they still thought that our cures, like those of their sacred men, were effected by incantation, and that one medicine must be able to cure every disease. Hence, when a man had got medicine for himself, he would say, "I want some medicine also for So-and-so." "Very well," I would say, "and what is the matter with him ?" "Oh," he would say, "I do not know ; I saw his brother as I came along, and he said he was very ill, and I was to ask you for some medicine for him." "But," said I, "unless you can tell me something about his disease, I cannot give you any medicine. You see this medicine chest ; you see all these bottles : these all contain different medicines for different diseases; you know that you suffer from more diseases than one. Now this medicine is to cure pains in the head, this is to cure pains in the back, this is to cure pains in the bones, this is to stop vomiting, this is to cause people to sleep : this is to cure one disease, and that to cure another. Now you must go to So-and-so, and tell him to come to me, and explain what is the matter with his brother, and then I will know what medicine I can give him, that it may cure him." It took years, however, to make them all comprehend the difference between the charms and incantations of their sacred men, and the medicines and the medical treatment of the missionaries.

From the first I opened my dispensary every day at one o'clock for all the patients that came ; and the attendance was smaller or greater according to the state of the public health, from one, two, or three, to twenty or thirty, or even more. A number of the cases, especially among children, were cured, a large number were benefited, and as it happens in all medical practice, in a large number of instances my medical labours were fruitless; but I examined every case carefully, and treated them all honestly, to the best of my knowledge and ability, and the result was, that the natives came to have unbounded confidence in my medical treatment ; and this department of my mission work tended greatly to increase my moral influence among the people.

I had always one and frequently two hospitals for the reception of indoor patients, one for the people of the upper or eastern end of my district, and the other for the lower or western part. These were very humble structures, mere huts, erected by the natives themselves under my directions, but they served a useful purpose. They stood at a convenient distance outside of our premises. The natives provided their own food and attendance; if it was a husband the wife nursed him and attended to him, if it was a girl the mother nursed her, if it was a boy both father and mother were in attendance. I visited the patient and administered the medicine; my wife supplied tea, biscuit, arrowroot, and other medical comforts: and the elders, deacons, teachers, and church members often went and made worship with them night and morning, and at other times, and sometimes brought a small present of food, and the results were satisfactory; the social influences, as well as the medical treatment, promoted the recovery of the patients, as the good feeling and cheerfulness thereby engendered were new and powerful curatives added to the sanitary conditions of the island and the hospital.

There is one point in relation to medicine on which I must say a word or two. It was one of our primary objects in the mission to avoid pauperising the natives, and to cherish in every way among them a spirit of self-respect and independence, and yet to make the mission as little burdensome as possible. We gave them nothing for nothing. We made them understand that they had no claim upon us for anything, and, as soon as we deemed it to be expedient, we made them pay for their medicines. In Samoa and elsewhere the missionaries did the same, but the Samoan missionaries made every native pay for his own medicines; but our natives were much poorer than theirs, and we found that with medicines as with books, it was better to lay a tax upon the entire community than to make each man pay for himself. Mr. Geddie and I, therefore, arranged that, week by week, the teacher or the chief should collect from two to four baskets of taro among the people of his district, according to their number, and bring them on the Wednesday, and then every native on both sides of the island was at liberty to go to each of the dispensaries respectively, as often as they required it, and obtain medicine for nothing. I had twenty-eight schools, hence it took twenty-eight weeks to go over these, and as we had a good many marriages during the year, and also other occasions, such as the opening of schoolhouses, at which presents, chiefly of taro, were always made, and at which times we always stopped the taro for the medicine, so it was seldom oftener than once a year that they had to give anything for medicine; and as the tax fell on every one, and on every one equally, it touched every one so lightly, that it was not felt at all to be a burden. To those who carried the taro I always gave a few fish-hooks, which rendered the labour less irksome; or, if they came from an inland district, where they could not fish, my wife gave them some needles and a portion of thread. These weekly contributions supplied our household—ourselves and the natives who lived with us—with the most important article of vegetable food that we required. Our friends at home supplied the medicines. The Rev. Dr. Goold's congregation in Edinburgh presented me with a medicine-chest and a set of medical instruments when I first went out to the mission in 1844, and as often as requested they refilled it. On one or two occasions the Rev. J. Kay's congregation in Castle-Douglas sent me a valuable supply of medicines, through the late J. Paterson, Esq., of the Apothecary's Hall. On all occasions our friends were thoughtful and liberal. We never made an appeal to them for medicine or for anything else but we met with a generous response.

The birth-rate since we went to Aneityum has always been high; but alas! the death-rate has always been higher. For about ten years before we left the island the birth and death rate stood something like this: birth-rate, $99\frac{1}{2}$; death-rate, $100\frac{1}{2}$. A reverse of this ratio would make us equal to what exists in India, where the birth-rate is equal to $100\frac{1}{2}$, and the death-rate to $99\frac{1}{2}$; and this going on for ages has resulted in the millions of our Indian Empire, instead of the steady depopulation of Aneityum. Some years after we left the island the disproportion between the birth and the death rate was still greater. But we are still hoping that, when the present transition period has passed, and Christianity, with its strongly conservative influence, has been fully and permanently established, there will set in, as in many of the eastern islands, where the depopulation was as great as it has been with us, a steady increase in the number of the inhabitants; and thus may "a little one become a thousand, and a small one a strong nation;" and may "the Lord hasten it in His time!"

CHAPTER XXIII.

CIVIL GOVERNMENT ON ANEITYUM.

WHEN the mission work was begun on Aneityum, the island was governed by six principal chiefs, and about fifty under chiefs. The name of a principal chief was *Natimarith*, from *Natimi*, man, and *arith*, high; a secondary chief was called *Natimi alupas*, from *Natimi*, man, and *alupas*, great. In heathen times the duties of the priesthood were discharged chiefly by the Natimariths. Each Natimarith, in his own district, was a kind of *Pontifex maximus*, or high priest; he presided at feasts, and performed certain sacerdotal duties; but when heathenism came to an end, their priestly vocation also terminated, and their civil power alone remained; but it became very much increased when it became based upon Scriptural authority. In heathen times there was no union, no united action among the chiefs. The normal state of society was for one part of the island to be at war with another part; for two districts to be at war with the other four, but not necessarily the same districts. On the south side of the island, Mr. Geddie's side, the principal district was Anelgauhat, of which Nohoat was the Natimarith, and after his death his son Lathella; on the north side it was Aneityo, of which Nowanpakau was the Natimarith. At first, when Mr. Geddie was settled, the three high chiefs on the south side were Nohoat, Yiapai, and Karaheth, all three men of

influence and of great force of character, who joined the
mission at an early stage, threw their influence into the
movement, and helped it greatly. Topoe, or Topwe, an under
chief, a brother-in-law of Nohoat's, was another power for
good; and Waihit, a famous sacred man, was for thirty years
a great support of the mission. The Natimariths on my side
were Nemet, Viali, and Nimivero, all three feeble men; but
we had three under chiefs, Tavita, Luka, and Napollos, who
proved admirable substitutes. Tavita's history I have given
elsewhere. Luka, in his heathen state, was a great warrior,
but a great savage; on the death of his son, a little boy, he
strangled his own sister, that her spirit might accompany the
little boy's to *Umaatmas*, the Land of the Dead, to attend upon
him there. When the first Samoan teachers were settled at
Ipekè, the district adjoining Aname, afterwards my station,
and were beginning to influence the young men, Luka became
very angry with them, and set off one day, followed by a party
of the heathen, and carrying a massive spear with which to
murder them. The two Samoans and their wives got word of
his intentions, and kept inside the house, barred the door, and
betook themselves to prayer. Luka came on, broke open the
door, and told them that he had come to kill them. They
calmly looked him in the face and told him they were not
afraid to die, but warned him to think what he was doing, for
that God would certainly avenge their deaths, either here or
hereafter. Luka raised his spear, but, as Milton, I think it is,
says somewhere, "Awful is the power of goodness," and a
higher authority says, "The wicked flee when no man pursueth,
but the righteous are bold as a lion," so their words troubled
Luka's heart; he was agitated, the cord with which he poised
his spear slipped from his finger, and the weapon when he threw

it fell powerless to the ground. A conversation took place, the teachers engaged in prayer, and Luka went home no longer a heathen, and in the course of a few Sabbaths he was attending the place of worship. He was one of the very first whom I baptized and admitted to the fellowship of the Church. When he was an elderly man, and we had difficulty in getting teachers to go to Tanna, Luka and his wife volunteered to go thither, as he was well known there, and had much influence with the Tannese, to assist Mr. and Mrs. Watt. After they went thither, they met with great opposition from the heathen. His wife was indeed poisoned by the wife of a Tannese chief, who intentionally gave her a poisonous fish to·eat, when she was sick, under the pretence that it was a good fish. On one occasion the heathen attempted to murder Luka; an armed party surrounded him, they levelled their muskets at his head, one bullet knocked off his hat, another one passed through his shirt, other three fell short of him, but the Lord protected him, and he escaped unhurt. Luka lived to a good old age at Kwamera, Mr. Watt's station, and died honoured and lamented. The people of Itath, the land where he was chief, followed his example, and all along took the lead in Christianity, education, and civilization. A very interesting account of Luka, written by Mrs. Watt of Tanna, appeared in the juvenile magazine, the *Dayspring*, for November 1879, published by Messrs. Parlane of Paisley.

Napollos was a third *Natimi alupas*, or common chief, one of the three mighties in my district. In heathen times he was a great warrior, possessed great influence, was a man famous both in camp and in council, in planning an attack or a defence, or in carrying it into effect. The shadow of his arm struck terror into the hearts of his enemies, and the sound of

his footsteps was recognised as the harbinger of death; he
had joined the Christian party before our arrival. Shortly
after our settlement, of his own accord, both he and his wife
came and lived beside us for two years, that they might get
all the instructions we could give them, both scriptural and
secular. It was to his land, and at his request, that I sent
out Yona, my first native teacher. Next to the mission
station, Ijasis, his land, and Itath, Luka's land, were the
most advanced, on my side of the island, both in scholarship
and Christianity. He died just immediately before our return
to the island with the New Testament, in 1863. Tavita,
Luka, and Napollos were all three very able rulers, which
indicated that they possessed in an eminent degree the higher
order of intellect.

The chiefs both supreme and subordinate were partly
hereditary and partly elective. If a chief died, his son, if
grown up, succeeded him; if he had no son grown up, his
brother or some near relative succeeded; his daughter never
succeeded the father: there was a tacit Salic law, minors and
daughters were always excluded; and eligible candidates were
always confined to certain families. Human nature is human
nature all the world over. On Aneityum, rank is recognised
and appreciated as much as among the British aristocracy, the
Spanish nobility, or the Princes of Germany. In the early
part of this century the Duke of Beaufort had six daughters;
they were all married; the Countess of Galloway was one of
them, and it was said of her that she made the poorest match
of all the six, so well were they all married. But be that as
it may have been, we could nearly equal this on Aneityum.
About that very time one of the Natimariths of Aneityum had
five daughters, who all grew up to womanhood, and each one

of them was married to a Natimarith; but I mention this for
another purpose. When we,were settled on Aneityum, Nemet,
one of our three Natimariths, who had been married to one of
these five daughters of that high chief, had two daughters but
no son. His eldest daughter was a young, giddy, thoughtless
girl of whom nobody thought anything. By and by, as she
was a high chief's daughter, Mrs. Inglis took her into her
boarding-school, where she remained for several years, and
developed into a tall, good-looking young woman, though still
somewhat reckless and harum-scarum. At this time, Solomona,
one of our best, cleverest, and most scholarly young men, asked
her in marriage, and she was willing to take him; but family
considerations interposed. He was the son of only a small
chief, a poor gentleman, whereas she, both by father and
mother, belonged to one of the highest families in the land;
and the whole family connection was arrayed against them. She
must marry nobody but a Natimarith, as her mother and all her
aunts had done before her. But when the family council was
assembled, Ritia gave them a bit of her mind; trusting to her
position, she spoke more freely than a woman of lower rank
durst have done. "When I was a child," she said, "you
treated me like a wild pig, and let me run about as I liked,
and seek my food where I could find it. You looked upon me
as a *nakli natmas* (literally a little devil), a contemptible
creature, utterly worthless. But now, when Mrs. Inglis,
after taking me in, clothing me, and educating me, has made
a woman of me, you come now and say that I must take a
man whom I know nothing about, and whom I care nothing
about, because his father is a Natimarith. No, I want Solomona, and I'll have him if I can get him." However, the
family influence prevailed, and, although there was neither uv

elopement nor a suicide nor any of those tragic endings with which the writers of fiction so often finish up their stories, Ritia was married to a respectable man; but when the measles swept over Aneityum she was one of the 1200 that died in that epidemic, purposely brought to the island by the traders.

We never assumed any civil power, we recognised and accepted whatever civil government existed; we instructed and guided the authorities as opportunities occurred. In all offences against life we counselled severe punishment, so far as the Scriptures sanctioned it; but in all offences against property merely, we counselled the use of mild punishments. The natives wished to punish indiscriminately: for the killing of a pig and the killing of a man they would have inflicted nearly the same punishment. In all cases we counselled prompt punishment, while public sympathy was with the authorities and not with the criminal. There, as elsewhere, but especially in such a state of society, if punishment is postponed, public sympathy begins to turn in favour of the criminal and against the law, and the ends of punishment are defeated.

A case occurred in New Zealand in the early days of its history, before the British Government took possession of it as a colony. At that time there were several whaling stations established along the coasts of those islands. Within what is now the province of Otago, one of those whaling parties had apprehended a native for some crime, and adjudged him to be hanged, but as the time for executing the sentence drew near, they became alarmed. Men-of-war were sailing in those seas, and the power of the criminal courts in Sydney extended to New Zealand, and they might easily get themselves into trouble. Meanwhile, one of their number, who could speak

N

the Maori language, went to the native, and persuaded him that it would be much more honourable for him to shoot himself, than to be hanged by the *pakeha* (foreigner). A loaded musket was introduced into the place of his confinement, and the native shot himself. In this way the whalers gained their end, and evaded the legal consequences to which they were exposing themselves, and of which they were now becoming seriously afraid.

In some of the eastern islands the missionaries, assisted in some cases by an English lawyer, prepared a civil constitution for the natives. But, as far as I know, these remained to a large extent a dead letter. At first we got the natives, as a beginning in legislation, to pass four enactments, which Mr. Geddie printed. One of these was to prohibit the sale of native women to white men, and which effectually prevented that practice. With these four Acts of Parliament, printing for the Government ceased. We very soon concluded that it was our best policy to let the framework of society remain as we found it; not to touch the common or unwritten law of the land; and as for statutory law, we thought that the ten commandments would be amply sufficient for all ordinary purposes. The natives understood their own customs better than any foreign legislation that we could introduce.

Our chiefs were not at all the important-looking men that many supposed them to be. They were not tall, gigantic men, like the chiefs in Eastern Polynesia. There was no court language, no class of words employed exclusively in speaking to, or of, chiefs, as in Samoa. They were not objects of dread, whose shadow even no man durst touch, as they were in Hawaii. They were plain, simple-looking men, whom no stranger would have recognised in a crowd; and as there was very little formality among the people, very little deference appeared to be paid to their rank. Still it was surprising to see the power of preserving peace and order over the island which they acquired after Christianity was accepted.   In heathenism it required very little authority to get men to commit murder and fight, to retaliate and take vengeance, because all their natural instincts led them in that direction; but, in a community newly reclaimed from heathenism, to keep men all quiet required vastly more influence of one kind or another.   There were few breaches of the peace, and when . any breaches did occur they were quickly punished by the chiefs.   The particulars of one instance I shall give by way of illustration.   A man belonging to an inland district had committed adultery with his neighbour's wife.   The woman's friends belonged to the other side of the island.   When they heard of this affair a few of them went to talk with the man about his conduct.   Like most evildoers, he was angry at this interference; and when they were near his house he went out to meet them, threw his spear among them, and wounded one man severely in the foot; had it struck him in the side it might have killed him.   In old times this would have led to a war between the two tribes; the one party to revenge the deed, the other party to defend the evildoer.   The chief of the district came to me immediately to consult with me what was to be done, as he expected all the friends of the wounded man to be at his house next day.   I advised him to ask some of the other chiefs to come and help him to punish the man, but not to attempt anything till he had plenty of help.   He immediately asked three or four of the nearest chiefs to assist him.   On the following morning, these all repaired to this assize meeting, each chief accompanied by a few trustworthy

influential friends. In this country such an offence would
have been punished by so many days' or months' imprisonment,
but there were no jails there, and all punishments required to
be summary. They adjudged the man to be tied and fined, a
very heavy punishment. They tied him hand and foot for
half a day, and fined him of a large pig, which they gave to
the friends of the wounded man. The man had just three
pigs, and he pleaded hard that they would take the least one;
but the chiefs were inexorable and took the largest. The
people from the other side went away well pleased, satisfied
that full justice had been done. I was always anxious when
such cases occurred, and in that instance I felt great relief
when the people returned from the trial and told me how the
chiefs had acted, and what the result had been. There was no
excitement, no high words; but everything was done with
order and dignity. As I have already said, in all cases where
property only was concerned, I always advised the chiefs to
adopt a gentle policy, to talk to the offenders, and to get them
to make restitution, employing moral and personal influence
rather than legal authority, to carry out, if possible, a paternal
government. But, in all cases where life was imperilled, I
counselled prompt and vigorous measures, such as would strike
terror into the hearts of evildoers, and I got the chiefs to
unite in helping one another, so that their authority would
not be disputed. We always aimed at two things with our
chiefs—that their government should be *good*, and that it
should be *strong*. And happily in every important case that
occurred, on either side of the island, acting on our advice,
they proceeded unitedly, and also carried public sympathy
along with them, and thus increased both their official autho-
triy and their personal influence.

For the sake of showing the working of our criminal courts, I may here give a report of two cases that occurred, the one on the one side of the island, and the other on the other : the one a case affecting life, the other a case affecting property. I shall relate the property case first, and as I wrote an account of it at the time it occurred, which appeared in the R. P. magazine, I shall quote from my own letter.

" Perhaps the most readily observed crime among the natives on this island is stealing, and I believe the evil is increasing. Not that the people are getting worse, but that the opportunities for stealing are more frequent and more favourable. There is more property to be stolen ; and there are more facilities for concealing it. But there is not now, nor has there been for a long time past, any stealing of food, as there used to be in heathenism, or as there is still on heathen islands. During the past year there has been no punishing for stealing on my side of the island. There have been several cases of stealing, most of them of a petty character, but as the thieves were not found out, there could be no punishment inflicted. The last case of punishment for stealing by natives belonging to my side of the island, was at our last Synod here, when the stealing of four white shirts belonging to the crew of H.M.S. *Basilisk*, and valued at 16s. 6d., was wound up, and the last of the fines paid. Why those washing such a quantity of clothes, as was spread out on that occasion, should have left them unguarded, while there were five or six boats' crews of whalers in the immediate neighbourhoood, is to me unaccountable. I do not think that they would have done so in Sydney. The opportunity here certainly made the thieves ; a single sentinel would have kept them all honest men. I have no serious fears about stealing ever becoming a formidable crime on this island.

"The case was this:—On the 9th September 1872, H.M.S. *Basilisk*, Captain Moresby, came into Aneityum harbour, on his way from the islands to the north of Aneityum to Sydney. It was the middle of the whaling season. Both the whaling stations had all their boats manned and afloat; almost all the thoughtless, reckless young men were collected at the harbour. The seamen of the *Basilisk* went ashore to wash their clothes, and they spread them out on the beach to dry, opposite a piece of dense bush, and five white shirts, or jumpers, were stolen by the native whalers. That same day, without knowing anything about the arrival of the man-of-war, Mrs. Inglis and I had gone round to the harbour, to be present at the communion on the following Sabbath. The first news we heard on stepping ashore was about this stealing. I was very much annoyed to think that the natives should be stealing from a man-of-war, a thing that they had never done before. Captain Moresby, who is the warm friend of missions, felt sorry that the fair fame of the Aneityumese should be thus tarnished. The better class of the natives were much grieved, and did their best to find out the thieves; they discovered one of them, and the stolen article was returned to the ship. Manura, a Tahitian, who was foreman in one of the establishments, imposed a fine of sixpence each on one of his boats' crews, who had been seen in suspicious proximity to the exposed clothing. But four of the articles could not be found.

"The *Basilisk* was to sail the following morning at 11 o'clock, and there was not time for the chiefs to discover and arrest the offenders. Mr. Murray, the missionary in charge of the station, and I, therefore, went on board in the morning,

to explain to Captain Moresby the circumstances of the case.
As Mr. Murray had been but recently settled, and still unacquainted with native character and customs, I undertook the
whole responsibility of the affair.   I said to Captain Moresby
that I would pay for the articles stolen, and take the chiefs
for my security for being paid.   He was unwilling that I
should run any risk in the matter; but I assured him that I
had no fears, I knew the chiefs and the people too well to
have the slightest apprehensions about not being refunded.
Inquiries were then made at the purser, and it was found that
sixteen shillings and sixpence would replace the articles stolen.
I accordingly paid the money, received a written discharge for
the debt from Captain Moresby, and saved the character of
the Aneityumese.

"As soon as the machinery of the law, as it exists on
Aneityum, could be set in motion, by Lathella on the one
side of the island, and by Nowanpakau on the other, the
thieves were discovered, and the stolen property found.   The
culprits were each fined to the extent of the value of the
article he had stolen, and the articles taken from them; but,
as there are no professional lawyers on Aneityum, each man and
his friends conducting his own case, the Bench adjudged no
law expenses in addition.   It was not, however, till the meeting
of the Synod in the following year, 1873, that the matter
was finally disposed of.   Mr. Murray dispensed the communion at that time, the chiefs from both sides of the island
were present, and a large assembly of people.   The chiefs met
on the Monday, and had up before them all the young men
chargeable with that or any other offence during the previous
year, and talked very earnestly to them.   The chiefs paid
me out of the fines, while the stolen articles and Manura's

sixpences were divided between the two principal Natimariths, and by them appropriated respectively, as part payment for two nets, one for each side of the island, which the inland people (the great net manufacturers of the island) were making for the shore people. This is a kind of public treasury into which fines of this kind are usually thrown, which, as all are benefited thereby, has the effect of enlisting public sympathy on the side of public authority. This is the nearest parallel case that has occurred on this island to the gigantic robbery on the Bank of England that was going on about the same time. But it is satisfactory to know that while both in Britain and Aneityum crimes may be committed, they cannot be committed with impunity. In both countries the arm of Justice is strong—strong to protect the innocent, and inflict merited punishment upon the guilty."

The next case was one affecting not property but life. It was not murder but it was culpable homicide, and had to be dealt with by the constituted authorities. This case occurred on my side of the island. It was this:—On the 30th May 1865 a native living at Anpeke, about two miles or more west from our station, whose name was Yakari, killed his wife Lavi by striking her violently on the side with the paddle of a canoe. In the morning he had told her to do some digging, but she, evidently thinking that there was plenty of time, instead of going to the plantation went to the school. As she came out of the schoolhouse he saw her, and, being a man of a vehement and hasty temper, he lifted a paddle and struck her a most severe blow on the side, meaning to produce pain but not to cause death; Lavi fell at once to the ground insensible. Some of the women gathered around her, and lifted her up; but, though not dead, she was unconscious. They took her into the house, but she expired in half an hour. Yakari was panic stricken; he was more taken by surprise than any person present. He had never dreamed of such a result; he stood petrified. Tidings soon reached me of what had happened. I sent word to the three Natimariths, requesting them to meet, and to bring their chiefs with them, that they might inquire into the matter. We all met at Anpeke. Every man of note on my side of the island was there, and a good many from the other side, for the news spread like wildfire. No trial was required; the facts were patent, and Yakari never attempted to deny them: the only question was about the punishment. I explained to them the difference between murder and manslaughter; that this was not a case of murder, but of what is called "culpable homicide;" that Yakari had killed his wife, but it was not through what is called "malice prepense;" he had not killed her intentionally. He had had no desire to kill her, or no thought of doing so; but his sin and his crime was striking her in such a way as to cause her death; that in Britain there was always a clear distinction made between murder and manslaughter. While capital punishment was inflicted on the murderer, a milder punishment was inflicted for manslaughter. In this case it would be contrary to the Word of God, and to the practice followed in Britain, to put Yakari to death; but as he had been guilty of a very great crime, they might inflict any punishment they thought proper upon him, only they must spare his life, and not do any injury to his body. I had now explained to them the Law of God, and the practice pursued in Britain, it was for themselves to carry out these principles, and punish Yakari as they thought best. I was not a chief, and I had no power to do more than explain to them the

Word of God. I suggested to them that Nowanpakau, as being the principal Natimarith, should preside, and that the other two Natimariths should sit one on each side of him, and that all the chiefs should assemble round about them. They should decide what was to be done. Nowanpakau would pronounce the sentence, and the chiefs would carry it out themselves. This was all done after I had left them. It was agreed that Yakari's arms were to be tied, a very painful operation, and the chiefs were to talk to him; his house was to be pulled down and burned; all his property and food were to be taken from him, and given to the chiefs, to be distributed among them by the Natimarith. He was to be banished for twelve months to the other end of the island, and made to live in the land of a particular chief, who was to be responsible for looking after him; and he was never to be allowed to take another wife; he had had two already, and he had been good to neither of them. The chiefs were unanimous, and the people supported them as one man. The uncertainty of the law was anticipated, and its delay was unknown on that occasion. There and then, on the spot, and on that very day, the sentence was carried out to the very letter. Before the sun had sunk in the western ocean, Yakari was being conducted to the land of his exile. He served out his term of banishment, then left the land of strangers, and returned to his own people; but when he returned, I never saw a more changed man. I do believe that his punishment was blessed of the Lord for leading to his conversion. His whole appearance was changed. During the previous thirteen years that I had known him, while for the most part of it he was nominally a Christian, his uniform bearing was that of a heathen; but during the following ten or eleven years that we were on the island he seemed to be another man; formerly he was for the most part sour, glum, and sullen; but afterwards there was a cheerfulness and alacrity about his religious movements that I had never seen before.   Generally he was twice in the house of God every Sabbath, and although he lived more than two miles distant, he was at the prayer meeting every Wednesday afternoon. He entered my candidates' class, was baptized, and became a member of the Church, and I never heard a word against him all these ten or eleven years.   In a small way it might have been said of him, as the Rev. Sydney Smith said of his distinguished friend and contemporary, the Hon. Francis Horner, that "the ten commandments were written on his face, and all the law on his gait and manner."   Most certainly civil government is of divine appointment, and in the lowest and least civilised communities, if acting on anything like Bible principles, the magistrate is the minister of God for good, proving himself to be a terror to evildoers, and a praise to them that do well.   And this we found to our happy experience on Aneityum.

CHAPTER XXIV.

NUP-U-TONGA OR FOREIGNERS.

In the Aneityumese language *nup* signifies people; *u*, *i*, or *o*, of; and *tonga*, foreign. This word is applied to all who are not natives. But it is not applied to all foreigners. The missionaries are *nup-u-missionary;* those belonging to men-of-war are *nup-u-man-o-war*, and all the better class of white people are *nup-u-Beretani*. The French are *nup-u-wiwi*. But traders and all common white people are *nup-u-tonga*. Everything foreign, everything not produced on the island, is *i-tonga*. When we went to Aneityum the *nup-u-tonga* were a numerous and influential class in those islands. Their influence had to be taken carefully into account. They at first appeared as sandal-wood traders, then as whalers, then as engaged in the labour traffic, and finally as general traders. At first the *nup-u-missionary* were as nothing compared with the *nup-u-tonga*. They were allowed to hold their place more by sufferance than by anything else. When I first visited the New Hebrides in 1850, there was a large sandal-wood establishment on Aneityum, supported by leading merchants in Sydney; the wood was collected on Santo and Eromanga, stored and cleaned on Aneityum, and once a quarter shipped on to China. £70,000 worth of sandal-wood was said to be collected on Eromanga alone. It was a sort of East India Company on a small scale, and not much more favourable to the mission, not much more kindly in their feelings towards Messrs. Geddie and Powell, when they landed on Aneityum, than that great Oriental Corporation was toward Messrs. Carey, Marshman, and Ward, when they located themselves in the Danish settlement of Serampore. But when my wife and I settled on Aneityum in 1852, the proprietor of that establishment had removed to Tanna, and shortly afterwards he removed to Noumea, in New Caledonia; and as the "gold fever" broke out in Australia about that time, in a year or two all the floating population were drawn away both from Aneityum and most of the other islands, leaving the mission in the full possession of the field, and by the time they began to return, we had gained such an influence over the natives, that we had no special difficulty in holding our own against them. Nevertheless, we had to act towards them, as missionaries have to do everywhere, with great circumspection, so that if we could not obtain their friendship and assistance we might disarm their hostility, and secure, at least, their neutrality.

For some years about that time our friends on both sides of the Atlantic, and elsewhere, had been bespattering us with greatly more praise than was for our general good. It is, however, a wise and merciful arrangement in Divine providence, that when pride buds, the rod blossoms, with which it is to be corrected (Ezek. vii. 10). We were kept happily free from the *woe* denounced against those of whom "all men speak well." With our fellow-countrymen either sojourning or sailing among those islands, we, in general, got on very well; they were for the most part obliging, and acted in a kind and friendly manner; and we endeavoured to reciprocate their kindness, and oblige and benefit them as we had opportunity. Still, at times, our work came into collision with theirs. Our operations interfered, or were supposed to interfere, with their interests. We used all our influence to get the natives to give up the use of tobacco, and to sell their produce and their labour for cloth and other useful articles, rather than for useless or pernicious luxuries. In former times tobacco was the staple article of payment, and it continued to be by far the cheapest that the traders could employ. They could not openly object to the natives refusing tobacco and preferring other articles, but many of them did not like it. All along, too, we set our faces against rum and other intoxicants. We also had been using our best endeavours to elevate the status of our chiefs, believing that no government was so bad as a weak government. We, of course, used no means but moral suasion to accomplish these ends. We instructed the chiefs on their duties, obligations, and responsibilities; and the people on their privileges, and the duties they owed to their superiors. These instructions produced results, not always to the liking of those who thought that the natives should, at all times, do just as they wished them, and no otherwise. If the natives were not disposed to sell always when they wished to buy, or to work when they wished to employ them, we generally got the blame of the refusal. Every inconvenience which they experienced, in their intercourse with the natives, was charitably ascribed to our interference, or to our teaching. There were no chiefs ever heard of on the island, it was said, till we made them. We protected the poor women, and that, in the eyes of some, was an unjustifiable restraint upon the liberty of the subject. For these and similar reasons, the scourge of tongues was frequently applied with great freedom to our backs, and occasionally, without any feelings of delicacy, even to our faces. This latter mode of flagellation, however, though more painful, was less dangerous; as the weapon being perceived, it was often practicable to parry the blows, or even make them recoil on the head of those inflicting them. For although we did not render railing for railing, yet, at such times, we had occasionally an opportunity, in the way of self-defence, of stating important facts, and publishing important truths and principles. Mr. and Mrs. Geddie, from their residing at the haven of ships, and coming oftener into contact with our European neighbours, were more frequently honoured with those buffetings than we were. Still, even we were occasionally drawn out from our obscurity, and made ample sharers in the same privileges. Like Christian and Faithful at Vanity Fair, Mr. Geddie and I were sometimes made to stand on the pillory together. On one occasion we sat for four long hours hearing ourselves abused, and listening to an enumeration of the injuries done to the commerce of those seas by the operations of the mission. They all readily admitted at times that religion was a good thing. They approved highly, they said, of religion in its proper place. But then the natives were getting too much of it. They evidently thought that religion should be administered on homœopathic principles, and that the doses both for the natives and themselves should be infinitesimally small. It would be a long story, and neither very interesting nor very edifying, to repeat all the outs and ins of the charges preferred against us during that four hours *sederunt*, with all the replies, duplies, and triplies brought out in the defence. One of the gravest charges was as follows:—"Why," said the leading speaker, not in joke, but in sober earnest, "if things go on at this rate, they will soon be altogether unbearable. This island will soon be what England was in the days of the Commonwealth, when—

'They hanged a cat on Monday,
For killing mice on Sunday.'

We shall have the times of the Covenanters back again."
We had nothing to say in reply, except a silent amen ! Could
we believe our own ears ?   Were we really accomplishing such
wonders, our enemies themselves being witnesses ?   Were we
making Aneityum to resemble Puritan England, or Covenant-
ing Scotland ?   England as it was in the days of Owen, Howe,
and Baxter, and Scotland as it was in the days of Henderson,
Gillespie, and Rutherford ?   It was worth sitting four long
hours in such a position to hear the matter wound up with
such a charge.   I simply hinted that it was in those times
that Britain rose from being a second or third rate nation
to take her place as one of the leading powers of Europe.   I
said that every reader of history knew that it was not till the
thunders of Blake—that old stern puritan—had humbled
the pride of Holland, and scattered the armaments of Spain,
that the song arose, "Britannia rules the waves."   These
charges, comparing small things with great, seemed to bear
such a strong family likeness to those drawn up at Jerusalem
by John, Annas, Caiaphas, Alexander and their company, and
those set forth at Ephesus by Demetrius and his fellow-crafts-
men, that we felt as if we were more akin to the Apostles than
we had ever before dared to suppose that we were.   We
thought that we understood better than we ever did before,
how it was that they rejoiced.   It is, however, a very simple
thing to play the confessor or the martyr when a man feels,
as we did, that his head is quite safe on his shoulders.

The world is slow to admit the claims of Christianity, and to
recognise the benefits that flow from its influence.   Even such
an enlightened statesman as the late Earl of Derby wished to

attribute the abolition of the *suttee* in India, and all the improvements in the administration of law and justice in the East to anything and everything but the Gospel. So our *nup-u-tonga* friends out there, though they wished to see the natives peaceable and honest, that life and property might be secure, yet when the Gospel had effected that change, either directly or indirectly, they wished to ascribe it to commerce, rather than to Christianity. It was all the effect of tobacco and gunpowder, —the love of the one, and the fear of the other. Even Richard Cobden believed that he would chain down the spirit of war by bands of calico, and bring about the peaceful days of the millennium by the potent influence of free trade. There, in our islands, it was to be ushered in by pipes, muskets, and clouds of smoke. Christianity, such as we taught them, some of our countrymen, professedly well versed in theology, declared was not the right Christianity at all, not the Christianity of the New Testament, but some puritanical, pharisaical imitation of it, which made the natives not better, but greatly worse. It made them (the natives) to have greatly less love for tobacco, and greatly less fear for gunpowder than they had before we went among them. It made them begin, at least, to think and act for themselves, which, it was assumed, they had no right to do, as the blacks were made only to be slaves to the whites, and whoever taught them anything else did them only an injury.

But we were more afraid of the *nup-u-wiwi*—the French—than all the *nup-u-tongas*, all the whalers and traders in the Pacific. These were our fellow-countrymen ; we had a common language, and many common sympathies, and except when under strong prejudices, false impressions, or great excitement, we found even the worst of them to be reasonable men.

O

Besides, the island trade was improving, a better class of men were investing their capital in it, and from various causes it appeared likely to be accompanied with more advantages and fewer drawbacks to the work of the mission than it had formerly been.

Occasionally, too, the power of the Gospel, was seen to operate effectually among some of those characters; the prayers of God-fearing mothers, fathers, sisters, and brothers, no doubt, followed them to the islands, where the Gospel unexpectedly met them, and brought down blessings, when more direct home influences could not reach them. We had one pleasing case of this kind, that of George Rodburn, with which I shall conclude this chapter. George's first appearance at our station was anything but encouraging to us. One Sabbath day, as we were coming out of church, the second year of our residence on Aneityum, a boat was seen coming in to our little harbour, steered by a white man, and rowed by a native crew. The cargo consisted of pots, pans, and buckets, boxes, bags, and bundles, an axe, a handsaw, and some miscellaneous articles. This was George Rodburn and his belongings. The reason why he had come to reside so near us was this. Before we settled on the island several seamen connected with the sandal-wood trade had bought young women from their relations or the chief of the tribe and taken them away to the other islands. Some of the young women belonged to our district. According to the recognised native custom, if a man bought and paid for a woman, she became out-and-out his property. Her relations had no more claim upon her. If she had not been paid for, her friends could have demanded her back. One of these young women, called Morana, had been sold to a *nup-u-tonga*, and taken away before our arrival on the island, but

he had left the islands, and before doing so, had sold Morana
to George Rodburn, and she was now his property. When he
came to Aneityum he bought a small piece of land from an
uncle of Morana's, close beside our station. Those men, when
a number of them were together, were generally bouncing and
troublesome, but when there was only one or two of them they
were always quiet and easily controlled, and liked to settle
down near a missionary, not for the sake of his religion, but
for the sake of his protection. They felt safe in the neighbourhood of his dwelling. George Rodburn was no exception
to his class; he was a tall, well-made Englishman, about forty
years of age, rather pale, and not very robust, though in
general he enjoyed good health. He got a house erected a
little way off the beach, just in front of my boat harbour, and
we found him a very quiet inoffensive, obliging neighbour.
He came to church to the native service, and Morana came,
not only to the church, but also to the morning school. I
found her a very capable woman. As she had been twice sold
to a white man, and was now according to native ideas recognised as George's property, I advised him to get married to
her, so that they might live together as lawful husband and
wife. To this proposal they both very willingly agreed, and at
one of our Wednesday public prayer-meetings the marriage was
celebrated; and thus, after several years of a very doubtful
status, George "made her again an honest woman," to use an
expression that has found its way into the proverbial literature
of both north and south Britain, being quoted both by Dr.
Jamieson in his "Scottish Dictionary," and by Dr. Goldsmith
in his "Vicar of Wakefield." I found that George was a very
poor scholar; his original education had been very limited,
and when a young lad, like Robinson Crusoe, he had run away

to sea; but as he had not enjoyed the early educational advantages of Defoe's hero, so he had not improved his book-knowledge at sea, but had in reality lost almost completely all that he had ever learned.   When he came first to reside beside us he knew very little beyond the letters of the alphabet. I offered to give him a short lesson daily, and I began him with the first primer of the English Sunday School Union.   I preferred those primers because the print was large and very clear, and George had suffered an injury in one of his eyes, and his sight was not very good, and further the books contained nothing but texts of Scripture.   On the Sabbath afternoons my wife and I had always a short service in English for our own edification.   To this I invited George, and he came regularly.   After a short devotional exercise, we read a portion of some approved author; at that time we were reading through the "Pilgrim's Progress."   As our time was limited I did nothing but read a portion of it without any comment, as I thought that would be most profitable to George.   Both Mason and Scott wrote notes to the Pilgrim, and it is reported that on one occasion Mason found a plain man reading his edition of the Pilgrim, and asked him if he understood what he was reading.   "Oh yes," said the man, "I understand the Pilgrim, and I hope soon to be able to understand your notes also."   I once had an experience of the same kind myself.   When we lived in New Zealand we had a young girl of about fourteen years of age as a servant. In the course of our reading the Old Testament at family worship, when I came round to Genesis, I thought that instead of reading the Scriptures alone, I would read only half a chapter, and read along with that Scott's commentary on the portion read at morning worship.   About a week after I began this practice, my wife one day asked the young girl if she understood what I read at worship. "Oh yes," said the girl, "I understand the Bible, but I do not understand the explanation." On hearing of this result I discontinued the reading of Scott's Commentary, and read only the Bible. In like manner, when George attended our meeting I never read anything but the Scripture and the text of Bunyan; but these seemed to impress George deeply. I often saw the tears trickling down his cheeks, and when he left the room, he was so overcome by his feelings that he could not speak. After he could read with ease the three primers of the Sunday School Union, I got him a New Testament in large print, and as, on account of other duties, I could not spare time on week days for his lesson, I gave him a weekly lesson, which I heard on Sabbath. I made him prepare a chapter of John's Gospel, which he read to me before we commenced our service on Sabbath. In this way he mastered the whole of that Gospel. And I had reason to believe that the Spirit of God made those simple means effectual for his conversion. At the end of four years, a severe epidemic of influenza passed over the island. George caught the disease, and succumbed under it. My wife and I had to accompany the *John Williams* on a four weeks' voyage round the islands, to assist in the settlement of Mr. and Mrs. G. N. Gordon on Eromanga. On our return home we found that George was dead, but before we left home she had supplied him with all needful medical comforts, and Williamu and the other natives, for he was well liked, had ministered very faithfully to his wants, had read the Scriptures to him, and prayed regularly with him, and at last laid him decently in his grave.

If I might be allowed a short digression here, I would say,

it appears to me, that the much contested question of the
Bible in common or Board schools might be easily settled on
such lines as I followed with George Rodburn.   Religious
instruction in schools, and the Bible in schools, may easily be
made quite distinct questions.   Religious instruction in schools
generally means denominational teaching.   But the Bible in
schools may easily be kept quite apart from denominational
religious teaching.   All our Bible societies circulate the Bible
without note or comment.   So I would have the Bible read
in schools, but always without either note or comment.   Our
authorised version is a *national*, not a *denominational* book; it
has nothing sectarian in it.   In England and Ireland the
Bible is part of the common law of the land.   In Scotland,
according to Chalmers in his "Caledonia," we never had any
common law, nothing but statute law; but the Bible is, as it
is in both England and Ireland, a distinct part of the statute
law of the country.   It is, as such, embodied both in the
Westminster Confession, and in the Thirty-nine Articles.
Moreover, it is recognised by all our Protestant denominations
as the supreme authority in faith and morals.   None of them
could or would object to the simple reading of the Bible in
schools; and whenever the Romanists objected to our authorised version, I would give them every facility for reading the
Douay version of the Old Testament and the Rheims translation of the New.   These are not equal as translations to our
authorised version; but with a few exceptions they are correct
readings, and Dr. Chalmers has said, that the most imperfect
version of the Bible ever made, if honestly executed, will
convey a sufficient amount of knowledge to secure the salvation of the soul; hence the reading of this version would be
immeasurably better than reading no Scripture at all.   As

for the secularists, as they recognise the Bible to be one of
the best and most valuable of the ancient classics, they could
have no reasonable objection to the simple reading of it in the
schools.   I would, therefore, have the Bible made a part of
each of the six reading standards, and allow proficiency in the
reading of the Bible to secure grants in the same proportion
as anything else taught in the schools.   I would have the
reading of the Bible—but the reading only, including specially
the proper names, a part of Bible reading often sadly neglected.
I would have this reading thoroughly taught in schools ; let
the children learn also to repeat the books, to know the
chapters and verses, and to find the places with ease and
readiness, thus giving children full ability to read and examine
the Bible easily.   I would leave it to the Spirit of God to
apply the truths of the word to the hearts of the readers,
according, as Dr. Williams says, to "the equity of the Divine
government, and the sovereignty of Divine grace," and I
would have no fear of the result ; religion and morality would
flourish, and sectarian strife about denominational teaching
would to a certainty come to an end.

But to return from this digression, and come back to
George and Morana.   They had two children, both of them
girls, but the eldest died before her father.   The younger one
grew up to womanhood, was taught, when old enough to
enter it, in Mrs. Inglis's boarding or industrial school for
girls, and before we left the island was married to one of the
best and cleverest of our young men.   As they lived close
beside us, and as her husband gave her every encouragement,
Morana attended all my classes, and also all Mrs. Inglis's,
became a good scholar, and willingly made herself generally
useful.   While George lived she learned to read the Ancit-

yumese New Testament much faster than he learned the English. As a native woman she was much cleverer than he was for a white man, although he was a man of average capacity. She was at times impatient with him, on account of his slowness in acquiring the Aneityumese language, and would say to him, "Why cannot you learn the Ancityumese as fast as Misi (the missionary)?" "Oh, Misi," George would say, "Misi is a learned man, and I am not a scholar, and can never learn your language as fast as he can do." And George was right; a man who has received a professional education, and learned one or more foreign languages, will, as a general rule, learn any of those native tongues much faster than a man who knows no language but his own. George was often making mistakes, both when he was speaking the language himself and when he was hearing it spoken by others, some of them rather amusing. On one occasion Setefano, one of our young men, came to my wife and said, "Misi, I would like very much to learn English, if you would teach me." "Oh," said she, "I will be very glad to teach you, but you know it is a very difficult thing to learn English; why do you wish to learn English?" "Oh," he said, "to be able to speak to George; he speaks the Aneityumese so badly, that the people will be angry with him. As you know, he always says *ahving*, when he should say *merit*. When he wants a man *to work* for him, he says he wants a man that he *may eat* him!" Now this language, to men who had been all canni-bals, and were now thoroughly ashamed of the practice, was the reverse of complimentary. On another occasion George came to me in a great rage, on account of the way in which the natives had been speaking to him, and of him. He had taken my boat to the other station, and brought her back with a native crew; but the natives, he said, had been making fun of him all the way back; they had been calling him a *cat*, and had repeatedly said that he was *a poosie*. I was surprised at this, because I had supplied him with half a dozen of our best young men; but I called in two or three of them, and asked them what they had been saying to George, and if they had been calling him *a poosie*. The lads looked amazed; they could remember nothing improper that they had said. At last one of them opened his eyes wide, and laughed, and said to me, "I think I know now how it happened. The wind was ahead, and we had to tack a good many times. George was steering, but I had charge of the sail. As often as we tacked and had to turn the sail, I called out to those in the cent. e of the boat *atpuse* (stoop down), that the sail might not strike their heads. George had not understood the word, and as we were talking and laughing he must have thought we were calling him *a poosie*." I explained to him these words and he was satisfied; but he evidently felt a good deal ashamed of the mistake that he had made.

After his death, in due time, Morana, who was still a young woman, was again married, but this time to a native, to Pitello, one of the best of our teachers. We moved our teachers about, very much as the Wesleyans do their preachers, but, wherever they were located, Morana proved herself to be a power for good among the women. During her second marriage, Morana, quite unconsciously to herself, solved a question a good deal talked about in those seas, especially among a class of men who professed to be well acquainted with science and philosophy. The view held by many was, that if a native woman lived with a white man, and had children to him, and if she afterwards was married to a native, she would have no children to him. Thus proving, as they held, that the blacks and the whites were two distinct species, and could not propagate families, as if they had been both only one species. But Morana, as I have said, had two children to George, and both of them as like him as they could be ; and to Pitello, her second husband, two or more, one a very fine boy, whom I distinctly remember, and who bore evidence of his paternity, as distinctly as the two girls had done; thus clearly proving, as far as that case could prove it, whatever those sciolists might say, that God " hath made of one blood all nations of men for to dwell on all the face of the earth," and that from the three sons of Noah the whole world has been peopled, as they were divided in their generations, after their nations, after the flood. Indeed, as I have said elsewhere, we may see in the South Seas those three great divisions of mankind— the Hametic, the Shemetic, and the Japhetic—in the Papuans, in the Malay-Polynesians, and in the Europeans, as distinctly marked as when Mizraim, the son of Ham, and his sons settled in Egypt; when Terah and his three sons, Abram, Nahor, and Haran, dwelt in Ur of the Chaldees, or when Javan, the son of Japheth, the father of the Samoans, took up his abode in the Isles of Greece, or on the shores of Asia Minor, and respectively increased, multiplied, and replenished the earth, every one after his tongue, after their families, in their nations. No treatise on ethnology is so clear and distinct as the tenth chapter of Genesis.

CHAPTER XXV

PERHAPS in nothing have the South Sea missions been more characteristic than in the extent to which they have employed native agency. And in none of those missions has this principle been more fully carried out than in the New Hebrides Mission. On Aneityum every convert, as far as it was practicable, was made a missionary. At both stations we had a training school for preparing teachers. When our arrangements were complete we had fifty teachers and their wives stationed on Aneityum; and we followed out an aggressive policy in regard to the other islands of the group. At a very early stage of our missionary operations we sent two teachers and their wives to Futuna, and the same to Tanna; subsequently we occupied Aniwa with other two. When missionaries were settled on Eromanga, Efaté, and Nguna, we sent Aneityum teachers with them to strengthen their hands and assist them. The teachers on Aneityum received no salary, except an annual present of clothing to the value of from ten shillings to a pound out of mission boxes, sent out from home—from Scotland and the colonies to us, and from Nova Scotia to Dr. Geddie. The teachers on the other islands received a salary of five pounds a year, out of a fund raised in the colonies, which was commenced by Mr. Paton in 1863, after he had raised funds for the purchase of the *Dayspring*. For several years before we left the islands there were from twenty to thirty Aneityum teachers and their wives settled on the other islands. As in another place I have described the work that was carried on by the teachers on Aneityum, so in this chapter I shall confine myself to the work that was done by our Aneityum teachers on the other islands of the group. The first island to which Mr. Geddie and I sent teachers was Futuna; and that we might enlist the sympathy of the whole people in the enterprise, we selected a teacher from each side of the island. The men selected were Waihit and Yosefa; the former from Mr. Geddie's side of the island, the latter from mine. Waihit was a somewhat extraordinary character. In heathen times he was a sacred man, a great disease maker, and a furious savage; and hence a man of great influence among his countrymen. He became one of the first converts to Christianity. No sooner was he converted himself, than he sought, with all the energy of his character, to bring his fellow-countrymen out of the darkness of heathenism into the blessed light of the Gospel. Mr. Geddie was of opinion that the first great impression in favour of the Gospel on Aneityum was made chiefly by Waihit. He evinced the same earnestness and decision of character on Futuna. He exposed himself to considerable danger by his fidelity. The natives of Futuna had a cruel and barbarous practice when a scarcity of food occurred, which I suppose would be often once a year, before the bread-fruit season came in. They killed a man, as a sacrifice to propitiate their deities and secure an abundant harvest of bread-fruit. The chiefs assembled, fixed upon the individual, and immediately thereafter killed him. When Waihit heard of their intentions, he remonstrated with them

to the utmost of his power, but it was of no avail; they were
only angry with him, and several who professed themselves
favourable to Christianity left off coming near him. As one
of these poor victims had been killed only a short time before,
we had sent our boat there to visit the teachers. Our natives
returned quite shocked with the horrid deed, and apparently
more impressed than ever with the excellence of the Gospel.
The Aneityumese had been cannibals, but they had never
offered up human sacrifices. Waihit had also severely reproved some natives of Aneityum, living on Futuna, for their
wicked conduct generally. One of them was so angry at him
for this, that he advised the natives to kill Waihit. When
he heard that his life was threatened, he firmly replied, "Oh,
I am not afraid; they may kill my body, but they cannot
touch my soul."

Yosefa, the other teacher, who was from my side of the
island, was a young man of high promise; he was one of
eight or ten young men whom the Samoan teachers attracted
to the mission before the arrival of the missionaries, Messrs.
Powell, Geddie, and Archibald, in 1848; and who received
Samoanised scriptural or other names, such as Williamu,
Seremona, Yosefa, Filipo, Hosia, Lazarus, Sabataia, Paulo,
Setefano, &c.; a practice we soon discontinued as tending to
barbarise the language and destroy its idiomatic characteristics. Several of them went and stayed, for longer or
shorter periods, with Mr. Geddie, to learn the Word of God;
and they all joined my first classes. Subsequently they all
became teachers, and, as a whole, their character and history
continued very satisfactory. Our first converts were always
our best. They joined us from conviction. Intellectually and
morally they were the best men; and they were the longest

under instruction : their number being limited at first, the missionaries had more time to instruct them than they had afterwards. But to return to Yosefa. There was something of romance in his subsequent history. Mr. Geddie and I had talked of sending teachers to Futuna, but nothing was definitely agreed upon till the arrival of the *John Williams*, and we had consulted the deputation on board, when a decision was at once come to. Yosefa had been engaged to a young woman, and it was agreed that they must be married there and then. It was the second year of our residence on Aneityum ; our new church was only being erected, and the temporary building in which we were worshipping was far too small for the company. It was the first marriage that I performed on Aneityum ; it was conducted with great publicity ; it was performed on the shore, in front of the mission premises, and in presence of a great concourse of natives. Mr. Geddie, the Samoan brethren, Messrs. Murray and Sunderland, Captain Morgan, and a number of the men from the mission ship were all present. As soon as the marriage was over the young couple were hurried into the boat, put on board the *John Williams*, and the next morning they were landed on Futuna. This marriage trip was a rough voyage of one night between Aneityum and Futuna, their honeymoon was a full month spent in a land of strangers, all savages.

Shortly after the landing of our teachers, H.M.S. *Herald*, Captain Denham, spent about a week making surveys of the coast of Futuna. Captain Denham took a deep interest in missions ; and to strengthen our infant cause on that island, he made particular inquiries after our teachers, had them on board, and made it appear to the natives as if to inquire after and see the teachers had been the principal object of his visit.

Waihit and Yosefa went on prosecuting their mission work for about eighteen months, when we sent Pita, one of our Samoan teachers, who had formerly lived as a teacher on Tanna, with a strong select crew in our best boat to visit our teachers on Futuna and Tanna. On their return we learned that, ten days before they reached Futuna, a white man who lived there had left Futuna for Aneityum, and that Yosefa and two other natives of our island, besides some natives of Futuna, had accompanied him in his boat. As the *John Williams* had not called at Futuna, Yosefa was going over to Aneityum to obtain supplies. Pita and the natives found that the boat had not been heard of either at Tanna or Eromanga. The only conclusion, therefore, that we could draw was, that, as the boat had not come to Aneityum, it must have gone down at sea, being probably upset in a squall, and all in her had perished. We also learned from them that two canoes had been lost about the same time, one coming from Futuna to Aneityum, and the other going from Aneityum to Tanna. But, after being regarded as lost for six months, Yosefa, the white man, and all the boat's crew found their way back to Futuna, having had a most singular escape. They had nearly reached Aneityum, when a strong south-east wind arose, and they could neither make Aneityum nor Tanna. There was nothing then left them but to let the boat drift before the wind. Most providentially the white man, to whom the boat belonged, was a skilful seaman. He tied all the oars in a bundle, and fastening one rope in the middle of the oars, and another to each of the ends, and making all three fast to the bow of the boat, he threw the oars into the sea. The oars thus fastened, kept the head of the boat to the wind, and served also to break the waves, that might otherwise have swept over and swamped the boat. In this way, with little or no food but a few uncooked yams, they lay-to and drifted before the wind for five days. They then made for and reached New Caledonia, a distance of nearly two hundred miles from Futuna. They landed at Balad, near the north end of that island. This was the harbour at which Captain Cook chiefly lay, when he discovered that island in 1778, and took possession of it in the name of His Britannic Majesty. They afterwards sailed along the north-east side of New Caledonia, till they reached the Isle of Pines, a distance of about a hundred and fifty miles. They were there hospitably received by an English family, Mr. and Mrs. Underwood, who had formerly lived on Aneityum. They all remained there for about four or five months, till a trading vessel called at the Isle of Pines, the captain of which gave them a free passage, and landed them all safely on Futuna. We could not regard that event otherwise than as truly providential. It made a favourable and a deep impression on the natives of Aneityum. It strengthened their faith in God. Such an escape was never known in the history of these islands in the memory of living man, and even tradition had never recorded any similar deliverance.

Shortly after the settlement of the teachers on Futuna, the island which Dr. Gunn now occupies, we settled two Aneityum teachers and their wives on Tanna, at the station presently occupied by Rev. William Watt and his wife. The one teacher, Talip, from my side of the island; the other, Yaufati, from Mr. Geddie's side. They were subsequently joined by others; they were all well received, and prepared the field for the settlement of the Rev. J. W. Mathieson and his wife, whose health failed them, and who both sunk into an early grave.

Some years later, in 1858, Mr. Geddie accompanied the *John Williams* as far as Eromanga, and settled two teachers on Aniwa, the island on which Mr. and Mrs. Paton have laboured so successfully, and of which labours, when last at home, Mr. Paton gave so many thrilling accounts, and stirred the hearts of so many audiences by the exciting accounts of the digging of his well, and other telling incidents of mission life and work. The names of the two teachers were Navallak from Umej, on Mr. Geddie's side of the island, and Nemeyin from Ijasis, on my side. When the *John Knox* was at Aniwa in December of that year, all things were going on comfortably; but when she visited the island in May of next year, it was found that Nemeyin had been killed a few weeks before, and that Navallak had barely escaped with his life. After a careful investigation the facts of the case, as near as we could ascertain them, appeared to be these: Some thirty years before, if not more, a canoe had left Aniwa for Aneityum. This canoe carried Naparau, the principal chief of Aniwa, and six or eight of his people. The object of the voyage was to pay a visit to Naumi, the Natimarith of Aneityo, the highest chief on my side of the island, between whom and Naparau there existed a league of hospitality. Instead of getting ashore at Ithumu, the place where Naumi lived, the wind carried the canoe five or six miles farther to the east, to a place called Ingarei, the chief of which land had no connection with the people of Aniwa. As soon as the canoe had escaped from the rolling waves of the Pacific, and was got safely within the snug little harbour of Ingarei, Naparau and his fellow-voyagers were attacked by the people of Ingarei and Ijasis, and were all killed and feasted on, except two who plunged into the sea and swam for about three miles, till they reached

P

a huge rock that rises above the waves near the shore, at a place called Ahaij. They climbed up on this rock, and lay concealed all day. In those days iron axes were unknown on Aneityum, and canoes were very scarce. The few that were made were hollowed out of trees with great labour by means of stone adzes, and were as rude, rough, and shapeless as any antiquarian could desire. During the day, however, they saw one man fishing in a canoe. They watched him narrowly, and carefully observed the spot where he drew up his canoe on the beach. At night, when all was quiet, they swam ashore; one of them climbed a cocoa-nut tree, and pulled a few cocoa-nuts to satisfy hunger; they plaited some cocoa-nut leaves to use as a sail. They then launched the canoe, and as the trade wind was blowing fair, they reached their own island without much difficulty. Great was the grief, and loud were the lamentations of the people of Aniwa, when they heard that Naparau and his followers were killed; and measures were at once adopted to insure revenge for his death. That it might not be forgotten, a piece of ground was marked off, and pieces of wood were stuck into the earth; and from that year onward, as often as these rotted they were renewed, to perpetuate the remembrance of the event. Had we known anything of this, we should never have sent to them a teacher from Ijasis; for among savage tribes revenge is surpassingly sweet. When we lived among the natives of New Zealand, and were in daily dread of Rangihaeata and the rebel Maories, two native women tried to comfort my wife one day, by administering to her the sweetest cup of consolation they could think of, "Oh, you need not be afraid," they said, "for if they kill you, your countrymen will *revenge* your death; but if they kill us, we have nobody able to take revenge." After the teachers were settled, some of the people of Aniwa began to inquire from what part of Aneityum they came. The teachers seem to have had some misgivings, for they evaded the question. But an Aneityum woman who was married to an Aniwa man inadvertently told an Aniwa chief the name of the district from which Nemeyin came. The chief shrugged his shoulders and said very significantly *yiah*, yes. Nemeyin felt very uneasy about this disclosure, but nothing further took place at that time. As the Aniwa people had received the teachers from us, they felt bound not to injure them. But there were two Tanna men living on the island, and married to Aniwa women. The wife and child of one of these men died. The teachers were accused of causing their death by witchcraft, and a plot was laid to kill them. And, although the Aniwa people would not kill the teachers themselves, they felt no objections, but were quite well pleased, that their revenge should be taken by the Tannese. Accordingly, on a Sabbath-day, in the end of April of that year, 1859, when the teachers were returning from a place at which they had been conducting worship with the people, they were waylaid and clubbed by those two infuriated Tannese. Nemeyin was killed dead on the spot, and Navallak was knocked down and rendered insensible. But on some women coming up, the two men ran off. They soon after left Aniwa and went to Tanna, where one of them was killed in a battle. Since then Aniwa has contained a martyr's grave. But for the sake of the Gospel, Nemeyin would never have gone to that island. He lost his life for the sake of Christ. When the *John Knox* reached Aniwa a few weeks thereafter, our natives were extremely grieved to find that the teachers had been so barbarously treated. Nohoat, the principal chief of Aneityum, was with them, and his whole heart was moved. He spoke so long and so loud to the people of Aniwa on the wickedness of their conduct, that when he returned to the vessel he was quite hoarse and exhausted. The exertion had evidently been too much for his strength, as he became ill that very night, and never again recovered, but died about a month afterwards. After the return of the *John Knox*, we sent over a deputation of our chiefs to examine into the case. At the head of them was Viali, the son and successor of Naumi, between whom and the people of Aniwa the old league of hospitality and friendship still existed. Viali and his people had the privilege of a harbour on Aniwa. The Aniwa chiefs said that they had no ill-will to the teachers, that the debt of revenge was now paid, that the memorial sticks were destroyed, and that no one else would be injured, and that they wished the teachers to live among them. On their return Mr. Geddie and I again consulted on this matter. We felt exceedingly reluctant to abandon the island, and we felt equally unwilling to imperil human life. But as Nalmai, an influential man in Viali's district, and his wife, were both willing to go to Aniwa, we sent them to occupy Nemeyin's place, and the subsequent history of the island has shown that, in this instance, as often in medical cases, a bold practice was a safe one.

The history of our native agency, as regards other islands, may be divided into two parts; from 1853 to 1862, and from 1864 till the present time. I have briefly sketched the initiatory steps taken in this work, I shall now, but still more briefly, refer to its subsequent history. After the murder of the Rev. G. N. Gordon and his wife on Eromanga, in 1861, and the breaking up of the Tanna Mission in 1862, nearly the whole of the New Hebrides Mission was driven back on

Aneityum ; and on the arrival of the *Dayspring* in 1864, we had to commence the mission anew, under far more depressing circumstances than those under which we had commenced it at first. But I cannot go into details. Aneityum was the only island from which we could draw our teachers ; and here our choice was limited. After that, as the result of successive epidemics of measles, diphtheria, hooping-cough, influenza, &c., the population of Aneityum had been reduced by one-half, and our teachers had borne their full share of all those calamities. After these things, there was for several years, as might naturally have been expected, a great reluctance on the part of the Aneityumese to go forth as teachers to the surrounding islands. Happily in time that feeling passed away. But there were other difficulties which our diminished population more or less intensified. It was not every man, however well qualified in other respects, that was eligible to be a teacher, that would have been accepted, or at least been of any service on heathen islands. Strange as it may appear, it was only members of aristocratic families, chiefs, or near relations of chiefs, that carried any influence on heathen islands. As I have said elsewhere, the natives, even the most heathen natives, are intensely human ; rank or position are as much worshipped by them as by us.

Some time ago, at a meeting of the London City Mission, the late Lord Shaftesbury said that, in the most radical districts of the metropolis, the people would rather receive a visit from a lord than from a labourer ; because they thought that the former had more in his power to benefit their temporal interest than the latter. Human nature is essentially the same in all ages and in all parts of the world. The argument of the loaves and the fishes, or the temporal blessings that accompany or flow from Christianity, the rudest savage can in some measure soon understand. Hence, in addition to some intuitive notions on the subject, the heathen soon observed that, as often as the *Dayspring* visited their island, it was the teachers who were chiefs that always received the largest presents of food and property from their friends on Aneityum; and on account of these, as well as of their high ancestry, they were disposed to treat them with respect. The value of the spiritual blessings secured by the Gospel is the very last idea connected with Christianity which the heathen—may we not add the human—mind wakens up to comprehend.

Moreover, we did not find it advisable to send young people as teachers; men in middle life carried most influence, and proved most efficient. Besides this, some very suitable men had unsuitable wives, or large families, whom they could neither leave nor take with them. Some men had no wives, and could not get them, because every marriageable woman was married, and we found it inexpedient to send unmarried men.

It will be seen that, in the circumstances, our choice of native agency was very limited, and that from one cause or another a large proportion of our best men were necessarily shut out from this department of missionary labour, and hence our teachers on the heathen islands, though in general among our best men, were by no means, as a whole, among our best scholars. They could all read the Scriptures with tolerable fluency, and could conduct religious services in an edifying manner, but some of them could not write at all, and others of them very imperfectly.

I am afraid that there is a false impression abroad in many minds with respect to our native teachers. When people hear of a valuable and an efficient native agency, they are apt to think of such men as Tigo Soga, Narayin Sheshadri, or Rajahgopaul, men who received a regular course of university education in this country; whereas the most of our native teachers could hardly pass an examination in the first three standards. The only book in which they would make a good appearance at all would be the Bible. But you cannot expect to command a high class agency for five pounds a year.

It may be asked by some, What is the special work which our teachers on those heathen islands do? From the name *teachers* being given to them, it might naturally be inferred by most people that teaching was their principal work, and that each one of them had charge of a school. This was the case on Aneityum, where nearly the whole education of the island was carried on by native teachers, under the direction of the missionaries. The same men who had been teachers on Aneityum or elsewhere still retained the name of teachers when they went to heathen islands, although pioneer, or some such word, would have better indicated their position. The first thing they had to do was to live among the people, and acquire a knowledge of their language. For a considerable time it was by their life rather than by any direct teaching that they exhibited Christianity to the heathen. As soon as they landed among them they kept the Sabbath : they worshipped God morning and evening : they were peaceable, industrious, well-behaved men and women. A few of the heathen were generally more or less favourable to them, and as a general rule they, sooner or later, worked their way to positions of some influence. The teachers, as they best can, conduct services at their respective stations, and, as soon as the missionary can supply them with books, education begins. Moreover, they are like a bodyguard to the missionary:

in times of danger they protect him, his wife, his family, and his all. They are his eyes, his ears, his feet, and his hands: they inform him of what is going on; they carry out his suggestions and his plans; they supply him with the only skilled labour beyond his own that can be obtained; they build his house and man his boat, and without them, in the midst of heathenism, he would often be very helpless indeed.

The teachers are an humble and only a subsidiary agency; and although, chiefly owing to the diversity of languages, they can do little evangelistic work, especially in the first stages of any mission, yet, in their own place, they are often very valuable assistants to the missionary. As a whole, they are an active, diligent, reliable, courageous, consistent, and workable body of men; and while, being so limited in their attainments, and so crippled by their surroundings and their conditions, they have not been able to do much by direct teaching, they have exhibited a considerable amount of it in their lives,—a mode of teaching that can never be mistaken. As I have already said, up to the time of our leaving the islands in 1877, there were generally from twenty to thirty Aneityumese teachers and their wives on the other islands.

Aneityum supplied almost all the new missionaries with the needed native help, for house-building and other work, and malo cooks and female nurses for their wives, and all that the Americans call "helps." We also supplied the *Dayspring* all the year round with six or eight of a boat's crew, and these all were always more or less satisfactory: although, as might have been expected, when the missionary knew no Aneityumese, and the teachers knew no English, and they were both speaking to each other in a third language, of which both were at first all but completely ignorant, misunderstandings were often occurring on both sides from no fault on either; all the more, as the missionary was totally unacquainted with the manners and customs of the natives, and their modes of thinking. Even my excellent colleague, Dr. Geddie, with all his singular aptitude for understanding and managing natives, was often singularly annoyed and perplexed with his Samoan teachers. Our eight years' residence in New Zealand, and our extensive acquaintance with the Maoris, gave us an advantage in this respect, which no other missionary in the New Hebrides ever enjoyed, and reduced to a minimum our difficulties on that head.   At first all the native agency was supplied from Aneityum, but latterly Tanna, Aniwa, Eromanga, Efate, and Nguna have not only been supplying themselves for the most part, but also affording native help to the newly opened stations to the north; and their modes of operation and their experience are much the same as ours was on Aneityum, and the processes will go on, and be repeated with varying success, till the whole group shall be evangelised.   That is our aim, and by God's blessing resting on our efforts, we assuredly calculate on success.

CHAPTER XXVI.

RAROTONGAN AND SAMOAN-TEACHERS.

In treating of native agency in the New Hebrides an important place must be allowed for Rarotongan and Samoan teachers. It was our brethren of the Hervey and Samoan missions that opened up the New Hebrides group. John Williams and Mr. Harris laid down their lives in their first attempt to carry the Gospel to the "barbarous people" of Eromanga. Messrs. Heath, Murray, and others, with noble promptitude, stepped at once into the breach. I have elsewhere detailed Mr. Murray's courageous but cautious efforts to gain a footing on Aneityum. Year after year, for more than twenty long years, those brethren, with ungrudging spirit, sent forth native teachers, male and female, to the New Hebrides, to the number of seventy or eighty; the very flower of their islands, physically, intellectually, morally, and spiritually, fully equipped with everything necessary to secure success; but unfortunately, from no fault of theirs, they were weak in one point, and that to a great extent defeated the whole scheme. Those natives could not stand the climate. The missionaries, though very naturally, miscalculated. Time and experience have been needed to correct this mistake. In the Eastern Islands the climate was healthy : the natives were all acclimatised. The same conditions existed in the Loyalty Islands, hence the teachers enjoyed good health there, as well as on their own islands, and they were successful in their labours. But in every island in the New Hebrides they suffered so much from fever and ague that it was found to be hopeless to continue their services. Several of them were killed by the natives; a number of them succumbed to the climate and died; but the majority had either to be removed to their own islands, or else found their way, chiefly by trading vessels, from the New Hebrides to the Loyalty Islands, where they recovered their health and their usefulness.

In the New Hebrides, it was only on Aneityum where the Rarotongan and Samoan teachers were really a success; because it was only there that they enjoyed a fair measure of health. There they were living beside the mission families, had their health attended to, and had medicine and medical comforts supplied to them when required, and hence disease was warded off and life preserved. During the first eight years that we were on Aneityum, Dr. Geddie and I had always eight Samoans or Rarotongans under our charge; for some years we had twelve, besides children. With one or two exceptions these all enjoyed a fair measure of health, but on all the other islands where any teachers were placed, their health was every now and again breaking down, and the result of their labours was next to nothing. In all those islands one of the first things to be attended to in connection with native agency is sanitation, or the conditions necessary for securing health. In the New Guinea mission the missionaries have had similar difficulties to contend with that we have had.

The teachers from the Eastern Islands were a valuable agency. They largely bridged over the gulf between the missionaries and our own natives. Their knowledge of skilled native labour was much greater than that of the

Aneityumese.   In planting, cooking, and all kinds of mechanical skill, they greatly excelled our natives, while they were greatly below European; and yet they were not so high but that the Aneityumese could successfully imitate them, and in this way they greatly assisted in promoting the civilisation of the natives.   In the manufacture of mats, in the plaiting of native garments, in the making of canoes, in the burning of lime, in the building of houses, in cultivating plantations, in the whole range of the arts, in all the processes of education, in all the arrangements for public worship, they were always sufficiently ahead of the natives to take the lead and set a satisfactory example, and in this way they were always a valuable help to the missionaries.   They were expert in teaching the natives what they themselves knew, and in acquiring a knowledge of what they themselves did not know —they were adepts in learning the natives in all the arts which they themselves understood, and displayed an aptitude in acquiring a knowledge of the arts practised by Europeans. They were a fine, tall, robust, stalwart race, and commanded respect from their superior physical appearance.   They were in those seas a race evidently born to rule, and hence Canaan was their servant.

But instead of dilating on the general character of those teachers, I shall confine myself to a brief account of two of them, Amosa and Pita, whom I had under my charge for about seven years each, and who I have reason to believe were fair average specimens of the whole class.   Amosa (Amos) and his wife were a very efficient couple.   They were trained up under the late Rev. Dr. Nisbet and his wife.   Amosa was an excellent carpenter, both for native and European workmanship.   In erecting our mission premises, in building

churches, in fitting up the Teacher's Institution, I found
Amosa to be a valuable help. With axe and hammer, with
saw and plane, with mallet and chisel, with gimlet, augur,
and screw-driver, with every kind of common carpenter's tools,
his were skilful and active hands; and with every kind of
skilled native work he was equally at home. He was a great
help in the making of doors, presses, sofas, bedsteads, tables,
and all kinds of plain furniture; he was also a well skilled
boatman.* Among the gifts granted by the Holy Spirit to
the primitive Church were Helps and *Governments;* Amosa
and his wife both possessed in an eminent degree the faculty
of government. They could rule the natives without oppress-
ing them. Like the missionaries they never interfered with
the civil power of the chiefs. But like the missionaries, in
addition to a general superintendence, and the exercise of
moral influence, they kept a boarding-school for the benefit of
the more advanced and the more promising of the young
people in their district. Amosa had generally six or eight of
the best young men whom he trained himself, and his wife had
five or six of the best young women under her special instruction. In this way they drew out the industry and developed
the skill of the young people; they dug the ground, and they
planted it, and had always abundance of food for the natives
living on their premises; hence the young people were con-

---

* In those primeval days of mission work the missionaries had not only
to build their own houses, but also to manipulate the most important
articles of furniture, with which their houses had to be replenished.
At that time there was no *Dayspring* making biennial visits to the
colonies, and no steamers making bi-monthly visits to the islands, and
supplying all the wants of the missionaries, even before they occur, so
that, as compared with those days, the present is almost like playing at
missions, instead of going at them in dead earnest.

tented, happy, and genial: they were thus able not only to support themselves, but, at times, also to make a present of food to chiefs and influential men around them, and so were helps and not burdens to the community. At Ahaij, the district of which Amosa had special charge for six years, he erected an excellent house for himself, two rooms of which were always appropriated for the use of Mrs. Inglis and myself as often as we visited the district; but he also erected a church 75 feet long, in the very best style of Samoan ecclesiastical architecture. In after years, when the most of those young people had become teachers, they were all noted for their readiness and aptitude in the erecting of schoolhouses and churches in the districts in which they were settled.

Pita (or Peter) and his wife were in some respects totally different from Amosa and his wife, though taken all round they were as valuable as they were; some would have said more so. Pita had neither the mechanical skill nor the organising faculty of Amosa, he was lower intellectually, but he was higher morally and spiritually. He and his wife were natives of Tutuila. He was one of the first three natives of Tutuila that were admitted to the fellowship of the church, and sat down with the Rev. A. W. Murray at the Lord's table. He was a man of position: his sister was married to Pomare, the heir-presumptive to the chieftainship of Tutuila, who was also one of the first three converts; he went to Tanna as a teacher and died there. For some time Pita acted as a teacher on Tutuila, his own island; then he was appointed to the New Hebrides, and was located at Port Resolution, on Tanna. In 1850, when I first visited Port Resolution in H.M.S. *Havannah*, Pita was at Port Resolution, although I did not see him. By and by Pita's life was in danger, and he had to flee to

Aneityum.   After a time he returned to Tanna, but a second time he had to flee to Aneityum for his life.   As at this time the Tanna mission was virtually broken up, it was arranged that Pita and his wife should remain on Aneityum to assist us at our station.   This they did for nearly six years.   They returned with us in the *John Williams* to Tutuila, when in 1860 we came home to this country to carry the New Testament through the press.   We found both of them to be valuable assistants.   They were, and deservedly so, well liked by the natives.   They were exemplary, God-fearing Christians; they were quiet, kind, and obliging, and the natives would have done anything for them.   Pita's wife was a kind, true-hearted, reliable woman.   I may mention one instance of her unselfish and thoughtful kindness to my wife.   On one occasion I went round to Dr. Geddie's station; Pita went with me in charge of my boat.   We intended to return on the following day; but next morning the weather had become so squally, and the sea so rough, that I at once gave up all thoughts of returning home that day.   But as the sea was often rough on the one side of the island when it was smooth on the other, my wife, not knowing how it might be on Dr. Geddie's side, and not very certain whether I might not attempt to return after all, had arranged to keep up an outlook.   About the middle of the day she went down to the beach, and saw one of our young men looking very earnestly at some object down the shore.   She called out to him, and said, "Samuel, what are you looking at so intently?"   He said, "O Misi, when the squall came up I thought I saw the boat, but since it cleared away I do not see it.   I am afraid it is swamped."   "The boat swamped!" said my wife, "if so, they will all be drowned."   "I hope not," he said; "the missionary may, but the rest can all swim."

"Oh," said my wife, "let us all run to Nohmunjap and see."
So off she ran. Pita's wife was also on the beach; she took
hold of Mrs. Inglis's arm, and ran along with her, and all the
natives about joined them. As they ran along in a state of
high excitement, Pita's wife was overflowing with sympathy.
Ek aiheuc vai euc ainyak, ak Misi, &c., "Great is my pity for
you, Mrs. Inglis; how my heart feels for you: my love, my
compassion for the missionary's wife. What will she do if Mr.
Inglis is drowned?" They ran on for about a mile till they
reached Nohmunjap, the nearest settlement, and had the
satisfaction to find that it was a false alarm; it was not the
boat, it was only a native canoe that the young man had seen;
but it was a wreck. The outrigger was broken by the waves,
the canoe was upset, and the natives were thrown into the sea;
but as they were all expert swimmers, nearly as much at home
in the water as on the land, they all got safe to the shore,
dragging the canoe with them. My wife said oftentimes afterwards, that after the excitement was over she felt quite
ashamed of herself, that she should selfishly have accepted to
herself all the sympathy of Pita's wife, and rendered none to
her in return; never for a moment thinking that if Pita had been
drowned along with her husband, Pita's wife would have been left
a widow as well as herself. But I presume that neither Pita's
wife, nor any of the natives, ever thought it possible that Pita,
an expert swimmer, as all the natives were, and so near the
shore, could by any possibility be drowned; but that I should
be drowned was, as they might think, not only possible, but
also highly probable, hence the sympathy not only of Pita's
wife, but of all the natives.

Pita was a man of a strong will, and at times very positive.
On one occasion he got the liver of a shark. Now, this was

very good for making oil of : the oil made from it was better
than train oil; but the liver itself was very poisonous. The
natives knew this, and they had often told Pita so. But he
had taken it into his head that he would eat the shark's liver.
The natives strongly opposed his doing so, and his wife im-
plored him with tears not to attempt doing it. "O Pita,"
she said, "if you eat this and die, what will become of me and
these children?" "Oh," said Pita, "sharks are not poisonous in Samoa, and why should they be so here?" Eat it he
would, in spite of all remonstrance, and eat it he did. The first
intimation that we heard of what was going on was about one
o'clock on the following morning, when a gentle tap was heard
at our bedroom window. On asking who was there, in a low,
timid voice Pita's wife said, " O Misi, Pita is dying; do come
and .pray with us." I arose at once, and followed her. I
found Pita very ill; his pulse had fallen to fifty. I gave him
first an emetic, and then a purgative. I had a bottle of
brandy in my medicine chest, and following the suggestions
of my medical books, I administered small doses of this daily
while it lasted. Next day he was a good deal better, and at
the end of some weeks he was all but well; but at the end of
two or three years, when we left him in Tutuila with Mr. and
Mrs. Powell, he was not exactly himself; he was fairly well,
but he had not fully recovered his wonted vigour. He lived
ten years after his return to Tutuila, and maintained an
eminently consistent Christian character. Mr. Murray has
supplied a very interesting sketch of Pita in his able and
valuable work, "Forty Years' Mission Work in Polynesia."
During the last ten years of Pita's life he devoted a tenth of
all his income to the cause of God, and in this way was quite
abreast of the Society that aims at securing proportionate

Q

giving. But I had no merit in instilling into his mind those good principles. He must have been taught them by Mr. Powell, or, what is not at all unlikely, he must have imbibed them at his conversion from the Rev. A. W. Murray, the proto-missionary of Tutuila. Mr. Powell wrote me a very touching account of Pita's death. While Pita went back to Tutuila, his native island, Amosa, who was a younger and stronger man, was settled on Savage Island or Niwe, and laboured there with much success. Both these families were warm-hearted, friendly, and grateful. As long as we were in the islands, as often as the *John Williams* made a visit to the west, we received from them letters and presents, articles of native manufacture prepared by their own hands. One year Amosa sent us a fine sofa, made by himself, the bottom and back plaited with the finest native cinet, and the frame made of the best native wood—black, hard, and heavy, almost equal to mahogany. It would not have been in accordance with Samoan etiquette, nor yet in keeping with our own ideas of Christian ethics, if, in these circumstances, we had not practised a little *giff-gaff;* but certainly it would have been the last explanation that I would have accepted, that the desire to send us those much-prized valuable gifts was in any way stimulated by the lively apprehension of any future obligations. All those teachers were a credit and an honour to the Society under which they were trained—the London Missionary Society.

CHAPTER XXVII.

It is always interesting to trace the beginnings of any important movements, especially when these seem very unlikely to succeed. Such was the beginning of the mission work on Aneityum. The natives, through whose instrumentality the mission first gained a footing on the island, were the most unlikely that any one could think of to be employed in such a work. But God is wiser than man.

The first teachers on Aneityum, named Tavita and Fotau-yasi, were located on Ipeke, the district next to Aname, my station, by the Rev. A. W. Murray of the Samoan Mission. Mr. Murray says, in his "Western Polynesia": "Let us try briefly to trace those movements which, under the guiding hand, and by the blessing, of Him from whom all good comes, have raised Aneityum to the distinguished position which it at present holds among the isles of the sea. It was during the third voyage of the *Camden* to Western Polynesia that Christian teachers were introduced to Aneityum. On that occasion the writer was privileged to make his first acquaintance with a department of missionary work in which he has been permitted to have a considerable share. Vividly was this feeling realised on the morning of March the 30th, 1841, when we approached Aneityum. We had succeeded on the preceding day in introducing teachers to the adjacent island of

Futuna. There we had experienced comparatively little difficulty, as on that island a dialect of the Eastern Polynesian language is spoken; but how were we to manage at Aneityum, the language of which was utterly unintelligible to us? We had made the best provision against the difficulty of which our circumstances admitted, having brought with us the chief Kotiama from Futuna to act as our interpreter.

"An odd character, indeed, was Kotiama to bring on such a mission—himself a heathen, and afterwards concerned in the murder of his own teachers, and, alas! a heathen to this day (1863). He was of essential service to us, however, as without him there was no likelihood that we should have succeeded in the object of our visit. When we drew near the island, canoes came off towards the ship; but the natives would by no means come on board. A good many years before an affray had taken place with a sandal-wood vessel in which two white men were killed and some wounded, and five natives were killed, hence this distrust and apprehension.

"All our efforts to induce the natives to come on board being unsuccessful, a boat was lowered, and Captain Morgan and myself went in close to the shore. After a while one character of note ventured near enough to our boat to receive from my hands a string of beads. Snatching the treasure, at the risk of his life, as he seemed to think, he immediately backed astern; but the scale was turned. His venture had succeeded—and having succeeded once, he might a second time—hence distrust soon gave place to confidence, and we were in a fair way to gain our object. The bold fellow who received the beads was Yatta, the chief of the district off which we were. I have seen many a heathen of a deeply degraded and savage character, but a more finished savage, to all appearance, and, as we afterwards found, in reality, I never saw. He realised most fully the idea one forms of the ferocious and bloodthirsty savage. And yet this man received and protected the messengers of peace. We made known our object, as well as we could, through Kotiama. The teachers intended for the island went on shore, and on their return they expressed themselves satisfied with the prospects, and were willing to remain. The reception they met with was interesting and encouraging. Large numbers of people were congregated on the beach. They expressed their pacific and friendly disposition by waving green boughs. Thus they welcomed to their shores the messengers of salvation, and the initiatory step was taken towards the wonderful revolution which has since been effected. 'Who hath despised the day of small things ?' "

Mr. Murray was prosecuting the Lord's work in faith ; he was "enduring as seeing Him who is invisible ;" he recognised the hand of God in the relations into which he had been brought both towards Kotiama and Yatta. They were, at that time, the two most influential men on their respective islands ; but the finger of God was working on behalf of the mission far beyond anything that Mr. Murray then knew, or perhaps ever knew—at least he says nothing about it in his book, and I never happened to hear him speak about it ; but there was a man on board the *Camden* at that time, though probably quite unknown to Mr. Murray, who was the most important link in this chain of events, and that was Nu-umsi, the Columbus of Aneityum, a brother of Yatta's ; he was the first native of Aneityum who had ever sailed away in a trading vessel, and gone beyond the adjoining islands and out of sight of Aneityum. He sailed as far as the Loyalty Islands, and on his way home called at Aniwa, and was left with

Kotiama on Futuna, one of the nearest islands to Aneityum. When the *Camden* called at Futuna, and it was ascertained that she was going to Aneityum, and would take Kotiama, and also take home Nu-umsi, there was great rejoicing; a great trading expedition would be at once arranged. The settlement of the teachers on Futuna would be at once agreed to; almost any terms would have been agreed to in the circumstances; such a fortunate event had never occurred in the memory of living man; a foreign ship was going to take them to Aneityum, and bring them back again. No wonder that Mr. Murray says, as we have seen, that they had experienced little difficulty in settling the teachers on Futuna; the wonder would have been if there had been any difficulty at all. Everywhere there would be excitement; a large quantity of property, chiefly mats and baskets, the staple manufacture of Futuna, would be collected and taken on board. Kotiama would have half-a-dozen of his leading men on board with him, and Nu-umsi would act as pilot. He would cause the vessel to be steered, not to Anelgauhat, the principal harbour, then unknown to all sea-faring men, but direct to Ipeke, the district over which his far-famed brother, Yatta, was chief. As soon as Yatta would learn that his brother Nu-umsi was on board, safe back from his hazardous travels, and that Kotiama, the great chief of Futuna, was there also, with a large quantity of mats and baskets, and that this was not, like the last ship that had called at the island, a fighting ship—that this was a ship of peace, and killed nobody—in these circumstances it would become as easy a matter to arrange for the settlement of the teachers on Aneityum as it had been on Futuna. I have an old copy of one of the numbers of the London Missionary Society's Chronicle of that date, which gives a woodcut of the landing of the first teachers on Aneityum. There is the ship's boat, Captain Morgan at the stern and Mr. Murray in the bow; two strong natives are each carrying one of the chests belonging to the teachers, while the teachers and their wives are wading ashore, and a wondering crowd are standing on the beach giving them a cordial welcome. Meanwhile, Yatta would be levying a large contribution of taro, bread-fruit, cocoa-nuts, horse-chestnuts, sugar-cane, and bananas, from his three lands—Ipeke, Aname, and Isav—to present to Kotiama and his friends, who doubtless returned to Futuna extremely delighted with the results of the expedition. It was an era, as the natives would account it, in the history of both islands. Mr. Murray, too, and Captain Morgan, as they had good reason, were much gratified with their success. In the readiness with which the teachers were received on both islands, they believed, in their ignorance and inexperience, that they saw on the part of the natives a great desire for the Gospel. It was, as they thought, the isles waiting for His law. It was Ethiopia stretching out her hands unto God. It was, however, just what had happened on the shores of the sea of Galilee 1800 years before; when the multitude followed Christ, not for His teaching, not for the gracious words which flowed from His lips, but for the loaves and the fishes: because they ate of the loaves and were filled. So this opening for the Gospel was caused by no desire for its heavenly blessings: it was caused simply by the mats and the baskets of Futuna, and by the taro, the cocoa-nuts, and the bananas of Aneityum. But, nevertheless, in both cases the Lord was overruling men's hearts, without their being conscious of it, for the establishment of His kingdom. The Lord's hand was as certainly present in con-

nection with the *Camden* as it was when He girded the loins
of Cyrus, and supported his right hand at the time he was
made the deliverer of Israel, though he did not know Jehovah.
It was the Lord that implanted the spirit of enterprise in the
heart of Nu-umsi, as certainly as He had implanted it in the
heart of Columbus.   He guided the heart of the captain of the
trading vessel to land him on Futuna, and not on Aneityum.
In this way he was ready for the service of the mission when
the *Camden* reached Futuna.   He was made the connecting
link between Kotiama and Yatta; the one the best man for introducing Mr. Murray to Aneityum, because Mr. Murray could
speak to him, and he was a man of influence; and the other
was the best man under whom to place the teachers for protection, as he was the most powerful chief in the district.
Nu-umsi had wonderful stories relating to his travels with
which to entertain his fellow-countrymen, and to occupy their
minds till the most perilous period for the teachers had
passed, and they were gaining a hold on the hearts of the
people for themselves on their own account.

Nu-umsi died before any of the natives professed Christianity, but the teachers, Tavita and Fotau-yasi, might have
conveyed to him sufficient knowledge to produce faith in
Christ.   Bishop Selwyn used to say, "We cannot tell how
little Scriptural knowledge is sufficient to save the soul of a
heathen."   The famous Mr. David Dickson, minister of
Irvine, used to meet the objection of those who neglected the
salvation of their souls, and said in excuse, "Perhaps we are
not elected, and therefore it might be of no use to try," by
saying, "But perhaps you are, and the one perhaps is just
as good as the other, and rather better, for it is certain that
you have been elected to the privileges of the Gospel;" so God,

who elected Nu-umsi to be the pioneer of the Gospel for Aneityum, might also have elected him to everlasting life, and the Samoan teachers might supply him with the requisite knowledge for producing faith; but, like the Psalmist, we must not meddle with things too high for us, for in his case the Judge of all the earth would do right. But Nu-umsi left two daughters, Naipora and Murivai, both young girls, who afterwards attended Mrs. Inglis's classes, became church members, were married to excellent young men, and exhibited exemplary Christian lives, so that Nu-umsi brought the Gospel, if not for himself—which we hope he did—yet at least for his children and his countrymen.

Yatta had still another work to do, which he did, like the former, quite unconsciously, but not so honourably. From the settlement of the teachers till the settlement of the missionaries, seven long years were to intervene, and God made provision for that event, and in so doing brought good out of evil, and made the wrath of Yatta to praise Him. On Ipeke there lived a man called Wumra, and his wife's name was Singonga. Wumra was among the first on whom the Word of God took effect. He began to keep the Sabbath, to attend upon public worship, and pray both in secret and in his family. In 1845 Mr. Murray, along with Rev. Mr., afterwards Dr. Turner, visited Aneityum. Wumra applied to them that he and his wife might be taken to Samoa, for the sake of being more fully instructed in the Gospel; but he had a stronger reason than this of which the two missionaries were in all likelihood not aware. Wumra was an elderly man, but Singonga was a young, clever, good-looking woman; and Yatta had cast his covetous eyes upon his neighbour's wife, and was plotting the murder of Wumra for the sake of ob-

taining Singonga. Wumra's application was successful, and
they were both taken on to Samoa, and lived for three years
at one of the mission stations, gained a considerable knowledge of the Samoan language, considerably increased their
acquaintance with Scripture, and grew in Christian character.
In 1848 they came· back with Mr. Geddie and the mission
party. But like the Holy Family, who, when they came back
from Egypt and heard that Archelaus reigned instead of his
father Herod, instead of settling in Bethlehem, went on to
Nazareth, so Wumra, when he heard that Yatta was still
chief of the land, and had two wives, instead of returning to
his own property in Ipeke, remained with Mr. and Mrs.
Geddie on the other side of the island, where Yatta durst
not show his face except at the risk of his life. Nearly five
years after this, Yatta came to me one day, as I was about to
sail to Mr. Geddie's station, to ask for a passage in my boat,
which I granted him, to visit his mortal enemy, now, like
himself, a Christian, and on the following day, the Sabbath,
the two walked to the house of God in company. That was
the first time that Yatta had ever been at Anelgauhat, although
only about fourteen miles distant. Not that he lacked the
opportunity to do so, for, in order to get some of Yatta's men
to work for him, the proprietor of the trading establishment
had repeatedly offered to send round an armed boat to bring
Yatta to the harbour, but he durst not venture; but when a
mission-boat was going, though quite unarmed, he went with
the utmost confidence. When Wumra returned Yatta was
still a savage. After we were settled beside him, the natives
showed us an old native oven in which Yatta had caused the
body of a young man to be cooked for cannibal purposes. But
eleven years of missionary influence had wrought a marvellous

change on the savage Yatta. Tavita (David), the Samoan teacher, and his wife, had both died, the first of the missionary staff who had fallen on Aneityum, and the teachers had bestowed the name of Tavita on Yatta, while they called his principal wife Patisepa (Bathsheba). Notwithstanding much that was not only unsatisfactory, but positively very wrong in Yatta's history, as might have been expected, he continued steadily to protect the teachers and the missionaries. As time went on he continued to improve, the truth evidently laid hold of him ; as I have stated elsewhere, he put away one of his wives, and was married to the other, and enjoyed domestic peace to the end of his days. When he died, some years afterwards, he was a candidate for church fellowship. His death was caused by something like sunstroke, and his illness was short. He left no son, but his daughter, Sina or Jane, was a remarkably fine young woman ; she was the first native girl that Mrs. Inglis took into her boarding-school, and one of the first native women whom I baptized and admitted into the church. She was married to one of the very best of our young men, but after she had two children she died, like her father, of what we afterwards found to be sunstroke. I never saw such genuine grief displayed by the natives as I saw and heard at her death ; the natives wail at every death. but there, as elsewhere, much of the mourning is quite formal ; but when Jane died, any one could perceive that the mourning was genuine, that the weeping and the wailing came from the heart.

But to return to Wumra and Singonga. As I have said they were still afraid of Yatta, and did not return to Ipeke, but remained with Mr. and Mrs. Geddie, which was a great advantage to the mission, as they were a couple specially prepared of God to assist the mission family in their first struggles on Aneityum. Wumra assisted Mr. Geddie in acquiring a knowledge of the native language, and Singonga was for a long time Mrs. Geddie's right hand woman. It was from Wumra that Mr. Geddie first got the correct word for *sin*, and possibly, though I am not quite sure of this, also the correct word for *soul*. During all the seven years that the teachers were on the island before the arrival of the missionaries the nearest word for *soul* that they had got was *shadow*, and they were daily exhorting the natives to seek the salvation, not of their *souls*, but of their *shadows*. Mr. Geddie got also other important words, such as unbelief, faith, salvation, &c. To acquire a knowledge of a foreign language in such circumstances as they were in involved a great amount of groping in the dark. It was not till Mr. and Mrs. Geddie had been five years on Aneityum, and we had been one, that he found out the native word for *perhaps;* and I think the missionaries were ten or a dozen years on Tahiti before they discovered some word that was equally common and equally important. The word for perhaps is *kit*, often followed by *et*, it is, and is pronounced so quickly, and is tripped over so lightly, that it eluded their observation, and they were continually being annoyed by the natives telling them, as they thought, falsehoods. They would have asked a native, "Where is So-and-so?" or "What is So-and-so doing?" The native would have answered, *Kit et apan aien, &c.*, or *Kit et ango aien, &c.*, "Perhaps he is away," &c., or "Perhaps he is doing," &c. They understood him to say, *Et apan aien, &c.*, "He is away," &c., or *Et ango aien, &c.*, "He is doing," &c. They often afterwards found out, of course, that the meaning which they attached to the answer was not true, and they inferred that the native was not speaking the truth, which often led to serious misapprehensions. It was therefore a great and important discovery when *kit* was found out and its correct meaning established; it was an acquisition that was highly prized, a discovery that was greatly valued, and could scarcely be overrated.

Kotiama, Yatta, and Nu-umsi were very unlikely agents for God to employ to carry forward His work of mercy in those heathen islands, but so were Judah, Jephthah, and Samson in the Jewish Church; and if salvation were of works, none of these would be eligible for heaven; but as it is of grace, the irresistible efficacy of this Divine power can accomplish anything; it can transmute the chief of sinners into the most eminent of saints, change the most ferocious of murderers to be the mildest and meekest of martyrs, and render the wildest of savages to be the gentlest of human kind; and this process is going constantly on wherever our missionaries are opening the Bible to the heathen in their own tongue.

CHAPTER XXVIII.

THE FRENCH IN THE NEW HEBRIDES, 1887–8.

In the volume which I published some years ago I had a chapter on "The French in the New Hebrides." This is a continuation of that chapter, bringing the history down to the present date. The general public are very ignorant about both the geography and the history of the South Sea Islands. Few would believe how ignorant both the British Government and the secular press of this country are about the French and the New Hebrides, till within the last few years, when the attitude of the French toward those islands, and their unjust and unjustifiable claims to that group, have awakened an interest in the subject that was never before thought of. Lord Harrowby, President of the British and Foreign Bible Society, has done much to enlighten the British Government on the question. Lord Roseberry has enlightened the Government and the public as well. The reports of our Mission Synod have diffused important information on this subject in Scotland, in Nova Scotia, in Australia, and in New Zealand; the journals, letters, and speeches of our missionaries, especially those of the Rev. J. G. Paton, have kept the subject before the public mind. The *Sydney Presbyterian*, edited by the Rev. J. Copeland, formerly one of our missionaries in the New Hebrides, by the frequent publication of short, clear, reliable statements, kept the churches of that denomination well informed on this question. The Colonial Government in Australia and New Zealand have been repeatedly calling the attention of the Imperial Government to the attitude of the French towards the New Hebrides; and the Foreign Mission Committee of the Free Church of Scotland have been knocking at the door of the Foreign Office in London with all the persistency of the importunate widow; all of which things have been reported to the authorities in Paris, so that the French Government, like the unjust judge, for the sake of peace, have at last most reluctantly succumbed, and with a very bad grace, on the 15th of March 1888, they removed the troops they had stationed at Havannah harbour and on Malikula; and the life and property of their respective subjects in the New Hebrides are to be secured by a mixed commission of captains of British and French men-of-war. All claims for the annexation of the group by France are thus abandoned in the meantime, but how this dual protectorate may work is still uncertain. If the French still wish to occupy the New Hebrides, as there is too much reason to fear that they do, it will be easy for them to fabricate a reason for doing so. Before they left Malikula the French soldiers stole a pig, and when the natives remonstrated they shot one of the native chiefs. They left two Romish priests on Malikula against the will of the natives, and it will be easy for these men, in accordance with French policy, to lodge a complaint against the natives; and as far as the French may have it in their power, judging from all their past history in the South Seas, it will be the wolf sitting in judgment on the lamb, and it would require no prophet to foresee the verdict. The Australian journals, the missionaries on the New Hebrides, and the supporters of the mission at the Antipodes, are not sanguine as to the success of the working of the mixed commission. It is extensively believed that it is the chagrin felt by the French at their being obliged to remove their troops from the New Hebrides that has led them to wreak their spite on the missions of the London Missionary Society on the Loyalty Islands in the west and on the Society Islands in the east. The Rev. John Jones of Maré is the last victim of this Rome-inspired persecution. He was for thirty years one of the most peaceable, inoffensive, and law-abiding missionaries in the South Seas. The French had worried him and fettered him all those years to an extent that is almost incredible. One restriction after another was imposed upon him. He was forbidden to teach, he was forbidden to preach, he was prevented from exercising almost all pastoral or mission work, so that latterly he was confining himself almost entirely to his own house, and doing almost nothing but translating the Scriptures into the Maré language. But Rome saw the danger to her interests from the existence of an open Bible. In Tahiti, before the French took possession of the island, the natives had been supplied by the missionaries with a translation of the whole Bible, and so attached had they become to the Scriptures, that those of them who had become Papists demanded the Bible so determinedly from the priests, that, as they had no translation of their own to give them, they were obliged to procure the Protestant translation from the agent of the Bible Society, lest their converts should, as they threatened them to do, return to their former faith and again become Protestants. So, while engaged in translating the Scriptures, Mr. Jones was surprised to be informed, by the officer of a boat's crew from a French man-of-war, that they had come to take him off the island, and that if he did not

leave the station with them in half-an-hour they would
remove him by force. Mr. Jones hastily packed up his MSS.
of the Bible and a few necessaries, and went on board in the
custody of the French officers. No charge was formulated
against him. When he asked to be informed of what crime
he was accused, his captors could only inform him that they
had instructions to take him off the island; in a loose, informal way he was accused of advocating the annexation of
Maré to Australia, but no proof has been produced in support
of this charge. He was not tried either on Maré or on New
Caledonia. He was simply removed and sent adrift. When
Festus, the Roman Governor, consulted King Agrippa about
Paul, he said, "It seemeth to me unreasonable to send a
prisoner, and not withal to signify the crimes laid against
him." But these professedly Christian Frenchmen, members
of the only true and infallible Church, as they believe, standing
avowedly in the very van of European civilisation, are, in
their notions of justice, greatly behind those old heathen
Romans. A short time ago a deputation from the London
Missionary Society waited upon the Marquis of Salisbury and
laid Mr. Jones's case before the Government, but with what
result I have not yet heard. But from the policy they have
been pursuing, we can easily see the *animus* with which the
French regard Protestant missions; and if they had succeeded
in annexing the New Hebrides islands, judging of the future
from the past, the fate that would have awaited our mission
and our missionaries could have been easily foretold. On
their present lines of policy the French greatly want the New
Hebrides. New Caledonia is already strained to its utmost
capacity for sheltering the convicts and *recidivists*, and more
are being poured in continually. Guiana is "found too

unhealthy for them," and they are to be transferred to New
Caledonia. The Australians are shocked with the proximity
of such a community. Their feeling towards their French
neighbours was strongly and unmistakably expressed by one
of the deputation from Victoria to the Free Church Assembly
at Inverness. The relations between Australia and New
Caledonia are so strained, that a little more pressure would
end in a rupture. The *recidivists* are constantly escaping
from New Caledonia and finding their way to Australia, and
more and more alienating the Anglo-Saxons from their Gallic
neighbours.

To show how highly honourable Her Majesty and Her
Majesty's Government act in regard to treaty obligations, and
how very careful they are not to wound the tenderest sensibilities of the French in reference to the New Hebrides, I may
quote part of a letter that I received from a gentleman in
Glasgow, Mr. H. Barrett, who has been gratuitously acting
as agent for the Rev. H. A. Robertson, of Eromanga, in dis-
posing of the arrowroot prepared and contributed to the
mission by the natives of that island, and who also obliged
me in the same way by selling some of our Aneityum arrowroot. He says in his letter—

"4 NATIONAL BANK BUILDINGS, QUEEN STREET,
"GLASGOW, 21*st September* 1888.

"DEAR DR. INGLIS,—It may interest you to know that some time
ago I sent a few packages of the Eromanga arrowroot to Her Majesty
Queen Victoria, through the Secretary of State for the Colonies, and
to-day I have received the following note from Downing Street :—

'I am directed by Lord Knutsford to acknowledge the receipt of
your letter of the 1st instant, stating that you had forwarded to Her

Majesty at Balmoral Castle a package of arrowroot, on behalf of the Christian natives of Eromanga, in the New Hebrides.

'I am to acquaint you that the arrowroot has been duly received by Her Majesty, and she has commanded me to convey, through you to the Christian natives of Eromanga, her thanks for their present.

'I am to add that Her Majesty has accepted this gift in order not to cause disappointment among the Christian natives, but in no way as an act, however slight, of political importance ; the independence of the New Hebrides group being respected by Her Majesty's Government and France.   I am, sir, your obedient servant, R. H. MEADE.'

"I shall send our friend Mr. Robertson a copy of this, and I trust the effect for good on the natives will be appreciated by him.   With kind regards, yours very truly,   HU. BARRETT."

I am greatly pleased that Her Majesty has inserted such a distinct caveat in her letter, disowning on her own part, and consequently disallowing all political action on the part of our missionaries, and I trust that the French authorities will take notice of this action on the part of Her Majesty.   I will instruct the agent of our mission in Sydney, the Rev. Robert Steel, D.D., to forward a copy of this letter to Noumea to the Governor of New Caledonia, whom some French residents in the New Hebrides, but happily, to his credit, without effect, have been urging to annex the New Hebrides to New Caledonia, that he may see that our Government grant no favours to the missionaries but such as they grant to all loyal, peaceable, faithful, and law-abiding subjects, and we ask for no more.

CHAPTER XXIX.

THE Rev. J. C. (afterwards Bishop) Patteson first visited the New Hebrides along with Bishop Selwyn. He was a fine, tall, well-made, good-looking man, the very type of a high-class English gentleman. When the service of the Queen, in some department or other, is the great object of ambition among the sons of our nobility and gentry, we account it a great matter when men like Selwyn and Patteson, who, by their talents, character, and social position, can easily obtain the highest places in Church or State, cheerfully devote themselves to missionary work among the heathen. It is not their own work alone that is important, but their example stimulates and encourages a large number of average men to engage in the same work, and they in this way give a great impulse to missions. Most visitors, when they come to the islands direct from Sydney or New Zealand, and thus pass at once from the highest state of civilisation to the low type of our most advanced Christianity, are greatly disappointed with what they see among the natives, and express themselves in language the reverse of flattering to the feelings of the missionaries. It is gratifying, therefore, to find such an appreciative estimate of what he saw on our island put on record by Mr. Patteson. Aneityum was the first island in the South Seas on which he landed, and it was under our roof that he spent his first night on shore. The *Southern Cross* on that occasion had brought us two boxes of mission supplies from friends in New Zealand. Bishop Selwyn came round to my station to land these boxes; the sea was rather rough, but he came as near to our harbour as he durst, and, when the Tahitian went out in his whaleboat, he lay-to a little to windward, as near the shore as possible, and Mr. Patteson and Mr. Harper, a son of the Bishop of Christchurch, came ashore with the boxes.

The following extract is from the Bishop's journal, as given in Miss C. M. Yonge's " Life of the Martyr Bishop."

"The *Southern Cross* reached Aneityum on the 14th of July 1856. This island was occupied by Mr. Inglis and Mr. Geddie of the Scottish Presbyterian Mission, who had done much towards improving the natives. Small canoes soon began to come off to the vessel, little craft, consisting of no more than the trunk of a tree hollowed out, seldom more than a foot broad, and perhaps eighteen inches deep, all with outriggers—namely, a slight wooden frame or raft to balance them, and for the most part containing two men, or sometimes three or four. Before long not less than fifteen or twenty had come on board, with woolly hair and mahogany skins, generally wearing a small strip of calico, but some without even this. They were small men, but lithe and supple, and walked about the deck quite at ease, chattering in a language no one understood except the words 'Missy Inglis,' as they pointed to a house; presently another canoe arrived with a Samoan teacher, with whom the Bishop could converse, and who said that Mr. Geddie was at Maré. They were soon followed by a whaleboat with a Tahitian, a Futuna man, and a crew of Aneityumese.

"The Futuna man had expended his energies upon his hair, which was elaborately dressed after a fashion that precluded the possibility of any attention being bestowed upon the rest of his person, which was accordingly unencumbered with any clothing. The perfection of this art apparently consisted in gathering up about a dozen hairs and binding them firmly with grass or fine twine of cocoa-nut fibre (not from cocoa-nut fibre, but from the inner rind of the bark of a bush that grows inland, and is tough and pliable as a strong thread), plastered with coral lime. As the hair grows, the binding is lengthened also, and only about four or five inches are suffered to escape from this confinement, and are then frizzed and curled like a mop or a poodle's coat. Leonard Harper and I returned in this boat, Tahitian steering, Samoan, Futunan, and Aneityumese making one motley crew. The brisk trade-wind soon carried us to the beach in front of Mr. Inglis's house, and, arrived at the reef, I rode out pick-a-back on the Samoan, Leonard following on the back of a half-naked Aneityan. We soon found ourselves in the midst of a number of men, women, and children, standing round Mr. Inglis at the entrance of his garden. I explained to him the reason of the Bishop's being unable to land; that he alone knew the harbour on the other side of the island, and so could not leave the vessel.

"Then, having delivered the boxes and letters we had brought for him from Auckland, we went into his house, gazing with delight at cocoa-nut trees, bananas, bread-fruit trees, citrons, lemons, taro, &c., with bright tropical colouring thrown over all, lighting up the broad leaves and thick foliage of the trees around us.

"The house itself is built, after the fashion of these islands, of wattle, plastered with coral lime, the roof thatched with the leaves of the cocoa-nut and pandanus. The fences of the garden were made of cane, prettily worked together into a cross pattern, the path neatly kept, and everything looking clean and tidy. We sat down in a small well-furnished room, and looked out upon the garden, verandah, and groups of men and women standing outside. Presently Mrs. Inglis came into the room, and after some discussion I was persuaded to stay all night, since the schooner could not reach her anchorage before dark; and the next day the water casks were to be filled. An excellent dinner was provided—roast fowl with taro (a nutritious root, somewhat like potato), rice and jam, bananas and delicious fruit, bread and Scotch cheese, with glasses of cocoa-nut milk.

"Afterwards he showed us the arrangements for boarding young men and women, twelve of the former and fourteen of the latter. Nothing could well exceed the cleanliness and order of their houses, sleeping rooms, and cooking rooms. The houses, wattled and plastered, had floors covered with native mats, beds laid upon a raised platform running round the inner room, mats and blankets for covering, and bamboo cane for a pillow. The boys were, some writing, some making twine, some summing, when we went in; the girls just putting on their bonnets, of their own manufacture, for school.

"They learn all household work—cooking, hemming, sewing, &c.; the boys tend the poultry, cows, cultivate taro, make arrowroot, &c. All of them could read fluently, and all looked happy, clean, and healthy. The girls wear their native petticoats of pandanus leaves, with a calico body. Boys wear trousers, and some had shirts, waistcoats, and a few jackets.

" We walked about a small wood adjoining the house, through which a small fresh-water stream runs. In the woods we saw specimens of the various trees and shrubs and flowers of the islands, including those already noticed in Mr. Inglis's garden, and the bread-fruit tree, and sugar-cane, and a beautiful bright flower of scarlet colour, a convolvulus, larger than any I had seen elsewhere ; also a tree bearing a very beautiful yellow flower.

" We then returned to the house, and shortly afterwards went to the church, which is at present used as a schoolhouse, though the uprights of a larger schoolhouse are already fixed in the ground.

" Men, women, and children, to the number of ninety-four, had assembled in a large oblong building, wattled and plastered, with open windows on all sides ; mats arranged on the floor, and a raised platform or bench running round the building, for persons who prefer to sit after the English instead of the native fashion.

" All that were called upon to read did so fluently; the singing was harsh and nasal enough, but in very good time ; their counting very good, and their writing on slates quite equal to the average performances, I am satisfied, of a good English parish school. They listened attentively when Mr. Inglis spoke to them, and when, at his request, I said a few words, which he translated. The most perfect order and quiet prevailed all the time we were in the school. At the end of the lessons they came forward, and each one shook hands with Leonard Harper and myself, smiling and laughing with their quick intelligent eyes, and apparently pleased to see strangers among them.

" By this time it was dusk, and we went back to the mission-

house and spent a pleasant evening asking and answering
questions about Aneityum and the world beyond it till
8 P.M., when the boarders came to prayers and two or three
persons who live about the place.   They read the third
chapter of St. Matthew's Gospel in turns, verse by verse, and
then a prayer by Mr. Inglis followed.   At 8.30 we had
private family prayers, and at 9 went to bed.

"*July* 16.—We got up at 4, and were soon ready for our
walk to the south side of the island.   Mr. Inglis came with
us, and ten or twelve natives.   For the first half-mile we
walked along the beach among cocoa-nut trees, bananas, and
sugar-cane; the sun, not yet above the horizon, tinging the
light clouds with faint pink and purple lines; the freshness
of the early dawn, and the soft breeze playing about us,
gladdening at once our eyes and our hearts.   Soon we struck
off to the south, and, passing through taro plantations, began
to ascend the slopes of the island.   As we walked along we
heard the sound of the logs beaten together summoning the
people to attend the various schools planted in every locality
under the management of native teachers; and we had a
good opportunity of observing the careful system of irrigation
adopted by the natives for the cultivation of the taro plant.
Following the course of a small mountain stream, we observed
the labour with which the water was brought down from
it upon causeways of earth carried in baskets from very considerable distances.   Occasionally the water is led round the
head of various small ravines ; at other times the trunk of
a tree is hollowed out and converted into an aqueduct, but
no pains have been wanting to make every provision for the
growth of the staple food of the island.

"The last school here, on the north side of the island, is

about two miles from the coast, and from this point the path
is very steep, stony, and slippery, and occasionally requires
the use of hands as well as feet ; but to our amazement, and
advantage too, as it turned out, two natives attached themselves to us, and were always at hand to catch us if we
slipped, and help us up a rock or carry us across a stream—
willing, good-natured fellows, laughing and chattering away,
and waiting upon us in a style that I had hitherto supposed
to be exclusively Oriental.

"The scenery of the uplands of this island is excessively
beautiful ; rich masses of forest, with deep intersecting valleys,
undulating slopes, brakes and woods, streams and torrents,
and, occasionally, glimpses of the lower plains by the seaside ;
the clearings for cultivation, the cocoa-nut trees on the beach,
the lagoon and the coral reef, and the broad open sea beyond.
We reached Mr. Geddie's station about 11, and found the
Bishop seated a quarter of a mile from the settlement taking
shore sights, to the amazement, no doubt, of the dozen
natives who were grouped around him ; Hoari (George), the
New Zealand boy, very happy in the possession of a good
piece of sugar-cane, the men engaged in fetching water, the
vessel lying in the lagoon, and all looking as comfortable as
if the island had for centuries been the rendezvous of traders
and missionaries. Scarcely could one credit the fact that
eight years ago there was not one Christian upon it. Nohoat,
the principal chief of the island, came from his house to meet
us, and with him some three or four Tanna men, their faces
painted red. Nohoat has lately been behaving very well, and
showing a disposition to leave off native customs. Some of
these people are going as pioneers to the two islands which
can be seen from Aneityum, Tanna, with perhaps some

6000 inhabitants, and a volcano in active operation; and Futuna, with about 600.

" From this scene of hope and encouragement the *Southern Cross* sailed on the 16th, and, passing Eromanga, came in sight of Faté."

From this time till 1864, when we obtained the *Dayspring*, and no longer required his visits, he generally called once a year at Aneityum and the other islands where we had missionaries located, bringing letters or supplies, as the case might be, and taking up our mails to the colonies. Yea, up to the time of his lamented death at Nakapu in September 1871, there was nothing but the most cordial relations between him and us: and no higher tribute was paid to his memory than that recorded in the minutes of the New Hebrides Mission Synod in the following year.

Some, who were fond of drawing comparisons, likened Bishop Selwyn to the Apostle Paul, and Bishop Patteson to the Apostle John, the one a man of strong character, on whom feeble natures liked to lean; the other a man of singular amiability, to whom gentle natures went out in love and clung to in affection.

CHAPTER XXX.

RANGI AND HIS SON THOMAS AMOS.

For about twenty years Rangi was an outstanding figure in the New Hebrides, and filled a large space in the public eye among those islands, at first in connection with the sandalwood trade, and latterly as an agent in the labour traffic. He was a Malay, a native of Singapore, and a British subject. He first became famous in those regions while living among the natives in New Caledonia, before the establishment of the French power on that island.   A trading or sandalwood vessel was seized there by the natives, and some white men belonging to the crew were murdered. Rangi was accused of being deeply involved in the plot.   He was got hold of by the white men, tried, and condemned to be hanged.   But here the traders paused ; they saw danger to themselves ; they were afraid lest the authorities in Sydney, or elsewhere, might call them to account for their proceedings.   The law allows no British subject to inflict capital punishment, unless he act on Her Majesty's authority duly conferred.   I knew a captain in those seas who gave the use of his vessel to a party of white men to hang a native whom they had adjudged worthy of death.   He and his crew took no part in the proceedings ; they retired to the fore-part of the ship and left the after-part to those conducting the execution.   But no sooner did the vessel reach Sydney, whither the report had preceded him,

than the captain was arrested and lodged in prison on a
charge of murder being committed on board of his ship.   The
law recognises the deck of every British vessel as British
.territory, and holds the captain responsible for all that is done
on board.   This captain was tried and condemned to so many
years of penal servitude.   He was a man well connected, and
strong influences were brought to bear on the Government on
his behalf, and his punishment was first commuted, and subsequently remitted ; but the authority of the law was vindicated.
It was by overlooking this principle that the mistake was
made the other year by the missionaries of the Established
Church of Scotland at Blantyre in Livingstonia, and also,
about the same time, by the Rev. Mr. Brown of the Wesleyan
Mission in New Britain, who, with the aid of some white men,
as well as some Christian natives, waged war against the
heathens.   The captain of a man of war, who was sent by the
Government to examine into the case, exonerated Mr. Brown,
as acting simply in self-defence, although the public thought
that he went greatly beyond that, and when the matter came to
be discussed in the House of Commons, although no action was
taken in either case, the law was announced with unmistake-
able clearness.   And we who have lived in heathen lands know
the value of such a law.   But for this stringent enactment every
over-zealous, strong-headed, imprudent missionary might soon
get himself and his brethren into trouble, and possibly ruin
the mission ; and every runaway sailor might profess that the
natives had made him a chief, and that he could punish and
kill natives at his pleasure.   But Rangi's captors were wise
in their generation.   Fear led them to spare his life, and self-
interest counselled them to utilise his abilities.   Finding that
he was a man who might be turned to good account for the

sandalwood trade, they concluded that the most satisfactory
and salutary punishment they could inflict upon him was to
send him to Eromanga to collect sandalwood. The results
showed the shrewdness and sagacity of their views and the
practical worldly wisdom of their policy. Rangi was a man of
great energy, not at all scrupulous or squeamish about the
means he employed to attain his ends, and in the collecting of
sandalwood most successful; he was by far the best agent the
traders ever employed on Eromanga.

It was firmly believed by some that he was the chief insti-
gator of the murder of Rev. G. N. Gordon and his wife; but
as the evidence on this point was conflicting, he may be allowed
the benefit of the doubt.

When the traders left Rangi on Eromanga, they kept him
well supplied with "trade," or material with which to buy
sandalwood.   In the eyes of the Eromangans he was a wealthy
man.   In those days any man could obtain a wife if he could
only pay the price.   Rangi set to work at once, and, as opportunity offered, bought one chief's daughter as his wife after
another, till he had as many, according to report, as sixteen,
all slaves in reality. But the fathers and relations of his
wives, from motives of self-interest, all supported Rangi.   In
this way he was virtually king of Eromanga—he was the
"uncrowned king" of that Emerald Isle—and he thus held a
monopoly of the sandalwood. He could buy it when and
where he liked; no other person had any chance in competing
with him.   Eromanga was virtually a gold mine to the traders.
For a few foreign shells, mostly from Fiji, but prized like
diamonds by the chiefs for armlets, costing about a dollar
each, a boat-load of sandalwood could be obtained worth
£40 in China. The sandalwood collected on Eromanga, as

currently reported, realised no less than £70,000 in the China market, and the most of that sandalwood was gathered in Rangi's time, so that from a money point of view his had proved a valuable life to his captors.

When the sandalwood was exhausted on Eromanga, Rangi went to Efate to see if any could be found there, but there was none; but the labour traffic commenced about that time, and he at once became an efficient agent in that trade. When he went to Efate he took with him *ten wives*, all natives of Eromanga. He had previously had an Aneityum woman as his wife, who had one son to him; but he had left this wife when he went to Eromanga. He had also bought an Efate woman as his wife since he had gone thither. He was living in a low swampy locality, and four of his wives had died before he was killed. He had been on Efate about three years when he was murdered, which was in the end of May 1868.

A month or six weeks after the murder of Rangi, Mr. Cosh, our missionary on Pango, Efate, now minister of the Presbyterian church of Balmain, Sydney, and I, went in the *Dayspring* into Havannah Harbour, where Rangi had lived, as a deputation to open up the mission station now occupied by the Rev. D. Macdonald. The account we received of his murder was this :—One day an inland native came to Rangi's house; he had hid his tomahawk beneath the root of a tree near the beach, had gone in, and got Rangi out, pretending that he wished to make a bargain about the cutting of some grass for a new house which Rangi was about to erect; he then slipped away for his tomahawk, hid it under his arm, came quietly in behind Rangi, as he stood unsuspicious of danger, and struck him a fatal blow on the back of the head. Having dispatched Rangi, he coolly wiped the blood off his hatchet, put it again under his arm, walked up to the house, and with the same weapon killed one of Rangi's wives.   The other five Eromangan wives and his eight children would also have shared the same fate—would all have been murdered—had not Marek-mel, the chief of Isema, the nearest village to Rangi's house, been present, and interposed his authority for their protection, and stayed the slaughter, and taken them all home to his own house.   The two bodies were disposed of as is usually done by cannibals.   Rangi's property, which was very considerable— it was even said that he had £150 or £200 of money in the house—was all plundered by the natives who had planned his murder.

As to the facts of the murder, and the identity of the murderer, the accounts we heard were all substantially the same.   But as to the cause of the murder—the reason on account of which he was murdered—the evidence was very conflicting.   We heard three distinct, independent accounts —one from the natives, another from a native of the Loyalty Islands, an agent for the labour traffic, who lived in the Harbour, and who spoke intelligible English, and a third from a white man who knew Rangi well.   The first account was that Rangi had been carrying matters with a high hand among the natives, that he had become specially disliked by two chiefs in the district, that one day the daughter or niece of one of those two chiefs, whose husband had been away in Queensland for three years, was at the well for water, and was coming home, when Rangi met her in the path and insulted her; she ran home, and told her father or her uncle that Rangi had shown bad intentions towards her.   The chief's anger was inflamed; he said Rangi should die for that.   A plot was laid for his life, an inland man was employed to carry it out, and in a month thereafter Rangi was a dead man.

The second account said that three gentlemen belonging to the labour traffic had bought a large piece of land contiguous to Rangi's establishment, with the view of cultivating cotton, coffee, and sugar; that Rangi was employed as interpreter and agent in the transactions; that he paid ten muskets, so many webs of calico, so much powder and shot, so much tobacco, so many pipes, so many pounds of beads, &c., to one chief; to other two chiefs he paid each one half of the above quantity; and that the one of these chiefs, though he professed to be satisfied, was not, and knowing that Rangi had a large quantity of goods in his house, he resolved to kill him and get hold of his property. He therefore sent for an inland native, a man who had been implicated in the capture of a vessel called the *Mary Ira* and the murder of four white men about two years before that time. This chief broke off the head of a yam and a piece of a kava plant, and said to the man, "You eat and drink these, and kill Rangi." When he had accepted these, his honour was pledged to undertake the deed, and in due time it was accomplished.

The third account was, that when Rangi was collecting sandalwood on Eromanga, numbers of Efate men were taken thither as labourers; that Rangi had often charge of them, and treated them frequently with the greatest harshness and severity—made them work whether they were well or ill, and if he did not shoot any of them, he killed them with hard usage—and that he was still displaying his old spirit, as far as he had opportunity, and that the natives of Efate had for a long time resolved to kill him. "A terrible murderer," said our white informant, "was that Rangi." Some one, aware

S

of the feeling against him, told him to be on his guard.   He
replied that he was not afraid of the natives, as he had plenty
of powder and shot.   It is probable that there was a portion
of truth in all these three accounts, that all these different
causes more or less conspired to bring about the result.

Mr. Cosh and I went ashore and visited Rangi's house.   He
had had a large establishment.   It was surrounded first by a
strong fence of wooden posts, six or seven feet high, resembling
a New Zealand *pah ;* outside, but close to this, was a strongly
wattled reed fence ; the whole quite ball-proof, with loopholes
at regular intervals for shooting out at with muskets.   But
it is treachery, rather than force, that has to be guarded
against when living among natives.

We found four of Rangi's wives and seven of his children
living under the protection of the Loyalty Island man on the
other side of Havannah Harbour.   The fifth wife had been
taken away in a vessel by a white man, and one of the children
had died the day before our arrival.   Rangi had sent his boy
—his son by the Aneityum wife—to Brisbane, for the sake of
his education, as we were told.   When we were at Dillon's
Bay the Eromangans had urgently requested us to bring back
Rangi's wives to their own land.   We did our best in this
work of humanity.   We found the poor women very anxious
to get home, and we brought away three of the wives and
three of the children.   We left one wife and four children.
The Loyalty Island man wished to keep the two eldest boys,
who were about six or seven years of age, and they wished to
stay with him ; their mothers were dead.   But as the fourth
woman, who had two children of her own, both quite young,
was coming to the boat, one of the boys began to cry violently
for her to stay with him, and as he could not be pacified, and

as we were in the midst of heathen natives, we thought it best to push off with as many as we could get quietly, especially as our time was limited. The woman who appeared to be Rangi's chief wife carried a double-barrelled gun ; when she got into the boat she fired off, into the sea, first the one barrel and then the other, with as much coolness as if she had been an Amazon.   The woman that stayed behind carried a large revolver. We weighed anchor and put out to sea. On passing Pango Mr. Cosh was put ashore at his own station, and I brought the three women and the three children on to Eromanga, and left them with Mr. and Mrs. M‘Nair.   Their Eromangan friends, being mostly Christians, appeared to receive them with much kindness.

Mrs. M‘Nair, now Mrs. Dr. Turner, writes me and says : " Most distinctly do I recollect the time when you landed the women and children from the *Dayspring*.   Their support was almost—entirely at first—thrown upon us.   So we set about finding employment for the women.   The chief wife we took into our family as servant.   She was a clever and most useful woman ; but as she could not or would not work with the Eromangan girls, out of consideration for them we had to part with her after a time.   We thought we traced her in the Ellis group in 1876, as the wife of a white man there. Thomas Amos was a child about a year old, a plump, heavy-looking boy, with festering sores about his mouth and face, the little mouth always open, and round as a dollar : his mother was made assistant laundress.   The third woman was lame, and one mass of sores, so she got patch-work to sew or little garments to make for the small Eromangans, and so helped to maintain her independence."

Our merchants are princes, and our traffickers are the

honourable of the earth.   They magnify their office, extol
their calling, and boast loudly of the blessings that they con-
fer upon mankind.   That they accomplish a vast amount
of good, no one either doubts or denies.   But, unhappily, the
result of their movements is not always, as they wish us to
believe it to be, an unmixed good.   In the outskirts of
civilisation, and among wholly uncivilised races, the agents
they employ are often men of very doubtful character.
Rangi's employer was a merchant prince, a man honoured
by the mercantile aristocracy.   Rangi himself was a type of
one class of evangelists whom commerce employs among those
islands to civilise the natives and prepare them for Christianity, and of one detachment of the pioneers whom we
have to follow in planting the Gospel among those dark and
deeply degraded races.

If one might be allowed to compare the small with the
great, the present with the long past, the lines composed by
Sir David Lindsay of the Mount on Cardinal Beaton of St.
Andrews, and, more than a century later, applied to Arch-
bishop Sharp, might now, at the end of other two centuries,
be not unfitly applied to poor Rangi :—

> " As for the Cardinal, I grant
>   He was a man we weel could want ;
>   God will forgive it soon.
>   But yet in sooth, the truth to say,
>   Although the loon be weel away,
>   The deed was foully done."

But happily, in connection with Rangi we have a very
pleasing episode to relate.   At times grace interposes and
cuts off a sinful entail, so that the sins of the fathers are not
visited upon the children.   Josiah was the grandson of

Manasseh. The younger son of Kasuaui, the murderer of John Williams, laid the foundation stone of the Martyrs' Memorial Church at Dillon's Bay, Eromanga; and the youngest son of Rangi, called Thomas Amos, came to this country and was learning to be a printer, with the view of his being sent back to Eromanga to take charge of the mission press, and train up a staff of printers from among his own countrymen to print elementary books for all the islands, and in this way compensate, as far as possible, for the evils done by his father.

His coming to this country occurred in this way. When I brought three of Rangi's wives and three of his children from Efate to Eromanga, the youngest of those children was a boy of about a year old. His mother and he, with a sister about two years older, continued to live on the mission premises, first with Mr. and Mrs. N'Nair and subsequently with Mr. and Mrs. Robertson. The mother abandoned heathenism, and placed herself and her two children under the instruction of the missionaries. Both mother and daughter, I understand, have faithfully improved their privileges, and, if I am not mistaken, Mr. Robertson has admitted both of them to the fellowship of the church. Thomas Amos, the youngest son of Rangi, grew up a very smart boy, and attracted the attention of Lieutenant (now Captain) Caffin, R.N., an excellent Christian man, who was at that time in command of the *Renard*, the Government gunboat stationed on the New Hebrides to watch the labour traffic. He was often at Eromanga, and saw a good deal of the boy. On one occasion when my wife and I were in the *Dayspring*, we were wind-bound for about a week at Dillon's Bay, and there made the acquaintance of Mr. Caffin, whom we met with every day

at the mission-house. When Mr. Caffin was leaving the
New Hebrides, with the consent of the mother and of the
boy himself, he brought Thomas Amos home with him, with
the view of having him educated in this country and sent
back to Eromanga as a missionary to his own countrymen. He
expected to be able to get him educated free, or at least at a
reduced rate, at some college or institution here. But he was
disappointed to find that there was no institution into which
a lad of this kind could be received. The Rev. Grattan
Guinness would have received him into his Missionary College
in London, but he was too young for any of the classes in
that institution. But he promised to take him in when he
was sixteen years of age. Captain Caffin kept him boarded,
at his own expense, in an excellent private school near
Norwich, for about four years. He then transferred him to
Mr. Guinness's college, where he remained a year. But after
consulting with Mr. Robertson and myself, by whose advice
he has been always guided, it was thought that we could not
turn his acquirements to better account than by apprenticing
him for five years in a first-class printing establishment in
Leominster, Herefordshire, so that he might return to the
islands not only a good English scholar, but a thoroughly
trained printer. He was three years at the printing. Captain Caffin, who undertook the whole responsibility of his
support, always saw that his religious training was carefully
attended to, and that he was always surrounded by the best
of Christian influences. When I learned that Captain Caffin
was himself alone bearing the whole expense of his support
and education, I offered to raise £10 a year among my own
personal friends to assist him. This I did for seven or
eight years, chiefly through the aid of a few good Christian

ladies deeply interested in the New Hebrides Mission, who cheerfully gave me a pound a year each.   Mr. Robertson also collected £10 among his friends when he was home in Nova Scotia.   Captain Caffin's religious principles are of the type of Moody and Sankey's.   His father was one of their committee of management when they were first in London about fourteen years ago ; and when he and his second in command came ashore on Eromanga on the Sabbath evening to our mission service, they left the men on board singing Sankey's hymns.   He is also a brother-in-law to the well-known Rob Roy MacGregor, who sailed down the Jordan and other rivers in his canoe, and who, when an infant in his mother's arms, was rescued, in the Bay of Biscay, from the burning of the *Kent*, East Indiaman.   Great and marvellous are the doings of the Lord God Almighty.

Man proposes, but God disposes.   Our sanguine hopes are often sadly disappointed.   In less than two years Thomas Amos's curriculum of study would have been completed, his apprenticeship would have been ended, and he would have returned to Eromanga a fully qualified printer, prepared to devote himself, all his time and all his acquirements, to serve God in the work of the mission.   But God had otherwise appointed.   He was an active lad, social in disposition and overflowing with animal spirits.   He took an active interest in all the innocent athletic sports usually carried on in English public schools, such as cricket, football, &c.   But even in the best conducted of these games there is danger, as the newspapers are every now and again informing us.   In the end of last year, while playing at football, he accidentally received a kick on the ankle ; but he apprehended no danger, and hence paid no particular attention to it for some time ; but when the doctor examined it, he found that the case was a serious one, and he was at once placed in the hospital. There he was attended by the best medical skill and nursed with the greatest care that the institution could supply; but the bone had been injured, the foot had to be amputated, and the patient succumbed after the operation. Those islanders have not the robust constitutions that the inhabitants of this country possess : under favourable circumstances they enjoy good health and attain to an average length of life, but if they meet with any accident, or are exposed to any unfavourable conditions of life, they have not the sustaining energy nor the recuperative power that white men possess.

But it is satisfactory to know that during the eight or nine years that he lived in this country—in Norwich, in London, and in Leominster—he maintained a highly consistent Christian character, he made fair progress in learning, he was acquiring a satisfactory knowledge of printing ; he was everywhere well liked and highly esteemed, he was a general favourite among his companions; he lived respected and he died lamented. On the Sabbath after his funeral the minister of the church in which he worshipped in Leominster preached an impressive sermon, and improved the occasion and the circumstances of his death in a way that was calculated to benefit the audience and leave good impressions on the community among whom he had lived. When many shall come from the east and from the west, and from the north and from the south, and shall sit down with Abraham and Isaac and Jacob in the kingdom of heaven, may the children of the kingdom not be cast out into outer darkness.

TWO NATIVES OF ANEITYUM.

CHAPTER XXXI.

LASARUS AND ESTER.

TAKING them unitedly and all round, Lasarus and Ester were the most useful couple that we had in the mission. She was certainly the most outstanding woman we had on our side of the island. At the time we were settled on Aneityum, Lasarus was one of a galaxy of young men, about ten or twelve in number, who had abandoned heathenism and placed themselves under Christian instruction. Williamu, being the

oldest, was the most outstanding of this band. Lasarus was
the least conspicuous, because he was among the youngest.
They all became pupils in my advanced class. It is only
relatively that I call them advanced, for the best of them
could read only a very little; but they were all eager to learn,
and did learn well. In due time they all became members
of the church, and also teachers. For many years they were
my chief helpers, both for skilled manual labour and mission
work proper. We often observed that those natives who
were the first to give up heathenism and profess Christianity,
always proved in the end to be the best Christians, while
those who hung back to the last were always less satisfactory.

Lasarus's father had been the chief of Itath, a district
about a mile from the mission station. But as he died when
Lasarus was a boy, the chieftainship devolved upon his uncle,
Luka. When Lasarus reached manhood, the office should
have reverted to him, and some of his friends urged him to
claim his right. But power is sweet, and so Luka did not
offer to resign; and as he was an able and a popular ruler,
Lasarus refused to disturb an arrangement that was working
satisfactorily, and hence he let well alone.

When we settled on Aneityum in 1852 Lasarus was a
young man apparently about twenty years of age. He
became a very regular, a very diligent, and a very successful
scholar. In 1855 he and Ester were married, and I appointed
them to take charge of the school in his own land, Itath,
where they gave great satisfaction both to me and to the
people. His being the former chief's son went far to strengthen
his position and increase his influence. In 1858, when Mr.
and Mrs. Paton were settled at Port Resolution, on Tanna,

we sent Lasarus and Ester with them as their servants. To
the utmost of their ability they performed their duties. But
they suffered so much, Lasarus especially, from fever and
ague, that we had to bring them home at the end of a twelvemonth. From that time forward they lived on our premises,
in charge of the young women and girls attending Mrs.
Inglis's boarding school or school of industry. In this
department of mission work they were very successful. By
his prudent and consistent conduct, his kind disposition, and
his quiet but dignified manner, he maintained a mild but
unquestioned authority over all under their charge. Sometimes Ester would have said to Mrs. Inglis, "I am afraid that
So-and-so, that girl that came last week, is stealing. I think
there are some lumps of sugar going away, and I suspect her,
for I am sure that none of the other girls would do such a
thing. But I will watch her quietly; we will not say anything
about it just now, but if the thing goes on I will speak to
Lasarus, and he will soon stop it." Mrs. Inglis kept all her
general stores carefully locked up, but she always left in the
safe tea and sugar and sundry eatables sufficient for everyday use, and the girls were put upon their honour as to their
honesty, and they invariably behaved well. If this state of
things continued, and if proof was found that this girl could
not, as the Church of England Catechism expresses it, keep
her "hands from picking and stealing," on the Sabbath
evening, when Lasarus was catechising the girls, he would in
a quiet and apparently accidental manner make some strong
and striking remarks on the sin of stealing. There would be
no public exposure or no open reproof of any one; but
breaches of the eighth commandment would immediately cease
to be observed. In our absence from the island for some

months, first to New Zealand and afterwards, during another year, to Victoria, they had charge of all the premises and all our property, and on our return everything was found safe and in good condition.

Christianity has introduced new principles into family life on the island; one of the most prominent of these is companionship. In heathenism there was little companionship or sociality between husband and wife; they were not equals; the man was a tyrant and the woman was a slave. It is totally different there now, and few husbands and wives on the island exhibited more of the Christian element in their family relations than Lasarus and his wife; he was a faithful husband, a kind and affectionate father, and one that ruled his own house well.

He was never strong for heavy work; but in all kinds of light skilled labour, whether native or European, he was a ready workman. He was also skilful and expert in steering and managing a boat; from that and his trustworthy character, I often employed him as my helmsman when I was travelling by sea. For some years before he died he was my chief pundit when I was translating or correcting translations. After our return to Ancityum, poor Williamu, who previously had rendered such valuable help in this department of mission work, was of little service to me. And among the natives the number was very limited who could render any assistance in translating. They were good readers and intelligent men, but they would allow almost anything to pass without a check. But Lasarus possessed in a high degree what might be called the critical faculty. If you gave him the ideas, he could always tell you when the sense was clear and the language grammatical. Lasarus felt a deep interest in the translating of the Bible : he evidently loved the Word of God. During his latter illness, when I called in to see him or to give him some medicine, I invariably found him either reading the Scriptures or having some portion of them beside him. He had helped forward the work of God very materially on Aneityum, but his life and his labours were cut short. He was still in the prime of life, a little over forty years of age. He was never a robust man ; he was often laid up for a few days or a few weeks with intermittent fever or other island ailments, but during the last year of his life we had been remarking that his health had been unusually good. About the beginning of March, however, a kind of influenza passed over the island ; almost everybody had it more or less severely. Lasarus took it, and was very ill: once and again, however, he was nearly well, but caught cold and relapsed. The week before his death he seemed to be quite better, and was beginning to work. But he got himself wet, and all the unfavourable symptoms returned with increased severity, and never abated till he died on the 7th of May 1873.

He was quite sensible to the last. When I told him that all hope of life was gone, and that Christ was now his only refuge, he called to his wife, while I was speaking, to listen well to what I was saying, as his ears were becoming dull. When I went out she repeated to him what I had said. Yes, he said, it was all true ; he felt he was dying—his only hope was in Christ. And having given her one or two brief directions about their property, he urged on her to look well after the children, especially the two youngest. He was never demonstrative as to his religious feelings—none of the Aneityumese were—but there, as elsewhere, there were some whose Christianity was so apparent in their everyday life that no

one doubted its reality. Lasarus was one of those; if twenty
years and more of unblemished, exemplary Christian conduct
be satisfactory evidence, he had that evidence in his favour.
Cecil says of John Newton that he has heard him say, when
particular inquiries were being made about the last expressions
of some eminent believer, "Tell me not how the man died, but
how he lived."   Lasarus was one of the quiet and faithful in
the land, a man of peace, universally respected, esteemed and
beloved.   I have rarely, if ever, seen among the natives grief
for the dead more undoubtedly sincere, or sympathy for the
living more certainly genuine or more extensively displayed.

Ester, as I have said, was the most outstanding woman on
our side of the island.   She was a woman of high rank to
begin with; she was nearly related to some of the highest
chiefs in the land, and this was an advantage to her.   Social
position tells as much out there as it does at home.   The Rev.
Mr. Anderson has written two interesting books, the one
"The Ladies of the Reformation," the other "The Ladies of
the Covenant;" a third might be written on "The Ladies of
the Disruption and the Free Church," and a fourth also on
"The Native Ladies of the South Sea Mission."   Women of
royal and aristocratic families have, by their example and
influence, done very much to advance Christ's kingdom on
their respective islands.   Ester belonged to this class of
women.   When we went to Aneityum in 1852 she was then
a girl of sixteen.   Her father was not dead, but her mother,
heathen-like, had left him and become the wife of another
man.   Ester had left her heathen relations, had professed
Christianity, and was living with Amosa, the Samoan teacher.
The first we heard of her was this: A few weeks after our
arrival, one day while she was assisting some other Christian

women to prepare thatch for our house, word came that her
stepfather was dying. It was the custom on Aneityum in
heathenism to strangle every wife on the death of her husband, that her spirit might accompany his to the other world,
and wait upon him there as she had done here. Ester knowing what would befall her mother, threw down the thatch,
sprang up in a moment, and ran for nearly two miles with
the hope of saving her mother's life. Christian influences had
saved some lives before this time, and it was believed that,
had she been in time, she might have been successful. But
alas! she was too late; her poor mother was strangled, and
stretched out beside the dead body of her husband, and both
were ready for being carried off and cast into the sea.

As soon as arrangements could be made for Mrs. Inglis
opening her Girls' Industrial Boarding school, Ester became
one of her pupils, and was with her for three years. At first,
like many high-spirited girls, she was wilful and wayward,
but as soon as Mrs. Inglis could speak to her intelligibly in
her own tongue, and bring the truths of Scripture to bear on
her conscience, an improvement began, and she became singularly docile, and her consistent conduct for eight-and-twenty
years showed that she had received the truth in the love of
it. She had good natural abilities, and became an excellent
scholar as far as the three R's were concerned. She loved the
Bible, and along with several other women, in the course of
seven years, committed to memory and repeated accurately
the whole of the four Gospels, the Acts of the Apostles, and
the Epistles of Paul, from Galatians to Philemon both in-
clusive—that being the whole of the Bible at that time printed
in the Aneityumese language. She was a good singer, and
often led the psalmody in the church. She was uncommonly

well handed; for washing and dressing clothes, and for
general housework, she was equal to any white woman. She
was particularly well liked by the natives, especially the
native women. She was always generous with her food, and
that among natives is the most highly appreciated of all the
virtues; while stinginess or greediness in regard to food is
looked upon as the worst trait of character with which any
one could be charged. At first Mrs. Inglis was often annoyed
with idle gossiping, native women coming in and sitting in
our backyard, especially in the forenoon, when they came too
soon for medicine, which was always dispensed at one o'clock.
She took counsel with Ester, and they agreed that they would
provide some native work for this class of visitors to do. So
whenever any woman came likely to remain for an hour or
two, Ester would go up to her, give her a banana, or a piece
of taro or breadfruit, and say to her, *Ak etwak, aiheuc vai
nyak aiek, um ago nauritai haklin inigki*—"Oh my sister, have
compassion on me, and do this little piece of work." Of course
the woman complied, and began at once, and wrought on till
the bell rang, when she came to me, got her medicine, and
went home, well pleased with herself and the treatment she
had received. But lazy gossips soon learned to become shy of
our premises, and Satan found no idle hands to employ in
mischief-making, as described by Dr. Watts. Ester was
always grave, though ever cheerful; and although she was no
gossip, yet, as our station was always the centre to which
information came, she was always well informed as to what
was going on over the island, and when she heard of anything
which she thought it was right for us to know, she instantly
told Mrs. Inglis, and she again told me. If I thought it
necessary, I at once took action, and quietly brought influences

to bear on the weak or the wicked, who might respectively be the passive or the active instruments of evil, and thus often-times mischief was prevented of which the general public knew nothing. She was well known to all the missionaries, and highly respected by every one of them. Her blythe and open countenance, and her frank and courteous deportment, made her a general favourite; while, on account of her kind and unselfish disposition, she was especially beloved by the missionaries' children. After the death of Lasarus, she was again very suitably married to Laapayi, a widower, a man of her own age, also a chief and a teacher. They continued to take charge of the girls till we left the island in the beginning of 1877. At that time they were left, along with two other families, in charge of the mission premises. During the vacancy of two years and a half, till the settlement of Mr. and Mrs. Lawrie, Ester's character came out to great advan-tage for conscientiousness and firmness. When a missionary could not be got at home to supply our place, Mr. and Mrs. Watt, of Tanna, were appointed to our station; but when the case came before the Mission Synod, the other missionaries refused to sanction their removal, lest the Tanna Mission should be injured thereby. The people of my station were extremely disappointed, and while their hearts were sore they said, "We, the people of this station, have gone to assist every missionary on the group; we have gone as teachers, as boatmen, as builders of houses, as cooks, as servants; we have gone to do everything for them, and now they will not give us a missionary. What is the use of us looking after the mission house and the mission premises, and the furniture, and keeping everything safe and in good order, when we cannot get a missionary to live in them and look after us?

T

Let the houses go to the dogs, and let the pigs look after them." And but for Ester this proposal might have been carried out; but she stood up and firmly opposed it; which for a woman to do, even of her social position, showed courage far beyond ordinary; and she carried her point. The premises and the property were safe and in good condition when Mr. Lawrie arrived on Aneityum.

Ester died in 1880. In her last illness everything that skill and kindness could devise was done for her by Mr. and Mrs. Lawrie, but it was of no avail. They asked her if she had any message for Mr. and Mrs. Inglis. She said, "Send my kind love to them, and say that I will look for them in heaven." She had nine children; of these three, two sons and a daughter, survived her, and are still living. Her daughter, whose name is Yegreimu, is married to an excellent young man, and she is very much to Mrs. Lawrie what her mother was to Mrs. Inglis. "There shall be a seed to serve Him."

The object of our mission is to raise up, out of degraded savages, men and women of the type of Lasarus and Ester; and though only a small number may be equal to them, there are on all the islands more or fewer of the natives similar in Christian character, while a leavening process is going on year by year, beneficent influences are in operation, and the evangelisation of the whole group at no distant period is now a moral certainty.

CHAPTER XXXII

INHALAVATIMI means literally Man-child, but when used as an adjective it expresses great endearment, equivalent to dearly beloved. As a proper name it is generally abridged to Nalvatimi; and as this is the shortest form, and as it is as good as the other, I shall employ it in this sketch.

When we went to Aneityum Nalvatimi was a boy of twelve or fourteen years of age. His father, Katipae, was one of the leading men in Isav, a land next to Aname, on which the mission station stood. I at once began a class in the alphabet, and Nalvatimi was the eldest of fourteen boys whose names I enrolled in that class. He was a quiet but rather a soft boy, but as time went on he developed in energy. The class met daily for a twelvemonth; the progress was steady but not very rapid. At the end of that time H.M.S. *Herald*, Captain Denham, R.N., came into the harbour at Anelgauhat, on her way to Fiji to survey that group; but, being prevented by strong head-winds, the captain put in to Aneityum, which he was also to survey, and he improved his enforced delay by going on with that survey at once. Mr. Chimmo, the first lieutenant, who had command of the steam tender attached to the *Herald*, conducted the survey and laid down the coasts of Aneityum for several miles out to sea. While engaged in these operations he employed several natives to assist his own men. Among those thus employed was Nalvatimi, who, with his active and obliging deportment, so took Mr. Chimmo, that he engaged the boy to go with him as his own personal attendant. Some said that Mr. Chimmo wished him that he might show off his young active black servant to his friends and fellow countrymen when he returned home at the end of the voyage, for Nalvatimi was a handsome, well-made, good-looking lad; his grandmother had belonged to Futuna, so that he had some Malay blood in him. When the survey was completed, and the tender had come to anchor in the harbour, two seamen were appointed to prepare Nalvatimi for the voyage; they washed and scrubbed him, cropped and combed his hair, and dressed him in a serge shirt and a pair of dark trousers, and then took him to his master, quite civilised looking. "Here he is, sir," said the men, "clean, cropped, and clothed; what shall we call him?" I did not learn whether he was named Tom, Dick, or Harry. But if he got a name, it must have been some name of one word, short, easily pronounced, and easily remembered by the sailors; for I scarcely ever met with a seaman who could tell you the surname of any of his mates. If you asked him the name of any one of them, he would generally say, "Well, sir, I do not know; they always called him Jim," or Jack as the case might be, "but I never heard his other name." It was of little consequence to Nalvatimi what name was given to him, as it was never used. As soon as his father and mother knew that he was to be taken away by Mr. Chimmo, they were extremely distressed; he was their eldest child, and they were strongly attached to him. The father came at once to me, asking me to write a letter to the captain, that he might stop the boy from going away. I sat down and wrote a note to Captain Denham, who was a good Christian man, a kind friend to the native races, and who during the whole of his stay in those seas took a deep interest in mission work. I sent the letter by Katipae, the lad's father. As soon as the captain had read my note, he gave orders that the lad should be discharged and given over to his father, and then wrote me a very courteous note, thanking me for what I had done and saying that he would allow no boy to be taken on board by any officer without the full and free consent of his parents. During the five-and-twenty years that we were on Aneityum, we had generally a visit of a man-of-war once a year. And it is but just to say that the captains of all these vessels were kind and friendly to the missionaries and their families, and the most of them fully sympathised with the objects of the mission and rendered us every assistance in their power. The natives of Aneityum always looked upon the captain, the officers, and the crew of every man-of-war as their friends. They were, in their opinion, different from other ships, and closely akin to mission ships.

Nalvatimi returned to school, and made steady and satisfactory progress. We had an industrial school for the young men as well as the young women; some of them lived on the premises, and some lived at home. By-and-by Nalvatimi came to live on our premises, and, with some others, week about or month about, as the case might be, he was first one of our cow and goat-herds, at another time he had charge of the poultry, and by-and-by he was one of Mrs. Inglis's cooks. It was found to be the best arrangement to change them from one occupation to another, weekly or monthly as the case might require.

Some time before we left the island in 1859, Nalvatimi was

married to Thiganua, and, along with Lasarus and Ester, they remained on the premises as servants to Mr. Copeland, and gave him great satisfaction.

When we went to Aneityum in 1852 Thiganua was a little girl of about ten or eleven years of age. She belonged to an inland district. She was an orphan; both her father and her mother were dead. She had one brother some two or three years older than herself. Her brother and she came to live with some Christian relations near the mission station; their inland relations were all heathen. We first knew her more particularly about a year after our arrival, when she came to live with Tutau, a Rarotongan teacher, and his wife, who remained at our station for about a twelvemonth to assist us in the work of the mission. Tutau's wife was an excellent, active woman, but of a quick temper. Thiganua was always timid. One day the teacher's wife had spoken rather sharply to her, and, native-like, she ran off, first to the bush and then to her friends. Tutau's health did not agree with our climate, and shortly after this he and his wife left Aneityum in the *John Williams*, and went to Lifu, where he soon recovered his health, and Thiganua came to live with us, and stayed with us till she was married. She proved a very active, well-conducted girl, learned to read, write, cypher, sing, sew, wash and dress clothes, and do all kinds of household work. She had an excellent memory, and was one of Mrs. Inglis's class that committed to memory the Scriptures as fast as they were translated and printed.

In 1864 I stationed them as teachers at Ohuul, one of our principal inland districts, where the people were much scattered, and where both the imparting and the acquiring of knowledge were carried on under difficulties. Several teachers had laboured there, but all of them with very little success; consequently the natives were far back in their education.   The people took to them at once, and the improvement which they effected was marked and permanent.   Her influence on the women was great and lasting : their attendance at church and school became more regular, and quarrelling among families grew less; and from its being one of our worst and most backward lands, it became one of our best.   We had a number both of men and women from that district who applied for church membership, and who were in due time admitted into the fellowship of the church.   For nearly ten years after our return to Aneityum she was one of Mrs. Inglis's never-failing assistants.   If any special work had to be done—if the mission vessel brought a crowd of visitors, if extra female help was needed, either for an emergency or for a length of time— Thiganua had only to be sent for to secure her cheerful, reliable, and well-skilled assistance.

She was never robust—the seeds of consumption were lurking in her constitution—but she enjoyed on the whole a fair measure of health.   She had six children, four sons and two daughters; five of them died before her, at different ages, from one to six years of age.   Her remaining child, a fine boy of five years of age, died a few months after her, of inflammation of the brain, caused by exposure to the sun— a not unfrequent cause of death on the island.

She was intensely attached to her children ; when her fifth child died, she felt the death so much that we were afraid of her mind giving way ; and it seemed to enhance the attractions of heaven to her on her deathbed to think of meeting with her children in glory.

When we left Aneityum, in December 1871, to proceed to

Victoria on a visit, she was in rather indifferent health, but nothing serious was apprehended. On our return, however, on the 1st of May, after an absence of more than four months, we found her in the last stages of consumption. She was still at the station inland, but we had her immediately brought to a house which they had beside us, to see if anything could be done for her. But alas! she was beyond the power of human help; all that skill, or care, or kindness could do was to smooth the dying pillow, alleviate distressing symptoms, and render the descent to the grave something less painful. She died in about three weeks.

She died as she lived. She delighted in reading the Scriptures while she was able to read them, and in hearing them read when she became unable to read them herself. But her natural timidity never left her; she trembled as she entered the valley of the shadow of death; something like a chill came over her as her feet touched the waters of the mystical Jordan. One might have supposed that she was connected with one of the pilgrim families whom John Bunyan saw in his dream. Mr. Despondency might have been her uncle, and his daughter Much-afraid her cousin, for though, referring to their doubts and fears, they had entertained ghosts, as he confessed, when they first began to be pilgrims, and could never shake them off after, yet the root of the matter was in them, for when "they went up to the brink of the river, the last words of Mr. Despondency were, "Farewell night, welcome day!" and his daughter went through the water singing, although none could understand what she said. So it was much in the same way with poor Thiganua, for when she was reminded of the love of God the Father, the grace of Christ the Son, and the work of the Holy Spirit; how God justified the poor publican, how

Christ answered the prayer of the penitent thief, and how the angels carried the soul of poor Lazarus into Abraham's bosom, her fears were gradually dispelled and her faith was strengthened, and she expressed a strong desire that, at her death, the angels would come and take her soul to where the Father is, and the Saviour, and the Spirit, and her children.

Nalvatimi was one of the most scholarly and cultured of our native teachers; he had more of the logical faculty in him than most of them, he had a good gift in prayer, and aimed at method in his addresses.   I may insert here a portion of a letter written by Mrs. Inglis to Mrs. Kay, dated November 16th, 1868, and which was inserted in the R. P. Magazine for February 1869, in which she says: "Yesterday Mr. Inglis was away preaching at one of our out-stations, about seven miles distant, and the services here were conducted by the elders and teachers.   Williamu had charge of the first service, and gave a good address.   The second service was conducted by Nalvatimi, one of our teachers, who also gave a good address.   He began by saying: 'Long ago a man of this island went to the missionary to ask to be allowed to go to Tanna in the *John Knox*, and said that he could speak Tannese, and would help the teachers to speak to the people.   The missionary believed him, and allowed him to go.   On the next Sabbath day, when the teachers went to speak to the people of the different villages, this man went with them, and when they had spoken, and asked him to speak, he stood up, but his speech was very short.   He simply said, "Men of Tanna, men of Tanna, the word of Jehovah is true," and he sat down.   At the next village he said the same words, and the same at every village.   Now, I am like that man, my words will be very few.   I will read you a verse in 2 Cor. i. 22. "Who hath also sealed us, and given the earnest of the Holy Spirit in our hearts." A number of you have lately got the seal of baptism on your bodies, but have you got the seal of the Holy Spirit in your hearts? If you have not, the other will do you no good. When God made the world, He did not first make it and then think about it. No; He first thought about it, and then He planned it, and then He made it. He first made the earth and the sea, He then made the grass and the fruits, and then He made the fishes and the birds and the beasts, and then, when He had made these, and there was plenty of food, He made man, and He saw that everything was good. When the missionary made this church, he did not begin to make it without first thinking, and then marking and fixing the size and the shape. He first got us to clear the ground, and then he measured and marked the length and the breadth and the height, and then we made it as he marked it, and it was a good church. Some of you were seeking the seal of baptism, but the missionary and the elders and the deacons said, "No, you cannot get it just now; you must wait a little till we see what your conduct is." But you go away, and you shake your heads, and are angry at them, and say, "No, we will not come back to seek it any more." This is not good conduct. You want first to be marked as God's people, and then you will think what sort of people you will be. This is beginning at the wrong end. Think first what a Christian should be. Pray to God to teach you and seal your hearts by His Holy Spirit, and then come and seek to have the mark of God's children on your bodies, and do not behave in this foolish way.'

"Perhaps I cannot do better than add Williamu's address

here also. He was urging them very earnestly to prepare for death, and went on to say 'Nobody lives long on this island. *We* cannot keep away death. *The missionary* cannot keep away death. It is in the ground, and we cannot keep it from rising; and the ships that come here bring those diseases that have killed so many of us; but we cannot stop them in the sea, and keep them away from our shores. But, if we are prepared for death, it does not matter to us when it comes. It is true we are all Christians as to our bodies, but what good will that do us if we are hypocrites in our hearts? We are but a few people on this island, but many of us are hypocrites in our hearts. I went to Britain with the missionary. I saw what the land and the people are there. This island, what is it? It is nothing—it is just like one's hand; but Britain, it is just like the great ocean—it has no bounds; and the people are so many, they are like the sand on the sea-shore for multitude; but they are all good—none of them are bad; they have not two kinds of Christians there as we have here; they are all one in heart—they are all one in conduct. I did not see one bad person all the time I was there. Their conduct is all good—just like that of the angels in heaven' (!!!). This last comparison you will certainly look upon as a piece of Oriental hyperbole. But it was accepted here as literally true. The church was well attended, and the services well conducted."

Williamu met with few either in this country or in Sydney except the friends of the mission, and these were all uncommonly kind to him, and reasoning on the principle of *ex uno disce omnes*, he returned home with unmixed admiration for the goodness of our countrymen. Had he lived till now, and read certain numbers of the *Pall Mall Gazette*, he would have inferred that there was also another class who, if like

any angels, it was those described by the Apostle Jude. Had
it been deemed expedient to make him acquainted with the
dark side of social morality, my friend, the late Mr. William
Logan, author of "Moral Statistics," &c., by lifting the
curtain from the streets of our mystical Sodom, which he had
so fully explored, could have revealed scenes as repulsive as
any of those with which Mr. Stead had so rudely shocked the
mawkish sensibilities of modern Christianity. But here
ignorance was bliss, and to have increased knowledge in this
direction would have been only to increase sorrow.

But to return to Nalvatimi. After the death of Thiganua
he was married to the widow of an excellent man belonging
to Dr. Geddie's side of the island. She was a superior
woman, and on our leaving the island in 1876, to return
home, I appointed them to take charge of the school at
Aname, our station, where they remained till the arrival of
Mr. and Mrs. Lawrie. At that time he did a very important
work. When the arrowroot for the payment of the Bible was
made, it was all brought to the station to be dried; it was
only there that the necessary conveniences for doing so were
provided. The drying of the arrowroot was a very responsible
work. The value of the article depended very much on the
skill and care displayed in this part of the process. For three
years Nalvatimi, assisted by some other natives, had full
charge of the drying of the arrowroot, and it never was better
done even when my wife and I were on the spot. Mr.
Annand came round, saw it weighed, put up in casks, the
casks properly addressed, and all made ready for shipment.

In one of his Latter-day Pamphlets, written some thirty
and more years ago, Mr. T. Carlyle says (as I quote from
memory, I do not vouch for the exact words, only the sense):

"At Portsmouth," he says, "an old man-of-war is put into commission for a three years' cruise. She proceeds to the Cape, thence to the Antipodes, or wherever the behests of the Admiralty require her to go. At the end of the time for which she is commissioned she returns to Portsmouth, drops her anchor, and reports herself to the Admiralty. Two of their Lordships go down, inspect her, and depone that all is right on board. Now," says Mr. Carlyle, "notwithstanding the low tone of moral principle in these degenerate times, in this age of shams and hypocrisies, there must be a good deal of truth in that old man-of-war, when at the end of three years she comes back, with the exception of tear and wear, as good as when she went away."

So it was to us, and to all the friends of the mission, a very satisfactory result, and a strong proof of the reality of their religion, that for three years the whole of our natives made the same average quantity of arrowroot for the payment of the Bible, and the quality equally as good, when they were left solely to themselves, as when we were living in the midst of them. And Nalvatimi's presence and influence had much to do with this result, especially with the quality of the arrowroot.

Inwaijipthav is a long deep inland valley, opening up into two deep narrow valleys at the top. The valleys are the deepest and the hills are the steepest that are to be found on the island. We had a terribly hard battle to fight there with heathenism. The sacred men were esteemed the most powerful on my side of the island; the valley was difficult of access, and hence not easy to be visited, and in this way the people were about the last to profess Christianity. Finally they all came in, and I had three schools stationed among them. The central schoolhouse was used on Sabbaths and on Wednesdays as a church. I visited the station once a quarter on Sabbaths myself. Every other Sabbath the service was conducted by the elders, deacons, or teachers. During the vacancy things had gone back, and Mr. Lawrie, as soon as he knew exactly how matters stood, placed Nalvatimi and his wife at the principal school, with the view of resuscitating the cause of education and religion in the valley. A new interest was at once awakened. Assisted by his friends and the people of the place, he went vigorously to work; the schoolhouse was repaired, and a new teacher's house was erected; the earnest-minded were encouraged, the lapsed brought back to church and school, and the work was going on prosperously, when a providential calamity placed a serious check on the cause. Their house stood on the edge of a stream, close to a steep mountain, but the site was deemed perfectly safe. A storm, however, came; it rained for days. The ground was thoroughly saturated with water, the brooks swelled into rivers, the wind blew a hurricane, and one night when darkness set in a slight earthquake was felt. Suddenly there was a roar and a crash which awoke the sleeping inmates. It was a landslip up on the mountain above them. Down rolled the avalanche, sweeping everything before it and carrying Nalvatimi's house into the stream. Nalvatimi struggled out he knew not how, but his poor wife was killed at once and buried beneath the ponderous mass.

Some time after this Nalvatimi offered his services as a teacher for Tanna, and when I last heard of him he was settled in one of Mr. Watt's outlying stations near Kwamera. From time immemorial there existed between the Kwamera district and the district to which Nalvatimi belongs something like a league of hospitality, such as existed in ancient

Greece, so that he would be safer there, and possess more influence, than anywhere else on Tanna. When Mr. Paton and I visited Kwamera in the *Dayspring* in 1865, with the view of reopening the Tanna mission after Mr. and Mrs. Mathieson had been driven from the island, Nalvatimi was with us, and greatly facilitated our intercourse with the natives. He was their friend, and they trusted him. Had Nalvatimi gone away with Mr. Chimmo, what a loss it would have been to himself and to the mission. But the labour traffic has deprived us of hundreds of young men who might have been equally benefited and equally useful. But the bones of many of them lie in Queensland or Fiji.

CHAPTER XXXIII.

WILLIAMU.

As Williamu accompanied my wife and me to this country in 1860, to assist us in carrying the Aneityumese New Testament through the press, he was well known among the members of the Reformed Presbyterian Church, and to some extent also in the Free Church and elsewhere. A short notice of him will therefore, I believe, be acceptable, especially to those who still remember him. Perhaps more than any other native he was identified with the history of Christianity on Aneityum from its commencement till the time of his death. As I have elsewhere stated, the first attempt to introduce the Gospel into Aneityum was made in 1841. On the 30th of March of that year the Rev. A. W. Murray of Samoa settled two teachers on Ipeke, the district next to Aname, afterwards my station. Williamu, then a lad of fourteen or so, attached himself to the teachers, along with some other lads of his own age or a little older. Persecution soon began, for these lads were often scolded, and at times beaten, by some of the old chiefs and priests for countenancing the new religion. But Williamu's heart was drawn towards the teachers, and in spite of threats and blows he still clave to Christianity. He received the name of Williamu in this way. The Samoan teachers had a great difficulty in pronouncing Aneityumese words, hence they were eager to change Aneityumese names

Williams

into Samoan ones. Williamu is the Samoan form of Williams. A great many of the Samoans took the name of the famous missionary, John Williams; but as the South Sea natives have only one name, instead of Ioane Williamu they dropped the John and retained Williamu only. The subject of our sketch being one of the first converts on Aneityum, the Samoan teachers honoured him by calling him Williamu. Williamu is, therefore, not the native name for William, as some have supposed, but for Williams, or of all that could be utilised of John Williams.

In 1848 the Rev. John Geddie and his wife, and Mr. Archibald, a catechist, and his wife, arrived at Aneityum from Nova Scotia, accompanied by the Rev. T. Powell and his wife, of Samoa, who remained with them for a year to assist in establishing the mission. Mr. and Mrs. Geddie were settled at Anelgauhat, on the other side of the island. Mr. and Mrs. Archibald occupied what afterwards became our station, but they did not remain long in the mission. Williamu attached himself as firmly to the missionaries as he had done to the teachers, and when help at boating or housebuilding was needed his assistance was always forthcoming. At times, when Mr. Geddie could not obtain the requisite native help at his own station, Williamu and a few other young men went round to his assistance and tided him over those early difficulties.

In 1852, when my wife and I joined the mission, after having been eight years in New Zealand, Williamu, among others, gave us a hearty welcome; and when we entered our new house—a half-finished building of two small apartments, the chief materials for which I had brought from New Zealand; and which Mr. Geddie and I, with the assistance of the natives,

U

had erected—Williamu, to show his interest in us, brought us a present of a fine large pig of ten or twelve stone weight.

Three weeks before our arrival, during a visit of the *John Williams*, Mr. Geddie, assisted by the missionary deputation, had formed a church and admitted thirteen members. Some time after our arrival he saw his way clear to baptize Williamu and another young man of kindred character named Seremona (Solomon), the first-fruits of the mission on my side of the island. No more were baptized for eighteen months.

As Williamu lived near the mission station, he availed himself to the utmost of the means of grace and the opportunities for education. At the Sabbath services, the week-day prayer-meeting, the morning school, the Bible class, and the Teachers' Institution, he was in regular attendance; and his profiting was in accordance with his diligence. He was among the first of those whom I placed out as teachers. He was a good singer, and acted for a long time as our chief precentor. He was one of the first band of deacons that were elected, and he subsequently became an elder. When we were building our church, which is still standing at Aname—though bearing the scars not only of time, but of hurricanes, earthquakes, and tidal waves—Williamu was located as a teacher at the extremity of my district, nearly ten miles distant. But one day, when the building was roofed and nearly finished, and was beginning to stand out in its proper dimensions, he paid us a visit. On going into the church, and seeing the progress that had been made, he was so astonished and delighted with what he saw that he ran up and down the building, and leaping every now and again in an ecstacy of joy, cried, " Wauho ! how you have been working here ! We at the end of the island have been doing nothing." Williamu had wrought remarkably well at the church during the first stages of its erection; but preparatory and foundation work did not show like the finishing processes, and hence he was led to prize the work of others more than his own.

When he arrived in this country he was amazed at what he saw. As he sailed up the Thames he tried to count all the ships, and counted to the extent of about three hundred, but he abandoned the task as hopeless: a fleet of the Newcastle coal craft had just entered the river. When addressing the Reformed Presbyterian Synod in 1860 he said, "This is an extraordinary country of yours. I have seen so much since I came here that I am weak with wonder."

There were several things that struck Williamu very much in this country. One of these was the remarkable kindness of the people. Of course he was always living among our friends, or the friends of the mission, and was everywhere treated with special kindness; and he very naturally drew the conclusion that everybody was as kind as those with whom he was coming in contact. Hence reference was often made in his letters to the kindness he received and the abundance of the food with which he was supplied. He considered it necessary to assure his friends on this point, and he felt that he could do so honestly. There is nothing natives are so afraid of as suffering from hunger, and nothing that they prize so highly as having plenty of food. On our arrival at home we stayed for a short time at my father-in-law's. My wife's brothers and sisters and other friends were gathering in day by day to see us, and there was a generous, though neither an extravagant nor a wasteful hospitality being exercised. Williamu, however, soon began to be alarmed for the consequences. I may here notice in passing, that at first

Williamu got his food by himself. He was so shy that he objected to sit at table with us or with others; but by-and-by, when we explained to him that it was causing more trouble to give him his food by himself than along with the family, a sense of duty, and an unwillingness to give any extra trouble, led him to suppress his timidity, and to take his place at the family table; and when there, with an almost intuitive perception of what was proper, he conducted himself as if he had all his life been mingling with good society. So, about the end of the first week, he came to Mrs. Inglis one morning and said, " Misi, will you tell your mother and your two sisters that they must not give me so much food to eat." She said, " Why ?" " Oh," said he, "you know we have been feasting every day now for a whole week, and the food will certainly soon be all done. Tell them, therefore, to give me less, or they will have nothing to give to the visitors who are coming to see us." On Aneityum the natives can get up an abundant feast that will last for one, two, or three days; but after the food collected and cooked for a feast is consumed, the process cannot be repeated for some time; and Williamu thought that it must be the same here. But on being assured that there was no danger of the provisions being exhausted so soon, he felt relieved, and continued to take his share in the daily feastings without any misgivings; and he was, no doubt, glad when he found that there would be no necessity for either himself or the family being reduced to " short rations." But his thoughtful and unselfish spirit was none the less evinced by this proposal.

He was also much impressed with the *goodness* as well as the *kindness* of the people of this country. But here again he drew general conclusions from very limited premises. From what he saw of the ministers and elders, and their families, with whom, almost exclusively, he was becoming acquainted, he not unnaturally concluded that the whole community were equally good.   After our return to Aneityum a young man, a native, went up to Sydney in a trading vessel.   He remained in Sydney for some weeks, and lived on board the vessel.   He was a sharp, intelligent lad, and observed the state of society around him.   When he returned to the island he told the people that it was not true what the missionaries had told them about the white people.   There were no good people in Sydney ; they were all bad, there were none of them married ; they drank and swore, and did everything that was bad ; they were worse than the heathen on Tanna and Eromanga.   As he went on repeating these statements, the better class of the people were grieved, and some of them came to Williamu to ask if these things were so, and if these words were true. Williamu was as much surprised and shocked as the other natives at these representations, and said to them that they were quite untrue.   " I do not know," he said, " where Mataio was when he was in Sydney, or what he saw, but I know this, that I saw none of that conduct, I saw none of those bad people ; I saw none but good people.   All the people that I saw were good ; they were all as good as the people of Beretani " (Britain).   Comparison could go no further, it could rise no higher.   In Williamu's estimation greater excellence could not be found on earth than was to be found among the people of Beretani.   But both were right ; the one had seen the very best, the other the very worst phase of Sydney society.   Had each of them seen both sides, they might have said of Sydney as Cowper said of London, that it contained

"Much that we love, and more that we admire,
And all that we abhor."

But modern Sydney is doubtless better than ancient London.

He was greatly delighted with the loyal, law-abiding character of the people in this country ; and when the volunteers appeared before the Queen in Edinburgh in 1861—although it was a small affair compared with the review in the same place on the 25th of August 1881, the moral effect of which told upon every government in Europe—yet it filled Williamu with admiration. Some one had given him a picture of that review, and he looked at it with delight. Just to think that at the word of the Queen all the young men of the country should assemble before her, and say that they were ready to do whatever she commanded them ! To him—a chief, who had often had his patience sorely tried with wilful, stubborn, refractory young men, the Queen seemed to enjoy the most desirable of all the earthly conditions of existence. The thoughts of his heart evidently said, "Oh happy Queen ! Oh model young men ! "

He greatly admired our jails. They have no such institutions on Aneityum ; but he thought it was a capital idea to shut up in a strong, secure house the wayward and disobedient, and to keep them there till they are brought to their senses and become content to lead quiet and peaceable lives, hear the words of the chiefs, and obey the commands of the Lord.

He was often puzzled with many things which he saw in this country, and I was frequently in the same predicament that Pollock says, in "The Course of Time," he was placed in with the children, when he was called

" to answer curious questions, put
In much simplicity, but ill to solve :
And heard their observations strange and new."

The low position of the sun in the sky in winter was what he could not understand. To him, born and brought up on Aneityum, three degrees within the tropics, where for one day twice every year the sun passes over our heads, and we are among the *askiai*, the people who at noon have no shadows, and where the sun, even at the shortest day, is high up in the heavens—to him this phenomenon was perplexing. Hence one day, about midwinter, he came to me and said, " Misi, what is the matter with the sun just now ? For some time back he seems always as if he wished and were trying to get up to the top of the sky, but was not able. He just creeps along low down near the earth, and then sinks into the sea or drops out of sight." This was a simple question, but not so easily answered to one who knew so little of astronomy as did Williamu.

At another time he would come with a question of social or domestic economy. " Misi," he would say, " can you tell me about this ? On Aneityum there is always plenty of waste land, and if a young man wishes to marry he can go into the bush, choose a piece of land, fence it, dig and plant it, then build his house and bring home his wife. But how does a young man do here ? There is no waste land where he can erect his house. All the land is occupied, not only on the shore, as on Aneityum, but everywhere inland it is the same, up to the very tops of the mountains. The people here are so many, they are like the sand on the seashore." How to deal with our surplus, ever-increasing population is a question that has exercised more minds than Williamu's. But to him the simplest and most satisfactory solution of this complex and difficult problem was emigration to America, Australia, New Zealand, or some of our colonies.

We had great comfort in Williamu all the time we were at home. The majority of natives who accompany missionaries to this country are spoiled through the well-meant but injudicious kindness of friends; they become lifted up with these attentions, and forget themselves. Williamu entirely escaped that danger, but another trial awaited us. Just as the work was being brought to a close, his brain became affected, his mind gave way, and he became partially insane. Most providentially it was not till the last sheet was passing through the press that he entirely broke down. His brain was naturally weak, or rather, he was of that fine, high-strung nervous temperament which, though of the highest value when well, is easily deranged; and he supplied another illustration of Dryden's oft-quoted couplet—

> " Great wits to madness nearly are allied ;
> And thin partitions do the two divide."

Some time before we left the islands to come home, Williamu had an attack of fever and ague, and every day, as certainly as the fit came on, he became delirious, but the delirium always took a religious turn. He came always into the house in which our young men lived and read the Scripture to them, and then took away a young lad, a cousin of his own, into the bush, and gave him an earnest exhortation to follow that which was good. When the fever left him the delirium ceased. It is not uncommon for delirium to accompany fever and ague. Shortly after his arrival in this country he had a slight attack of fever and ague accompanied by delirium. But for two years he continued quite well. For some months, however, before we left this country to return to the islands, symptoms of brain disease began to show themselves, and at last, as I have said, he quite broke down.

During his illness there were certain aspects of his case that struck me forcibly. He became very timid, very proud, and intensely selfish. When his intellect became clouded the moral nature seemed to be subverted. When the brain became affected and the judgment lost its guiding and controlling influence, the moral sense or the conscience evidently became weakened. When Williamu was well he was kind and unselfish in a pre-eminent degree, but when his mind gave way he thought of nobody but himself. I am told that insane people are invariably timid; Williamu seemed to be always more or less in a kind of terror. Naturally he was very humble, now he became extremely proud. His selfishness also was quite a new feature of his character. Formerly, when we were travelling together on railways, without his ever being told, he was the first to look after umbrellas, travelling bags, portmanteaus, and luggage of every kind. But after he became unwell, while he was as active as ever in looking after his own things, he paid no attention to ours. He would deliberately lift his own umbrella and leave ours lying in the carriage, as if he had had no connection with us. But our experience was not exceptional. When the Rev. John Hunt —the celebrated Wesleyan missionary, the apostle of Fiji— had finished his translation of the New Testament, the native who had acted as his pundit became quite insane; not only so, but, as a consequence of his insanity, he abandoned Christianity and went back to heathenism; he threw off his European clothing and dressed like a savage; reason was suspended, and he was no longer accountable either to God or to man for his actions. Williamu never went so far, or anything like so far, as this. But nevertheless, acting under medical advice, we had to hurry off to the islands, as the most

likely means for securing his recovery; and this course was to
a great extent successful. We had some trouble with him
after his return to Aneityum, but after a time he settled
down comparatively well. A stranger could have observed
nothing wrong with him, but we who knew him formerly saw
that he was much altered. Our friends at home thought that,
after what he had seen and learned in this country, he would,
on his return, be a great help to the mission; and they were
prepared to have allowed him a salary, that he might be fully
employed as a native missionary. But God had willed otherwise, and these hopes were never realised. And we felt
thankful indeed that he remained quiet, and continued to
conduct himself with exemplary propriety. He frequently,
as in former days, led the singing, now and again he prayed
in public, and sometimes gave an address; but I durst never
employ him as my pundit while translating or revising lest
his brain might be thereby affected. He inclined to live more
secluded than he had formerly done. But there was one idea
which he caught up strongly in this country, and to which he
gave practical effect all his life afterwards, and that was the
duty of being industrious. "There is no idleness," he said,
"in Beretani; every man and every woman works, and that
every day too. And why should we be idle here on Aneityum?"
And he practised as he preached. In this way he eschewed
the temptations of an idle life, promoted health of body and
serenity of mind, had always abundance of food, was always
able to help those who were in want, and never needed any
help himself.

He was upwards of fifty years of age at the time of his
death. He died on the 15th of August 1878. His last
illness was very short—only twenty-four hours. He was

attacked with severe cramps in his feet and legs. These became dead, and this deadness gradually crept over his whole body till he expired. He was in church the Sabbath before his death. The station was vacant, but Mr. Annand was round at Aname preaching for three Sabbaths at that time. After the sermon he asked Williamu to pray, which he did. He also led one of the hymns, both of which exercises he performed well. He was not at the prayer-meeting on the Wednesday afternoon, but came to the mission premises in the evening to see how the arrowroot, which they were preparing for the payment of the Bible, was being attended to. He always took a deep interest in everything connected with the Bible. He became ill in the night. On the Thursday he sent one of his friends to Mr. Annand for medicine, but he charged him not to say that he was very ill—his native modesty evidently rendering him unwilling to trouble the missionary. In this way Mr. and Mrs. Annand were not made aware that he was seriously ill till they heard the death-wail in the night. Though no report of his last words, if there were any, has reached us, I know, from the character of those around him, what their last words to him would be, that the last words he would hear on earth would be those of prayer and praise ; a prayer for grace, mercy, and peace, from God our Father and our Lord Jesus Christ; and the last song he would hear, before he heard the song of the redeemed in glory, would be, "I to the hills will lift mine eyes," or "Rock of ages, cleft for me," or "How bright these glorious spirits shine," or something similar.

Williamu was a striking example of the transforming power of the Gospel, and of what the Word and Spirit of God can effect in the heart and in the life of the lowest savage. He was an *intelligent* Christian; he had clear conceptions of the leading doctrines of the Gospel. He was a *consistent* Christian, and had enlarged views of Christian duty. He had an intelligent understanding both of "what man is to believe concerning God," and "what duty God requires of man." He was kind, unselfish, and generous. The first money he ever owned, namely, four dollars which he received from a trader for four rare shells highly prized by the natives of Eromanga, and with one of which a trader could purchase a boat-load of sandalwood, he gave as his contribution to the Bible Society.

In prayer he was reverent, fervent, fluent, copious, and Scriptural; and he was a good public speaker. It was, however, as a pundit, in assisting me in revising and editing the Aneityumese New Testament, that Williamu rendered the most valuable and abiding services to the mission. Many natives, otherwise active and intelligent, can render very little help to a translator; they fail to see what you want, or, if they see your difficulty, they are unable to tell you how it can be met. But Williamu was quick to perceive the idea you wished to express, and equally ready to supply the word or the idiom that was wanted. In this department of mission work his services were invaluable.

Our avowed object was to Christianise the natives. Civilisation followed as a necessary consequence. We did not profess to teach the natives any trades. But the work created by the mission developed among them a considerable amount of mechanical skill, and showed that among them, as among ourselves, there was a great diversity of natural gifts or of an aptitude to excel severally in different kinds of skilled labour. In most kinds of native labour Williamu was expert; but in some kinds of European work he did not excel, while in others he did. He was a very poor carpenter; some other natives left him far behind. But as a boatman, either for pulling an oar or steering a boat, he had few equals among the natives, and very few white men would have surpassed him.

The power of Christianity to civilise, as well as to sanctify and make men good, was notably exemplified in this case. For politeness he was a perfect gentleman; he was never vulgar or rude, or even awkward, either in company or at table. If a lady entered a room where he was sitting he would be the first to offer her a chair.

He was a good scholar, as scholarship goes on Aneityum. He was a correct, fluent, and tasteful reader. He knew a little of arithmetic. He wrote a fair hand, and had a special faculty for writing letters. When in this country he wrote a series of letters to his friends on Aneityum, and some to persons here, portions of which I am appending to this notice as affording a vivid picture of the "First Impressions of Britain and its People" on the mind of a South Sea Islander.

Though only a secondary chief, yet from his intelligence, sobriety of judgment, and general Christian character, his influence in the community was far higher than his social position.

At the time of his death he was a widower, but he left one fine little boy about ten years of age. His name was Simetone (Symington), so called after the leading ministerial family in the Reformed Presbyterian Church. Simetone died about a year after his father. He had always a very grateful remembrance of the kindness which he received in Britain.

We thus see that the Gospel of our Lord Jesus Christ is everywhere the same mighty saving power, whether among sages or savages, among Jews or Greeks, among Scythians or barbarians, among bond or free. "It is the power of God unto salvation to every one that believeth."

. But let no one suppose, after what I have said of Williamu, that his was an exceptional character among the Aneityumese. By no means. On my side of the island alone I could with ease have counted of men and women at least a hundred whose Christian character was as pronounced as his, whose general talents were equally conspicuous, and whose acquirements, as far as time and opportunities allowed, were in no way inferior to his. And on Dr. Geddie's side of the island they were as fully advanced as on ours. If ever the Spirit of God was seen working among a rude heathen people, it was on Aneityum. There was never any excitement or any unusual demonstration, nothing that in these times would be called a revival. Neither Dr. Geddie nor I preached anything sensational, and perhaps too little even of the emotional. It was the simple exhibition of God's Word and the regular observance of God's ordinances that produced the change. In their case "the kingdom of God was as if a man should cast seed into the ground, and should sleep, and rise night and day, and the seed should spring and grow up he knoweth not how" (Mark iv. 26, 27.) They were not all genuine Christians. The old roots of heathenism were ever and again cropping up. But they were as good Christians as could be reasonably expected in the circumstances. There existed a little leaven of Christianity which more or less leavened the whole lump. There was present the salt of grace which preserved from putrefaction the whole body of the people; there was a light of Divine truth among them which shed its illuminating influence over the whole population, which made

Aneityum a different island from any in the group, and rendered it the Iona of the New Hebrides. The Word and Spirit of God had transformed those wild, savage cannibals into a quiet, peaceable, intelligent, docile, and affectionate community, a loving and a lovable people.

CHAPTER XXXIV.

WILLIAMU'S LETTERS.

WHEN we arrived in this country in 1860 I suggested to Williamu that he should write home to Aneityum to some of his friends, and said that I would enclose his letters to Mr. Copeland or Mr. Geddie, as the case might require. This he consented to do. I did not expect that his letters would be either long or interesting. But I knew that, although they should be neither, like all letters written in similar circumstances and coming from a far country, they would be acceptable to his friends. I had taught him the art of writing, and he wrote a fair, small, copy-hand; but I was too busy, and had too many other things to attend to, to give him any lessons in letter-writing, or make him acquainted in any way with the principles or the rules set forth in the "Elegant Letter Writer." Beyond a few short notes, he had never written any letters at all. But during the two and a half years that we remained in this country he wrote a great number of letters, and I was surprised to find that the letters were both long, and, to me at least, interesting. As often therefore as I had time I translated the letters, and copied the translations into a book. These have been beside me ever since, and from them I have made the following selection. They are genuine letters, unaided compositions, the simple utterances of the writer's own thoughts. Like most strangers recording the impressions made upon their minds by a country and a people visited by them for the first time, he has made a good many mistakes. But as no one will go to these letters for information about this country, I did not consider it necessary for me to correct these mistakes; and hence I do not hold myself responsible either for the correctness of the facts or the soundness of the opinions. The letters are faithfully translated; I have neither added, subtracted, nor amended. I have occasionally left out a sentence or two, or even a paragraph, where I found that substantially the same statement had been made in another letter; I have occasionally transposed a sentence or two for the sake of preserving the connection. The letters were all written offhand. They are all first copies, none of them were corrected and then rewritten, and hence he had sometimes forgotten what he had intended to say, and afterwards brought it in in another connection. The letters are chiefly interesting as showing the first impressions made upon the mind of a native by what he saw and heard in this country, and the ability displayed in recording these impressions by one of the Christian natives of Aneityum, who are regarded by the special correspondent of the *Melbourne Argus*, the far-famed VAGABOND (see *Melbourne Argus*, May 1884, "Trip to New Guinea," No. III.), as "the greatest fools and the biggest boors he had met," and who were apparently, in his opinion, injured and not benefited by the missionary teaching which they had received. On this point I leave my readers to judge for themselves.

———

To Mrs. Snodgrass, Castle-Douglas.

NEWTON-STEWART, *Sept. 20th,* 1860.

MY VERY GOOD LADY,—I wish you well, and I thank you for your kind present to me, for the shirt which you sent me. It is big and it is good. I have no words to express my wonder. I never saw any kindness like this among my people. I thank you very much for the present.

I will now tell you a little about my country. Formerly, long ago, when we lived in heathen darkness, we showed no kindness to one another. We were like people who carried heavy burdens on their shoulders. We were a people laden with iniquity, we wrought all manner of wicked works. We never ceased, night nor day, to steal, and rob one another's plantations. We quarrelled, and there was never a year passed over us in which we did not engage in war and kill one another. We had this custom also, that when any man died they strangled his widow. We were earnest in offering up sacrifices to our false gods. We never ceased from doing such things as these.

Formerly there were two great epidemics on Aneityum. I saw the one, but I did not see the other. Around the whole island the people died ; they fell like the leaves from off the trees ; old men, and men in the prime of life, and young men and women, and big boys ; but there were no little boys or infants died. We performed heathen rites over them for a while, and threw them into the sea ; but we became so weak that we could not carry away the bodies, and there was no wailing, and no tears were shed, and we ceased to observe those customs by which we showed honour to the dead, the people in the land had become so few. Moreover, we never lived in peace one year. Our land was like a canoe tossed about between the winds and the waves. It was this from time immemorial, till the Samoan teachers came and lived among us. But even then we continued to believe in lies, and we were obstinate in resisting the truth. We said, "The Samoans have one way and we have another." But after that the missionaries came, and explained clearly to us the Lord's Gospel of peace, we gave up all these things ; and even those wicked men, whose bodies were always gashed with wounds received in fighting, are now whole and sound, like trees covered with fresh leaves, all the effects of the Gospel of peace. The women are now raised, and they are rejoicing, whereas formerly on account of our mad conduct they were killed round the whole island of Aneityum, so that now the land is like a wilderness, and the people are few in number, from our constantly fighting and killing one another. We are truly thankful for this good word of peace which has put a stop to all those evil practices which we formerly carried on.

When I came here with Mr. and Mrs. Inglis, and saw this country, I had no words to express my wonder and my joy. There are such crowds of people here ; the houses are all built close to one another ; the land is everywhere so well cultivated, and the conduct of the people is so good ; they all speak so lovingly to one another and live in such peace. Truly this is not the way that we lived among ourselves on the other side of the world.

My very good Lady, do not despise us. You are very many here ; do have compassion upon us, and let some more of you come and watch over us and instruct us. These are my words, and may the Lord bless you.   WILLIAMU.

To Mrs. Dr. Wilson, Glasgow.

NEWTON-STEWART, *Dec. 8th*, 1860.

MY VERY GOOD LADY,—I wish blessings on you. I thank you for your great kindness to Dora, my wife, in sending her the desk. I am very glad, and I thank you very much for your kindness. When Dora sees the present she will be delighted, and she will be surprised at your unexpected kindness, and she will thank you.

Besides this, I wish to tell you a little about the heathen customs that prevailed on our island before the missionaries came among us. We worshipped false gods ; we had heathen feasts ; we practised witchcraft ; we carried on war and fighting ; we robbed one another's gardens ; we quarrelled ; we said the spirits are powerful to give us all things. They gave us life, and they made the island for us. We sacrificed to them that they might give us plenty of food, and that they might save us when we died. We said there are two ways to *Umaatmas (the Land of the Dead)* ; the one goes down at the west end of the island, the other goes up at the east end. When the Samoan teachers came among us and explained to us a little of the Gospel, some of us said, " They have one religion and we have another." One party among us said, "That is the religion of their islands;" others of us said, "It is impossible to receive their religion and practise it; it is best to continue and worship the spirits." But the missionaries came and sowed the good seed among us; they were earnest in preaching the Gospel, and in turning us from our former practices, and in teaching us the way of righteousness. Now we are very glad and very thankful for the grace of God, in that He sent His servants to turn us from the ways of darkness and guide us into the light. At present we are glad and joyful on account of the Good Word. We are now living in peace, and have given up all those things that we formerly practised; namely, murder, witchcraft, idolatry, robbery, quarrelling, strangling of widows, war, heathenish feasts, and all these wicked courses. We are very thankful. If the missionaries had not come we should soon have been all dead on account of our wickedness. These are my words, and may the Lord bless you. WILLIAMU.

To Lasarus and Ester, Aneityum.

SCOTLAND, *August 4th*, 1860.

MY DEAR FRIENDS,—I wish you two well, also Inhalvatimi and Thiganua. I write this letter to you all to tell you about our travels and our health. We are all well just now. When we came in sight of Britain, we sailed along the shore for a whole day, and when night came we cast anchor and slept. On the following morning we sailed, and made for the bay. The ships on the sea around us were like driftwood on the water in the time of a flood. We could not see the shore, it was hidden by the ships. When we reached the bay a steamer came and towed us and brought us into the river. At low tide we anchored, and waited till the tide turned. The steamer then towed us, and brought us into a place where the water was shut in by a wall. We had come as far as from Aname to Anelgauhat. We again lay at anchor all night. In the morning they opened a gate, and we brought the ship into a place they call the docks. Here the ships were so crowded that we could not get far in, and we lay there till the Sabbath was over, and then the ship was brought into another place to remain. After this all the missionaries and the children went ashore; but Kausiri [another native of Aneityum who accompanied the vessel as a sailor] and I remained in the ship till Saturday. Then Mr. Inglis came back and took us away, and we three travelled in a thing that runs by smoke. They call it a steam-engine; it runs far faster than a horse—its running is like the flying of a pigeon. We came to the house of Dr. Cunningham, and stayed there over one Sabbath. After that Kausiri went back to the ship. But we took our luggage, and travelled by the railway till we came to Manchester, to the house of the brother of Mrs. Inglis. It is as far as from Aneityum to Efate. We slept there, and on the following day we travelled by railway till we came to Liverpool. Here we went on board a large steamer, and sailed for Scotland, as far also as from Aneityum to Efate. Here we came ashore, and rode in a thing they call a machine, which is drawn by a horse, and came to a place called the Mark of Shennanton [near Newton-Stewart], to the house of Mrs. Inglis's father. They were all living. We stayed there over three Sabbaths, and then took our luggage and went to Glasgow. But on our way we came to the sea (at Girvan), and stayed in the house of Mr. Easton. They were as kind to me as if I had been their own child, and took great care of me, and gave me plenty of food, and spoke kind words to me. The next day we came to Glasgow, which is as far as from Futuna to Efate. There we stayed in the house of Dr. Symington. He is a very good man, and his wife and children are the same. They were very kind to me, and took great care of me, and gave me plenty of food, and gave me a fine room in the house to myself. They wished also to look at me, but I was ashamed and afraid in presence of the people.

This Britain is a wonderful country; there is not the like of it in the world. It is all true that the missionaries told us about the things here in Britain. It is impossible for me to explain to you all the things in Britain, unless the letter were a thing that could carry Britain to you, so that the people of Aneityum could see it themselves. But it is impossible for me to explain it to you by words. The things in Britain are not like things made by the hands of men. Such are the houses, the ships, the roads, and everything. Many, many are the people. They are like the sand on the sea-shore. Every place is like Aname at the time of the Sacrament, when all the people on Mr. Inglis's side of the island, from Isia to Anau-unse, are gathered together. So many are the people, and so great are the crowds in the towns, that it is difficult for them to walk backwards and forwards, or pass each other on the streets, so many are the people. When I am walking with any one, he takes hold of me by the arm, lest I should lose sight of him for the crowd in the streets. And there are so many houses. If all Aneityum were covered with a forest, and if every tree were a house, that would not be equal to the houses in Britain. I dare not go about by myself, lest I should not find the house where I am staying. I am weak with wondering at the things which I see. This is my letter to you two. May the Lord bless you.

WILLIAMU.

To Dora, his wife.

SCOTLAND, *August 20th*, 1860.

O DORA,—My love to you. I write this letter to you to let you know that I am well; so are Mr. and Mrs. Inglis, and Mr. Geddie's children. Formerly we were staying in the house of Dr. Symington in Glasgow. Afterwards we travelled by the railway and came to Edinburgh, which is a very great city. Dr. Goold, the son-in-law of Dr. Symington, lives there. He is a minister, and has a great many children. We three stayed with him. They were very good to me, and gave me plenty of food. A gentleman, a friend of Dr. Goold's, took me and showed me through the houses where they make things— the house where they make axes and iron tools, the house where they make types, the house where they make pictures, the house where they print books, and a house where they keep most beautiful things. But it is impossible to explain them to you in this letter.

Moreover, the people of Scotland were meeting every day in a church, and making speeches about a great man who lived in Scotland long ago; his name was John Knox [the Tercentenary of the Reformation]. He expelled the false religion and brought in the true religion. They were holding these meetings to keep it in remembrance that he was the first to establish this true religion; and also to keep in mind all the good he had done, and also that they might thank the Lord for His mercy, that He had taken away the false religion and had given His Word to them and to us all.

We three left Edinburgh by the railway, and came to the house of a gentleman, Mr. Rowatt, of Currie-Vale, and stayed there over one Sabbath. Afterwards we again travelled, and came to the house of Dr. Symington in Glasgow, and stayed there. We then went and took farewell of Mr. Geddie's children at the vessel. They sailed to Liverpool in a steamer. From Liverpool they are to sail in a very large steamer to Nova Scotia. We three bade them farewell. They send their love to you. We left them and returned to the house. On the following day we travelled, and came to the house of a minister's daughter, Miss Symington, Paisley, where we took tea. We left there and came on to the house of Mrs. Inglis's uncle and aunt, Rev. Mr. and Mrs. Jamieson, Kilmarnock, where we slept. Next morning we again travelled by the railway, as far as if you were to leave Aname and go twice round Aneityum. We alighted at a village called Thornhill, and travelled in a thing drawn by a horse till we came to the village in which Mr. Inglis was born; its name is Moniaive. This was as far as from Aname to Anelgauhat. When we came there we stayed in the house of Mr. Proudfoot. Both he and his wife are very kind people. They were both very good to me. On the Friday there was a marriage there, and Mr. Proudfoot and I went to see it. On the Sabbath day all the people were very desirous to hear Mr. Inglis. I had to rise and go out of the church; my former illness, fever and ague, came upon me. First my legs were benumbed and then my hands. Mrs. Inglis and I went into the church, but she brought me back to the house. My illness, however, was not great, and it has now quite left me. On the next day, the Monday, we three came to the house of Mrs. Inglis's sister, Mrs. M'Geoch, Craignell, near New Galloway. This was as far as from Iteng to Itheg. We slept there. On the following day we came to the house of Mrs. Inglis's father, where we stayed at first, and we are staying here at present. Moreover, Mrs. Symington gave me a dress for you as a token of her love to you. It is put into Mr. Geddie's box. You must take good care of it and not give it away to anybody. My letter is finished. My love to you, and may the Lord bless you.

WILLIAMU.

To Dora, his wife.

NEWTON-STEWART, *October 15th*, 1860.

O DORA,—I wish you well. I write to tell you about my health. I am very well at present, and so are Mr. and Mrs. Inglis. Formerly we three lived in the house of Mrs. Inglis's father, but afterwards they two went to a town called Newton-Stewart, and rented a very fine house for us three. At present we three live here, and a girl, whose name is Agnes, for a servant. It is a very fine house; it is large, and has a number of rooms above as well as below.

I must also tell you this: when we were in Glasgow there was a meeting for three days of the Reformed Presbyterian Synod, in Dr. Symington's church. All the ministers and the elders and the missionaries were there, and a great congregation of people. They made speeches about the work of God throughout the world and in Britain. Mr. Inglis stood up and spoke, and explained to them the progress of God's work among the islands, and particularly on Aneityum. When the people heard him they rejoiced, and gave thanks to the Lord for His love and mercy to us all. When he had finished he called upon me to rise and speak. When I rose I was ashamed, and made a short speech and then sat down. When we three were on our way to Britain I never once thought that I would have to speak. I only thought that I would have to look. A great number of the ministers made speeches, and gave thanks to God for His love and mercy. They also made speeches about a revival, and the work of God in different countries. They also spoke about the Reformation 300 years ago, the time when they gave up the false religion and embraced the true religion, and became one and prospered. In every part of Britain the people attend church every Sabbath day, and never give over. The people of Ireland and the people of America do the same. They have great reverence for the Lord. There are no heathen here.

Now, Dora, I will tell you of a present sent you by a lady. Her name is Mrs. Wilson. Her kindness to you has been very great. She has bought you a desk. It is packed in a box sent to Mr. Geddie. Take good care of it, and be strong, and write on paper every day. Also be very careful lest some one should persist in begging it from you, and you should not know its value and give it away. Be sure you take good care of it. You know well that no one can get anything like this for nothing. The price of it is great; and very great was the kindness to you of her who bought it: therefore take good care of it.

On Tuesday the 20th September I received your letter, and also the ones from Mathima and Thioka. I read them, and I was glad you were well, and I thank God for His mercy to us all. Be you strong and pray to Him every day without ceasing.

I like this land of Britain very much. I am in very good health

and think I would like to stay here a good while : but I do not know
how my heart may continue to feel. I visit a number of houses, and
the people give me always good food to eat. I have as much food
every day as I can eat. All the people are kind to me, and wish me
to go and visit at their houses. May the Lord bless you. This is the
letter of me, WILLIAMU.

To Setefano, a native teacher, an intimate friend of his.

NEWTON-STEWART, *November 27th,* 1860.

O SETEFANO,—My love to you, my brother.' We three received your
letter on Tuesday the 20th of this month, November. I do sympathise very deeply with you on account of the death of your wife. I
felt just as you do on account of my child, which the Lord gave me
and then took away. I was exceedingly grieved, and my heart was
like the heart of a dead man. But when Mr. Inglis talked to me, his
words refreshed me like water. I thought, and I said to myself, my
child is like one calling before me in the way that leads to heaven ;
and if I am strong I shall yet see him : whereas had he remained with
me I might have been weak and not watched over him carefully in
the world, to keep him from those things that are evil.

I will now explain to you very shortly about Britain. This is a
most wonderful country for everything. They make roads for things
that run by smoke and boiling water ; they call them steam-engines,
but they call the roads on which they run railways. In places like
Mount Nathatahau they make roads underneath the ground, as if you
would go in at Itath and not come out till you came to Aname. Now,
Setefano, do not think that I am joking. I have travelled eight times
along with Mr. and Mrs. Inglis, and seen a great many places, as if
you would go to Futuna, and Tanna, and Aniwa, and Eromanga, and
Efate, and I have travelled under the ground where it was like darkness itself. This is a fine country. There is not a single spot in it
that is lying waste. It is all cultivated. The ministers have very
fine houses. They are high, and have a great many rooms in them ;
and the churches are splendid ; they are like two houses under one
roof ; the upper house is called a gallery.

Moreover, the people of Britain have consulted together, and they
have appointed men to protect the country. They call these men

volunteers. There are twenty thousand of these men. But these belong to the one half of the country only, which is called Scotland. I do not know how many there are in the other half and in all other places. These were all assembled in a city called Edinburgh. They met together and marched before Victoria, the Queen of Great Britain. When she saw them she was very glad.

Now, you teachers, see that you all obey Mr. Copeland, and do not be obstinate and self-willed, but hear him willingly. If he has no food, see that you, the teachers and the church members, bring him some. Remember me to Filip, and Solomon, and Napolos, and Yamtiu, and Luke, and Petelo, and Hosia, and Nowanpakau, and say that I am not forgetting one of them. Peace be with you all.

WILLIAMU.

To Thioka and Mathima, an uncle and a half-brother.

SCOTLAND, Nov. 24th, 1860.

O THIOKA AND MATHIMA,—I wish you well. This is my letter to you two, and to all the people of Aname, to explain to you two what I wish you all to do. I wish you to look well after my house and garden, and keep up a good fence round it. The women will gather reeds ; and tell Nako and Niau and Nityok to look after the garden, and weed it neatly. And do you, Mathima, look after my orange trees, lest they be injured ; and be careful also about the house, lest it be burned down ; and do not kindle too large a fire, lest the walls become black with smoke. Moreover, do not be idle, but be strong, and work every day. And do not be thinking every one of you about his own things only, but be helpful to one another ; and do not be quarrelling among yourselves, but live all in peace, and watch over one another, and hear one another's advices. I have told you twice now this, to look well after the pigs, that they do not injure the plantations, and thus break the hearts of the people. Take good care also of the sweet potatoes and the yams. Do not forget about them, but dig and make plantations ; and if they grow well, be kind to Dora and give her some of them. Besides this, be strong, all of you, and go to the school every day, and attend the church, and read in your own houses, and do not sit idle at home and think only about the things of this world. Live in peace one with another, and do not be soon angry with one another, or quick to revenge injuries, but be kind one to another.

The people are all very good to me here, and speak very kindly to me, but I do not understand well what they say. I get plenty of food, as much as I can eat. This is an extraordinary country. Many, many, are the houses, and the people, and everything; and the country is so large, it is like the ocean in extent. But you hear of no bad conduct in any place. The chiefs are all strong to put a stop to bad conduct. My love to you all.   WILLIAMU.

To Dora, his wife.

NEWTON-STEWART, *January 4th,* 1861.

O DORA,—My love to you. I write this letter to explain things to you, and to tell you that we three are well. Mr. Inglis and I are very busy just now with the translation. While we were on the voyage home we two began and corrected Matthew and Mark, and Luke and John, the Acts of the Apostles and the Epistles of Paul. And then when we came to Newton-Stewart we began and corrected all these books a second time, and we have not yet finished them. Mr. Inglis has a great deal of work to do. They were repairing the *John Williams,* and they were collecting money in every place to pay for the repairs. Mr. Inglis had charge of this work in Scotland, and he had to write a great many letters to the collectors to thank them for their kindness to the missionaries in collecting money to repair their ship. Moreover, when the corrections of the translation are finished, he will take it to London, where it is to be printed.

The cold is very severe in Britain in November, December, and January. When we arrived here in June, it was not cold. But the cold began in October, and snow fell, but it was not much. The water also was frozen and became hard, only it was but little. But when November came the cold was very severe, and a great deal of snow fell and covered all the ground. You could not see any growing thing. It was as if you had spread out white clothes and covered both the ground and the houses with them. But it was very beautiful and very white. You could just see the trees and the houses and the fences. The frost came down and the water was hard. What

Mr. and Mrs. Inglis told us is quite true, that the water becomes hard, and when the people go to get water they have to break it like glass, and then get water; they call this hard water ice. When December came the cold was dreadful, and the water frozen very hard; even the milk was hard in the dishes. One morning the servant took out the dishes from the breakfast, and left them unwashed till she did something else. When she went back to wash them they were all sticking to the table with the ice, and she could not move them. When she saw them sticking fast she laughed, and came and told me, that I might pull them off. But I was afraid lest I should break them. One morning she brought in some water from the well, and set it down; I was in bed, but rose about six o'clock—that is like at the false cock-crowing—and kindled a fire. I took the water pitcher to pour some water into the kettle, but it was hard. I laughed to myself, and then took the tongs and broke it just like glass. Another morning there was no water in the pitcher; the girl was from home, and had not brought in any. I kindled the fire, and then took the pitcher and went out to the cask that stands at the side of the house, but the water was frozen hard. I then went into the house, and took a large axe and broke the frozen water in the cask: it was like a flat stone; after that I got the water. Very great is the cold in Britain in November, December, and January. Your hands get benumbed, and you can do nothing with them.

Moreover, we three are living here; but we go to their houses and visit people, and feast with them; and they come and feast with us three. One day I went along with Mr. Inglis, that he might buy a coat for me. We went into the house where they weave cloth. I saw them weaving. It was wonderful beyond anything you ever saw, but I cannot explain it to you in a letter. Before this I had gone to a house where they make thread, belonging to Mr. Clark of Glasgow. It was a large house, and very high. There were six houses inside, all one above another. I could not express my wonder at seeing it. There were one hundred, yea, I think two hundred people, working in it, both men and women. In conclusion, give my love to the family at Umka, and also to Goai; and remember me to Mary, and Lathella, and Selwyn. These are my words to you.   WILLIAMU.

To Mathima, his half-brother.

NEWTON-STEWART, *January 29th*, 1861.

O MATHIMA,—I wish you well. I write this letter to let you know that I am well, and also that Mr. and Mrs. Inglis are well. Formerly we three went to visit a number of large towns; Glasgow, and Edinburgh, and Rothesay, (?) and Moniaive (??), and likewise a number of small places. Afterwards we returned to the house of Mrs. Inglis's father and stayed there. Then Mr. and Mrs. Inglis went to the town in which I am writing this letter, and rented a fine house for us three. We three are staying in it just now. It is a very good house. There are a great many rooms in it. There are five apartments below and three above. The walls are smooth and beautiful, and covered with painted paper. Moreover, it is fitted up with lights which they call gas. This gas is first made out of coal, and kept in a vessel like a very large cask, and then it goes under the ground in large iron pipes; it goes like wind; then it comes up into the houses and stays there always, and when it becomes dark then they light it every night. It is very very cold in Britain just now, in those months when it is warm in Ancityum. And when it rains it is like arrowroot; it falls in scales, and it is hard; its name is snow; and a dew falls which they call frost; and the water freezes and becomes like glass, and very hard; and the ground becomes all hard like stone, and the cold is fearful. Still I am well and strong, and can do anything.

Britain is an extraordinary country for everything, and for the good, upright conduct of all the people, all the married men and all the married women, and all the young men and all the boys; they work diligently every day. They never sit idle; young men and boys all work. They are not like the young men on Aneityum. Moreover, there are fine roads in Britain. There is one kind of roads, very broad ones, for carts, and omnibuses, and gigs, and coaches, and cabs. These are things with wheels; they are drawn by horses, and go very fast. There is another kind of roads for things that go by smoke. The name of this is a steam-engine, but the name of the road on which it goes is a railway. It is made by laying pieces of wood across, and by laying along above these long stones which they call iron. One of these roads is as far as from Ancityum to Efate.

Moreover, they have made a thing here which they call a *telegraph*.

It is made in this way. They erect poles on the ground, and then they fix wires along on the tops of the poles. Then they catch the spirit of the lightning and put it into a box. They can speak to people as far distant from one another as from Ancityum to the Loyalty Islands. They do it in this way. Suppose Mr. Inglis wanted to speak to Mr. Jones on Marè, he would speak to the man who has charge of the telegraph ; he would take the spirit of the lightning and send it along these wires, to convey Mr. Inglis's words to the man on Marè, who has charge of the telegraph there ; he would write down Mr. Inglis's words and give them to Mr. Jones. The words go as fast as a flash of lightning, just at once. My words are done. Peace be with you. WILLIAMU.

To Ester (wife of Lasarus) and Thiganua (wife of Inhalvatimi).
(These two families were living with Mr. Copeland in charge of the mission premises.)

NEWTON-STEWART, *July 1st*, 1861.

O ESTER AND THIGANUA,—This is Mrs. Inglis's love to you two, and her word to you two. She has asked me to write this letter to you two, and to say that she was very glad when she heard by Mrs. Geddie's letter that you two had had a baby each, and that you were nursing them well, and keeping them clean ; and also about the house, and that you are looking well after it. She says, just go on as you are doing, and look well after the house, that she may find all things as she left them. We three expect to return next year. Mrs. Inglis is just as she was on Aneityum. She had a pain in her breast, but she is well again. Mr. Inglis is well, and so am I. We three have an excellent house. There are a great many rooms in it, both above and below. But we have only one servant girl. Her name is Jane. But she is equal to five, yea ten, of you women on Aneityum. I say we have just one servant girl, but she looks after the house and every-thing in it. She cooks the food, she washes the dishes, she sweeps the house and she washes it ; she cleans the windows and she makes the beds ; she runs messages and she buys food ; she brushes the shoes and she cleans out the kitchen—it is just like another room. She takes care of both Mr. and Mrs. Inglis's clothes, and of mine also; she washes them and irons them all herself. Mrs. Inglis does not require to help her. She works away herself. She is quiet, she never gossips, and she is never angry; she is never sulky, and she never sits idle. She is not like the women of Aneityum. Quite a band of them go to the water to wash the missionaries' clothes, and they stay there, and bawl out, and laugh loud, and joke one another, and sing songs, and one says, "I am hungry;" and another says, "I am going to the sea to gather shell-fish;" and another says, "I am sleepy;" and another says, "I am tired;" and it is night before they have done.

Moreover, we went to the house of Mrs. Inglis's brother, his name is James [the late Mr. M'Clymont, Borgue House], and we stayed there four weeks. It is a beautiful large house, with a great many rooms in it, and it is surrounded by excellent fences. He has so many things, I cannot describe them to you—sheep, and cattle, and fowls, and a great many servants. We three stayed there, and after we left his house we came back to our own house at Newton-Stewart. We three have a beautiful garden. We have in it potatoes, and cabbage, and turnips, and pease, and parsley, and a great many gooseberries, and currants, and apples.

Besides this, one of Mrs. Inglis's sisters was married on Thursday, the 4th of July. Her name is Grace [the wife of Rev. D. Kellock, Presbyterian minister, Spencerville congregation, Ontario, Canada]. Mr. Inglis married them. We all met and feasted, and sang and rejoiced. They have splendid marriages in Britain, but I cannot describe them to you in this letter. Mr. Inglis is very busy every day with the translation [of the New Testament]. He is never idle. My love to Mr. Copeland, also to Lasarus and Inhalvatimi and the young men. Peace be with you. ‾ WILLIAMU.

To Sabataio (his cousin).

NEWTON-STEWART, *April 1st,* 1861.

O SABATAIO,—I wish you well. I received the letter from you two, and read it, and was glad to learn that you were all well. Let us be thankful for the grace of God to us, and that He is keeping us alive. Let us pray to Him daily that He may give each of us a heart to hate sin, and a heart to resist heathenism, and a heart filled with peace, and a heart full of light. I am quite well just now ; I have had no sickness except a slight cough, but Mr. Inglis takes good care of me, and gives me medicine.

They have finished the road here for the things that run by smoke [the Castle Douglas and Stranraer railway]. It was opened in March. The great men who are the owners of it travelled along it first. I went to see them. All the people were assembled. There might be a thousand people there. The running is far faster than that of a horse. The road is as far as from Aneityum to Efate.

Mrs. Inglis's grandmother died on Wednesday, 20th of March. She was ninety-one years of age. But they did not bury her soon. They waited till after the Sabbath before they buried her. Mr. Inglis and I attended the funeral. All her relations came. There might be two hundred people present. There were thirty-six machines drawn by horses. They took her as far as from Imtainga to Anau-unse. All the ministers and the elders were at the funeral. I go to the church every Sabbath and worship, and I hear a few of the English words that I know, but I do not understand the preaching.

Say to the people of Aname [his own land] that I always remember them, and that I wish them all well. Be you all strong, and work daily. Let no man stroll about, let no man sit idle. O Sabataio, my cousin, do you assist Thioka, and exhort these three young men that they may behave themselves well, and work diligently, and dig, and have plenty of food. This is my advice to you all, that you live peaceably ; and if any one stir up a desire for heathenism do not ye follow him, but abhor our former ways. You all know that if we revive the heathen customs that we practised long ago, we should be rebelling against God. Be you all strong, and work every day, and look well after your lands, that you may have plenty of food. And remember this, that if any one wishes to keep a pig, let him prepare a sty for it and put the pig into it, and not leave it to go at large, lest it break the hearts of the rest of you by its destroying your food. Also look well after the water-course for the irrigation, that it may be always in good repair. But if any one say, "Why is he talking so much about the things of this world?" I would say, no man can live on stones or on wood. We sustain our bodies only by the food which God freely gives us day by day. But if some one would say, "The things of this world are all vanity," I would say, are not the things of earth the gifts of God as

well as the things of heaven, and to be prized and used as His gifts?
This is my word to all of you. I wish you all well, both men and
women. My friends, be you all strong, and pray to God every day
that He may have mercy upon you and give you food to sustain your
souls and food to sustain your bodies. And pray for me that I may
explain correctly the language of our island, and His servant will
write it for us. All things are easy to God, and to Him all things
belong. This is the word of me, Williamu, to you, Sabataio.

To Dora, his wife.

NEWTON-STEWART, *June 20th,* 1861.

O DORA,—My love to you. I am thankful that you are well. We
are the same, we three are well. I will tell you how we have been
getting on. We lived in Newton-Stewart during the winter, but
when May came we three and a sister travelled by the railway
and came to the town of Dumfries. We stayed in the house
of the minister, Mr. Symington, over the Sabbath. We went to
church, and Mr. Inglis preached. On Monday morning we three
travelled in a thing drawn by a horse to go to the railway; a young
man named Mr. William Halliday drove us. We were too late for
the railway, and we stayed in the house of a woman whose husband
was dead to wait for the next train. The young man and I went
away to fish in a river, and when we came back in the middle of
the day he went away home to Dumfries; but we stayed till the
afternoon, and got a fine dinner, and then went by the railway and
came to Currie-Vale, to the house of Mr. Rowatt [the late Bailie
Rowatt of Edinburgh]. We slept there. On the following morning,
which was Tuesday, Mr. Inglis went to a meeting of ministers and
elders, which they call a Synod (the Reformed Presbyterian Synod).
They began their meetings on Monday, and continued them till
Friday. I went to the meetings, and Mr. Inglis told me I was to
rise and speak. I made a short speech. They meet to speak about
the work of God in Britain and throughout the world. They met
every morning in Dr. Goold's church, and continued their meetings
till late at night. They did not go out except to their dinner, and
at night every one went to his own home. On the day that they

Y

met, it was not observed that a window was open above ; Mr. Inglis
sat under it and caught a very bad cold, which continued for a fortnight, but he is again quite well. While we stayed at Currie-Vale
they were very kind to me ; they gave me a little knife, and the
daughter of Mr. Rowatt gave me a pair of scissors for you. Her
name is Agnes, and she is about the same age as Charlotte [Miss
Geddic]. She has a sister whose name is Maggie. She is about the
same age as Lucy. And they two have a sister who is about the
same age as Elizabeth. They have three brothers. While we stayed
there they taught me to sing and to play on the piano. We left
Currie-Vale on the Saturday, travelled by the railway, and came to
Castle-Douglas. This is the city of Mr. Kay (!!). We remained
over the Sabbath, and then went to Mrs. Inglis's brother's [Borgue
House] where we stayed one Sabbath. On the Friday after we came
to Castle-Douglas there was a great meeting [a soiree]; the church
was full. Mr. Inglis made a speech, and then called upon me to
speak. I told them about our heathenism and our folly long ago,
and also about our peace and happiness now. Mr. and Mrs. Inglis
stayed with Mr. Kay, but I stayed in the house of Mrs. Snodgrass,
a lady who was remarkably kind to me, she and her two daughters.
She sewed three shirts for me, and gave me a fine coat, and trousers,
and drawers. I was just like the child of them three, they were so
good to me. These are my words to you, O Dora. My love to you.

WILLIAMU.

Note.—At this time measles were introduced into Aneityum
by a trading vessel. The epidemic and its *sequelæ* swept off
one third of the population of the island, and among others
Dora, Williamu's wife, died. Mr. Geddie's church was also
burned down the same year, supposed to be the act of an
incendiary. Frequent reference is made to these sad events
in Williamu's subsequent letters.

To Mrs. Geddie.

NEWTON-STEWART, *August 24th*, 1861.

DEAR MRS. GEDDIE,—I wish you well. I write this letter to you to thank you for letting me know about Dora's death. But I cannot write well to you on account of my grief, nor can I explain to you the sorrow of my heart. My wife, Mary Ann, and I lived first together. But after she died, when I looked at Dora she was just like Mary Ann, and on this account I married her. But she too is gone from me, and my heart is very sad. But when I sorrow about Dora I do not repine nor question about her death. We are all subject to death and sickness. No one can run away from sickness and death in this world. I am grieved, however, that her life was so short, for her conduct to me was so good. She never grieved or vexed me. She attended to what I said, and she acted towards me in the same way that she did towards you.

Alas! for the island of Aneityum. The people are all dying, and it is becoming a wilderness. When we three first received letters telling us that so many of the people were dying we were very grieved. I was also afraid to receive a letter. And when the letters came on Friday last I was out in the garden doing something. When I came in to dinner I went up to Mr. Inglis's study to mend his fire, and saw letters lying on the table. When I looked at them I saw that they were letters from Aneityum. When they two went out from dinner, they went up to the study; but I was afraid to go with them to hear the letters, and I went and sat in my own room. When they had read the letters they called for me, and told me. We three were very grieved. Oh yes, Mrs. Geddie, I am still very grieved. But since they two have talked to me, and you also have written to me, my heart is resigned, and it says, "It is even so. The Lord has rebuked me and chastised me three times [by the death of his first and second wife and his son], and why should I be afraid of His hand?" Your words to me, and the words of Mr. and Mrs. Inglis, were soothing to me as its mother's milk to her child. And now I find that it is as you say. Your words are true.

We three are very grieved about your church which was burned. Woe to that wretched fellow! His father, the devil, put it into his heart to burn the church, that the hearts of the people might be weak towards the truth. What could make that foolish man think that he could drag the people of Aneityum back to heathenism, and that, being a fool himself, he could make them all to be fools too, and resist the word of the Lord respecting His holy house? Very great was Mr. Geddie's work in building the church, and he was assisted by all the people; very great also was their work in building. But that worthless fellow, who never put a hand to it, to go and burn it down. I am very grieved about his conduct.

Mr. Inglis is very busy just now with the translation. I am in good health, I have no sickness. Mr. and Mrs. Inglis are also well. Your words are very good respecting the things which Dora has left. I salute Mr. Geddie. My love to Ella. I mourn with Lathella on account of the death of Mary his wife. Who will take care of his motherless children? I pity the poor things! I also sympathise with Mataio for the loss of his wife. This is my letter to you, dear Mrs. Geddie. My love to you, my mother. WILLIAMU.

To Talep (at that time a teacher on Tanna).

NEWTON-STEWART, *Sept. 10th*, 1861.

MY DEAR UNCLE TALEP,—I wish you well. I do not forget you for a single day. I write this letter to you to let you know that I enjoy good health every day. Mr. and Mrs. Inglis are doing the same. I write also that I may tell you about my grief. Very very great is the grief of my heart for the death of my wife, and also of my rela· tions. The first letter we received told us of the death of Suaing, and Joane, and Viali, and Katipae. Our next letter told us of the death of Nemitangi, and Mala, and Nako, and Netwai, and the rest of the people who had died; and also that the sea had destroyed some of the houses of the missionary, and many of the schoolhouses, and that the church at the other side of the island had been burned down. This letter came here in July. In August we got letters telling me of the death of Dora, and Mary, and Naraki-inwai, and Mataio's wife, and the rest of the people who had died on the following month. When all this news came crowding on me, very great indeed was my grief, and so was that of Mr. and Mrs. Inglis. Our hearts contained nothing but grief, and we said, "What can this mean?" But it is the Lord's will towards us, and He is Lord over all men. Tell me if you three are well. Be strong, and pray every day to our Father in heaven for His Holy Spirit, and remember Jesus our Saviour, and let us not be feeble in our minds on account of these things. Let us not call in question His doings. He has chastened us by these deaths, and by the trials He has brought upon us: and He is still rebuking us. Alas! alas! for our little island. It is now almost a desert; the people are nearly all dead.

Remember me to your wife Elizabeth and your daughter Retia, and say to your fellow-labourers, Matthew and Singonga, that I wish them well. Be strong, my brethren, and let your hearts be established in love to Jesus your Saviour. Say to your fellow-teacher, Yaresi, that I wish him well, and the same to Nakau, his wife. Speak kindly to the Tannese chiefs, viz., Yaresi, and Namaka, and Taura, and Lauaua, and Naka, and Kaipapa, and Namua, and say that the word of Jehovah is certainly true, and that all things on earth are weak to save our souls. Let them be strong towards the words of truth, and give up those lying vanities that kill men's souls and send them to hell. Jesus only is the way and the truth, both for us and for the people of every land. Remember me to the missionary and his wife, Mr. and Mrs. Mathieson. I am sorry that my friends have not written to me as the missionaries have written to Mr. and Mrs. Inglis.

Moreover, Britain is a remarkable country for religion, and for the kindness of the people to one another and to strangers. The people all go to church every Sabbath day without ceasing, and they often meet also on week days. Into whatever house I go, the people are all so kind to me, and seem so glad to see me, but I am ashamed to be looked at. This is indeed a good land. There are such crowds of people here; the houses too are crowded close together in the towns; and the country is so large, it is just like the ocean, and yet there is none of it lying waste, there are so many people. But I cannot describe it to you in a letter. Moreover, Mr. Inglis has bought me a beautiful clock. It has a glass door, and in the inside there is a bell which strikes every hour. At one o'clock it strikes once; at two o'clock it strikes twice and then stops; at three o'clock it strikes thrice and then stops, and it goes on in this way at every hour till it comes to twelve o'clock, when it strikes twelve times and then stops. Are you two looking after the two yams that I gave you? My love to you three. May the Lord bless you. WILLIAMU.

To Sabataio.

NEWTON-STEWART, *September 30th*, 1861.

O SABATAIO, my cousin, I wish you well. I am well at present, and so are Mr. and Mrs. Inglis. We three are living here. But we go to a number of places, and visit the people and feast with them. I have a number of valuable things which the people have given me in presents. The people of this country are so good to me in giving me food. I never ask for anything nor yet for food, and yet I am never in want of anything, as I used to be on our island Aneityum.

Moreover, I say to you, tell the people of Ananie [his own land, where he was chief] that I wish them all well, men and women and children ; I do not forget you for a single day : but I say to you, be all strong, and assemble every Sabbath in the church, and pray to our Father in heaven without ceasing ; and do not be weak-hearted on account of those sorrows which you are now enduring. But think of this, that our days on earth are few, and think of that place where you are to abide for ever.

Besides this, be strong, and dig, and plant, that you may have plenty of food to eat. Do not sit idle, but look well after the water-course for irrigating the plantations. Do not neglect that. If you neglect the land, and do not work, and if I return, I will not follow your indolent ways ; but I will say that your former conduct was better than your present. Let us cultivate the land, let us leave the old plantations and form new ones, and drain the swamps and make good dwellings. When I come home I wish to build a new house, I wish you all well, and I long to see you ; but I cannot yet on account of the work for which I accompanied Mr. Inglis.

Be strong, all of you. If any one make you angry, do not take revenge on him, and do not follow his way, but exhort him, and live together in peace, and watch over your conduct, and do not provoke one another to anger. Do not talk proudly, and do not quarrel. Tell Nityok and Mathima to look well after my cocoa-nuts, and collect them for oil to me. When I return home I will see whether they have collected them or not. I wish you all to write me a letter, and tell me about things and what the people of Aneityum are doing, and how you are all getting on ; how you are attending the church and the school, and how all the people are behaving themselves, and everything about Aneityum. I sympathise with you in all your sufferings and in all your sorrows.

This is the letter of me, Williamu, to you, Sabataio. My love to you and to all the people of Aname. Be ye all strong.

WILLIAMU.

To Napolos, a chief of Aneityum whose wife had died.

NEWTON-STEWART, *September 5th,* 1861.

O NAPOLOS,—I sympathise with you, my brother, on account of the death of your wife. I do indeed sympathise with you on account of your grief ; your grief and mine are the same. The sorrow of all of us is the same. I am telling you of my grief, while I am living here in another land. When I first heard that death had come among you, and that so many of the people were dying, and that the two churches on the other side of the island had been burned down, and that a number of the people were becoming weak in their hearts, and that they were going back and observing old heathen practices, and making offerings to their old gods—when I heard of all these things my sorrow was very great. I was truly grieved, and I wept ; because when we worshipped vanities long ago, on account of our ignorance of the Lord, He had compassion on us, and sent His servants to us that they might show to us the only good way, even Jesus our Saviour ; and because that now when we know Him well we are rejecting Him and reviving those practices which we formerly observed. This is wilful disobedience. Why do men think evil thoughts of Him on account of those trials by means of which He has been chastening us, in order that we may obey Him and become like fruitful trees? It is not good for us to be angry with God to whom all things belong and we ourselves also. We must not call in question His doings. The doings of God which we see are mighty. All things and all men belong to God, and He doeth with us what seemeth good to Him. O Napolos, my brother, very great is my sorrow on account of the death of my wife and my relations. But I think the Lord is chastening me that He may send me up to heaven. Why should I rebel and be angry because He is rebuking me ?

The work of God prospers much in Britain. The ministers never cease to assemble the people, and to speak to them about the work of

God in all countries throughout the world. They know all about those trials that have come upon you. They sympathise with us, and pray to the Lord for us at every meeting and every day, and that without ceasing. I am grieved on account of the houses belonging to Mr. Inglis which the sea destroyed. They stood too near the sea ; also on account of the church, and the Teacher's Institution, and the schoolhouses. But it was all our doing ; we were sleeping secure, and never thought of the time that these things would come on us, and built our houses on the shore, and forsook the inland districts. But let all the people be strong and rebuild all their houses. Do not let them say that this work pains them, and help Mr. Copeland. You, and Kapos, and Yona, and Katipae, and Luka, and Yamtiu, and the rest of the people. Speak also to the people, and let the chiefs exhort all their followers in every district to work hard, that they may have plenty of food and build good houses for themselves, and keep their dwellings all clean. It is quite true that the missionaries tell us that we do not take proper care of ourselves. When any one is sick he lies outside at night exposed to the damp and the cold, or else his house is bad, and he breathes bad smells from the rubbish lying on the ground. Britain is a fine country ; the whole country is cleared ; the houses are excellent ; they clear away all rubbish from the ground ; and they work every day, and make their houses and gardens beautiful, and they have plenty of all things. But I cannot write any more to you. This is the letter of me, Williamu, to you, Napolos. My love to you, and to all the people who are living with you. Yours,

WILLIAMU.

To Mathima (his half-brother).

NEWTON-STEWART, *March 25th*, 1862.

O MATHIMA,—My love to you, my brother. I am very well at present. I have a great many clothes, and I wish to make you a present of something, but I cannot just now. I have also a number of English books. Moreover, I am learning to sing at present. A young man comes to teach me. His name is Mr. Vernon. He leads the singing in Mr. Goold's church, where we worship. Mr. Goold is a very good man ; he is very kind to me. Very great is Mr. Vernon's knowledge of singing ; he has taught me fourteen tunes which I know. He also goes over them again with me, that I may have them correct. He has been very kind to me. He made me a present of an instrument which sounds like a *natarau* [a native flute]. They call it an *accordion*. It is something like the instrument which Manura made. He also made me a present of a book which teaches us how to sing and play. They call it a music book. Very excellent is the singing in Britain; and so is all the worship. I am well at present, and so are Mr. and Mrs. Inglis. But Mr. Inglis has not done with his work yet, but they have commenced printing. It is being done in a great city which they call London. We three expect to be home in the end of the year.

Remember me to Nethnoware and to Yona, and say that I have not forgotten them. Say to them also, Let the chiefs of Aneityum be one in heart and live as brethren. Let their word be one, and their work one also, and let their conduct be consistent. Let them look well after all the people; let them speak soft words to their young men when they go astray, and bring them back by persuasion, but do not get enraged at them, and beat them, or scold them, or threaten them. We know that God only can punish aright those who refuse to do His laws. My friends, do not be weak in your hearts because you are few in number at present, but be strong and do your parts well, as those dwelling in the land, that our island may again revive and prosper. And be strong and help Mr. Copeland, and speak well to all the people, that they look after him, and remember the words where it is said, "The labourer is worthy of his hire." My words are done. Peace be with you.   WILLIAMU.

To Talep (his uncle, a teacher on Tanna).

NEWTON-STEWART, *March 25th*, 1862.

O TALEP, my best wishes for you. I am very well just now, and so are the two missionaries. The cold is very great here at present, but I am strong to work and to walk, and when Mr. and Mrs. Inglis visit their friends I go with them. We go to a great many houses. I do not know well what they say, but I go for the feasting. Very very great was the cold of the winter of 1861. The cold of 1862 has been moderate. I am strong to go to the church every Sabbath and also on week days. I had a cough, and Mr. Inglis was afraid of me, and gave me medicine, and took care of me, and made me stay in the house, and made me put on more clothes in the daytime, and gave me more blankets at night, and I live as they do. In the same way all the people are good to me here in this great land. Such is their way in this land of light. They treat me as if I had been born here, and as if I were the child of everybody in the land, their kindness to me is so great and their treatment of me is so good. They are not kind to me because I am a chief, or for anything they see about me. It is just the way they do in this land of light, from the grace of God in their hearts, and from the peace and truth and goodness which He has given them, and thereby made this land great, and made the people willing and able to believe on His name. We three have gone to a great many places where the people have asked Mr. Inglis to explain to them the condition of other lands, as they wish to hear about their way of living and their conduct. He also told me to speak and explain to them our conduct in the days of heathenism. I speak, and Mr. Inglis interprets in English what I say. I have spoken in eight churches, and explained our heathen customs that we clung to long ago. I spoke before great crowds, as many as are assembled on Aneityum at the time of the communions. The churches were full.

Moreover, it is good for us people of Ancityum to think earnestly just now, seeing that we have renounced all our sins in the presence of God, and have come to Him to receive eternal life through Jesus our Lord. O Talep, my father, I say this to you just now. Be very strong, and seek diligently food for your soul, that is eternal life; and pray to our Father in heaven every day for His Holy Spirit to abide with you, and love our Lord and Saviour Jesus Christ with all your heart, and read His Word every day that you may know the truth of His Gospel, and explain well this Word of His to those chiefs on Tanna—to Yaresi, and Taura, and Namaka, and Lauaua, and to the people who hear a little, and assure them that the Word of God is true, that their idols are lies, that the works of the devil are vanity, that his works bring men to misery, that he deceives us, and wishes that we may all go to his place of torment, that the Lord Jesus is the only true Saviour of us heathens in all lands. Urge the Tannese to be strong and keep hold of Christianity, and not let it go from them; and let them take good care of their two missionaries, Mr. and Mrs. Mathieson, and not to be angry with them. They two are teaching them the Gospel, the Word that will save their souls. Be you and Matthew strong, and assist Mr. Mathieson in his work; and let your two wives do the same to Mrs. Mathieson, and live all of you in peace. I am thankful to learn that you are all well.

Great is Mr. Inglis's work on the book, the New Testament, up to this month in which I am writing this letter to you. But they have begun to print it in London, which is the chief city in Britain, and is at the other end of the land. It is, as it were, at Espirito Santo; and we are here, as it were, at Aneityum. But the proof-sheets are carried backwards and forwards by a railway, a thing that runs as fast as a pigeon flies. We have been a long time here, but our stay will now be short; perhaps we may be home this year.

I am very happy living here. I am not crying for Aneityum; I do not long for any of the things in our land. I am fully satisfied with what I get to eat; I am not in want of anything. I am not as you were when you travelled and went to Sydney. You were so pained with hunger that you longed for the leaves of the trees, and no one gave you anything. It is not so here. Whatever house I go to, of their own accord they say, " How do you do? I am glad to see you; come and eat something." I have no voice to express my wonder at the conduct of the people in this land of light. Peace be unto you

WILLIAMU.

To Mathima and Kapos.

NEWTON-STEWART, *July 28th*, 1862.

My love to you two. I wish you two well. When we three were at the Synod in Glasgow Mr. Robertson of Blairbeth, at whose house we were staying, took Mrs. Inglis and me into his house where he makes cloth—the house where he makes cloth out of cotton—a very very large, high house. It is six houses inside from the ground to the roof; they call them storeys. The inside of it is as large as the whole enclosure around our church. It is as wide as from the fence at the back of the church to the road at the trees on the shore. And it is as long as from the fence at the bell-house to the lower fence at the Teachers' Institution. And there is another house joined to it, also a very large house; it has either six or seven roofs, I forget which. There is a chimney at the side of the house as tall as any of the cocoa-nut trees beside the teachers' house. The body of the chimney is as thick as the great inteijith (banyan) tree in Nityok's yard. There are six fireplaces for heating the water that is inside the boiler—a boiler like that which used to be between the two islands, between Inyeug and Nahringagas, which came out of some vessel; but it is long and full of water, under which they make fires. When the water boils it makes a thing to go round which they call a wheel. It goes round like those we saw on the outside of the steamer, but they were small, this one was very large. Moreover, when this wheel is made to go round by the steam of the boiling water, it sets everything agoing in every one of these houses, and the noise is like the noise of a waterfall. Everything is going round in every house, from the bottom up to the top, both the things for spinning thread and the things for weaving cloth. When everything is going round and the wheels are all making a noise, the ground is shaking just as if it were an earthquake. When all things are going, the thread makes itself in one place and the cloth makes itself in another place. None of the people make any with their hands. They just stand, and look, and watch it. None of them spin any thread with their hands, and none of them weave any cloth with their hands. This is the way they do in all the places where they make thread, and cloth, and blankets, and everything else. I cannot explain it to you. I cannot write about it. I could not wonder. I stood still and looked. When I went into the house in which they kept their cotton they showed me some that came from Aneityum. They asked Mrs. Inglis if it grew well on Aneityum. When she said that it did, they said, "You ought to plant it; we wish cotton very much." What do you think of this, Kapos? I think it will be an excellent thing for us. Do not think it is a little word this about the cotton, I say it is a big word. It has a body in it. There is a young man coming out with us three to explain it to us. Let us be strong and plant cotton, and gather it, and he will buy it from us and give us payment.

Moreover, when we came back from the Synod to the house in which we lived, we packed up all our things and left the house, and went to live in another house. We did this on the day on which all the people who leave their houses and go to new ones do so, that is on the 26th of May; they call it Whitsunday. It was on a Monday.

Salute Luka, and Yosefa, and Filip, and all the people of Itath.

Salute also from me, Beni, and Moana, and Lasarus, Inhalvatimi, and all the people of Aname. Salute also Seremona, and Faresi, and Yawila, and all the people of Ipeke. I wish them all well. Let them pray for us three. Peace be with them all; my words are done. WILLIAMU.

CHAPTER XXXV.

FOR a long period the Polynesian missions were highly popular, and deservedly so. Tahiti, Hawaii, and the South Seas were the watchwords at every missionary meeting. But for a number of years other fields have been attracting so much of public attention that the South Seas are falling greatly into the background. The continents are swamping the islands. The millions in India, China, Africa, and elsewhere are brought so prominently and so constantly forward, that the thousands in Polynesia are all but thrown into the shade. Those islands, it is said, were very good to begin with, or they may be very well adapted for small churches or small societies, but at this advanced stage of missionary progress, and for our large societies, the large continents, with their teeming millions, are the proper fields on which to carry on missionary operations. When you have continents containing hundreds of millions, why direct your attention to islands where the population is counted only by thousands? And then science, commerce, and politics, with plausible arguments loudly proclaimed and constantly reiterated, come in as counsellors to a sincere and simple-minded, rather than a shrewd, sagacious, and far-seeing philanthropy; so that the extent of territory and the amount of population, irrespective of more important considerations, are allowed undue influence in the selection of fields for missionary enterprises. While it is only the merest fringes of those great territories and the merest fractions of those vast populations that are being touched, of what benefit to the work of missions are those untold millions on whom no impression whatever can by any possibility at present be made? While we are attacking Satan's strongholds in detail, why not attack his weakest points first, other advantages being equal? And he is greatly weaker on the islands than on the continents. By all means let everything be done that can be done for the continents with their millions, ten times more than is being done, but by no means at the expense of the islands with their thousands. Could we count our missionaries by thousands but—alas! all our European and American missionaries amount only to three thousand; or could we count our funds by millions— but alas! all our annual contributions amount only to one million and a quarter—this mode of reasoning would be quite conclusive: but so long as we send forth our missionaries by units, or at most by twos, and collect our funds by hundreds, or at most by thousands, the most manageable and the most remunerative fields ought certainly to be chiefly cultivated. And when God in His providence is granting ten times more success in most of the islands than He is doing in most of the continents, and when missions can be carried on in Polynesia at half the cost at which they can be carried on in India, surely the claims of the islands are immeasurably stronger than the claims of the continents. And, did space permit, it would be easy to show that the hopes of science, commerce, and politics would be in a similar proportion more fully realised in the many isles of the sea than in the vast continents of which so much has been said. To scientific men what portion of Cook's voyages were so interesting as his descriptions of the South Sea islands? In botanical specimens those islands are remarkably rich. Aneityum alone contains about a hundred different species of ferns. When I was thinking of settling on Aneityum, the Curator of the Botanical Garden in Sydney, who had made a voyage on board a man-of-war in the New Hebrides, said to me, "Mr. Inglis, if you would only collect specimens on those islands you might immortalise your name." The entomologist will also find a highly interesting field for his researches. They are teeming with all varieties of insect life. Of shells and sea-fish the numbers and varieties are truly marvellous; while in the many and dissimilar languages, customs, and traditions of the inhabitants of those islands, the ethnologist will find ample materials for extensive and interesting investigations. In a commercial point of view, an island is of far more value than the same space of land, however fertile, in the centre of a continent. The sea is an open highway, and the Pacific is fast becoming one of the greatest thoroughfares in the world. It is surrounded by countries which are rapidly rising in commercial importance. It is the highway between China, Australia, New Zealand, South America, California, and Columbia. It is the greatest whaling-ground in the world. To say nothing of Colonial and British whalers, it is said that 400 of the 600 whaleships sent out from the United States are traversing the Pacific. It is only at Christianised islands that any ship is either safe or can calculate on obtaining supplies. As many as seventy vessels have called at Rarotonga in one year for supplies of wood, water, and fresh provisions. For all tropical productions those islands will become like the West Indies to our Australasian Colonies. Their political value to Britain is also great. Where is France intriguing so much at present against British interests as among those islands! France sees how rapidly those colonies are increasing in wealth, and, at the same time, how weak and unprotected they continue to be, and she is lurking in great strength among the islands, ready to seize any favourable opportunity for wounding our empire in that vulnerable heel. The missions in those seas, so far as they extend, are a source of political strength to Britain and the Australian Colonies. Perhaps no equal number of men, in the same position, are a source of more political strength to our Colonies than the hundred Protestant missionaries who are labouring in the South Pacific. But for the moral influence of the missionaries, New Zealand, with her 600,000 colonists, would in all likelihood not have been a British colony to-day; the natives would not have signed the treaty of Waitangi, and the sovereignty of Great Britain would not have been recognised by the Maoris. New Guinea would not have been annexed so easily had there been no missionaries on the spot. On account of all these and other advantages, as well as of the direct missionary work accomplished and anticipated, we appeal to the churches, and the individual members of the churches that support the New Hebrides mission, for increased funds, in order that we may conquer those islands for Christ; Satan has long held them under his dominion. But we have opened the campaign; and, if it is vigorously followed up, we have the prospect and we have the promise of ultimate and complete success, for "the kingdom is the Lord's," and "the isles shall wait for His law."

But we require men as well as money, perhaps men more than money for this work, although hitherto for this and all

Z

other missions God has given both in very equal proportions. Very few well-qualified men have ever been refused for want of funds to support them, and seldom has the mission treasury been overflowing and no suitable agents forthcoming requiring support. The Lord has not only supplied funds, but He has sent forth men with all the qualifications needed for the work; and doubtless, in answer to prayer, He will do so in time to come. In the mission-field, as elsewhere, there has always been and there still is a diversity of gifts, but it is the same Spirit, dividing to every man severally as He willeth; on one is bestowed the gift of tongues, and he is soon recognised among his brethren as a living Polyglot; he can chain the savage spirit of the heathen, as Paul did that of his own country-men, by the simple but magic-like power of their own tongue. On another is bestowed the gift of healing, and he is soon known, like Luke, as the "beloved physician;" his very shadow, like that of Peter, is supposed to have a health-giving influence, and, on this account the word finds readier access to many hearts. On another is bestowed the gift of government; like Moses, he can organise and rule, reduce chaos into order, and infuse such principles of scriptural polity into both ecclesiastical and civil institutions as shall conserve truth and freedom to succeeding generations. On another is bestowed the gift of mechanical skill, and tabernacles and temples for the worship of God rise up under his skilful hands as they did under those of Bezaleel or Huram. On another is bestowed the gift of song and music, and like David, he can call forth from ten thousand voices the high praises of the Lord. To another it is given to go down to the sea in ships and do the business of the Lord in great waters; he is at home on the ocean; to him the loveliest scene on earth is the isles waiting for God's law, and the most attractive representation of heaven is the hyaline sea, having its shores lined, as some eminent critics interpret the figure, with the innumerable company of harpers all singing the song of Moses and the Lamb.   To another it is given to traverse continents; like Livingstone, to carry with apostolic zeal the Gospel into the regions beyond where any other missionary has penetrated, and leave behind him at every step the seeds of Christianity, civilisation, and commerce, so that the wilderness is made to flourish and blossom as the rose.   On another is bestowed the gift of prophecy; he is a Boanerges or a Barnabas, a son of thunder or a son of consolation; when he prophesies, when he preaches Christ as the Son of God and as the Saviour of the world, when he exhibits sin in its nature and in its consequences, and salvation in its origin, in its purchase, and in its application, the heathen as of old are convinced, the secrets of their hearts' are made manifest, and they fall down confessing that God is in him of a truth.   To the most there is given a portion of several gifts, no one towering above the rest; prodigies are but few in number, because few such are needed; ordinary work is best done by ordinary men: such excite no special notice on earth, but the result of their efforts is added to the common stock of the world's benefits, the recording angel inscribes it to their account in heaven, and it is kept in remembrance before God. Every gift is needed in the mission field, none can be dispensed with and none are to be despised; and every man serves God best with his own gift.

In the South Sea Missions we have had a few very outstanding men, and we have had a large share of fully average men, both in the South Seas and in the New Hebrides missions.   But it seems to be a tacitly recognised principle at present, in all missionary circles, that the highest intellect, the highest scholarship, and the highest general ability must be quietly yielded up to India and to Africa, to China and to Japan, but that for the South Seas nothing above mediocrity is required; to a certain class of students it is looked upon as the reverse of.complimentary to ask them to go to the South Seas. We are still disposed to covet earnestly the best gifts, but we are nevertheless content if we can obtain men possessing the average amount of talent, of scholarship, of piety, and of common sense. With us, however, an indispensable qualification for missionaries and the wives of missionaries, is that they possess good health and a good constitution; that they be able to rough it, and be able, more or less deftly, to turn their hand to anything that may cast up. As Dr. Livingstone has well put it, and it holds as true of the New Hebrides as it does of Africa, "The missionary must be Jack of all trades without, and his wife must be maid of all work within." They must both belong to "the working classes." Average missionaries of this type, with their heart fully in their work, and the blessing of the Lord resting in an ordinary measure on their labours, are morally certain of success. They may go forth weeping, bearing precious seed, but they shall doubtless come again with rejoicing, bringing their sheaves with them.

THE END.

www.ingramcontent.com/pod-product-compliance
Lightning Source LLC
Chambersburg PA
CBHW030913270326
41929CB00008B/684